550 AP®
U.S. GOVERNMENT & POLITICS
Practice Questions

The Staff of the Princeton Review

PrincetonReview.com

Random House, Inc. New York

The Princeton Review, Inc.
111 Speen Street, Suite 550
Framingham, MA 01701
E-mail: editorialsupport@review.com

ISBN: 978-0-8041-2443-0
eBook ISBN: 978-0-8041-2442-3
ISSN: 2330-7064

The Princeton Review is not affiliated with Princeton University.

Editor: Meave Shelton
Production Editor: Beth Hanson
Production Coordinator: Blake Dennis

Printed in the United States of America on partially recycled paper.

10 9 8 7 6 5 4 3 2 1

Editorial

Rob Franek, Senior VP, Publisher
Mary Beth Garrick, Director of Production
Selena Coppock, Senior Editor
Calvin Cato, Editor
Kristen O'Toole, Editor
Meave Shelton, Editor
Alyssa Wolff, Editorial Assistant

Random House Publishing Team

Tom Russell, Publisher
Nicole Benhabib, Publishing Director
Ellen L. Reed, Production Manager
Alison Stoltzfus, Managing Editor
Erika Pepe, Associate Production Manager
Kristin Lindner, Production Supervisor
Andrea Lau, Designer

Acknowledgments

The Princeton Review would like to give special thanks to the following individuals for their hard work on and contributions to this book: Mike Hernandez, Peter Hanink, Eliz Markowitz, Bryan Cunningham, Jennifer Amerkhanov, Kevin Kelly, David Stradley, Chris Stobart, and David Stoll.

Contents

Part I
Using This Book to Improve Your AP Score

- Preview: Your Knowledge, Your Expectations
- Your Guide to Using This Book
- How to Begin
- Diagnostic Test
- Diagnostic Test: Answers and Explanations

PREVIEW: YOUR KNOWLEDGE, YOUR EXPECTATIONS

Your route to a high score on the AP U.S. Government and Politics Exam depends a lot on how you plan to use this book. Start thinking about your plan by responding to the following questions.

1. Rate your level of confidence about your knowledge of the content tested by the AP U.S. Government and Politics Exam.

   A. Very confident—I know it all.
   B. I'm pretty confident, but there are topics for which I could use help.
   C. Not confident—I need quite a bit of support.
   D. I'm not sure.

2. If you have a goal score in mind, circle your goal score for the AP U.S. Government and Politics Exam.

   5   4   3   2   1   I'm not sure yet

3. What do you expect to learn from this book? Circle all that apply to you.

   A. A general overview of the test and what to expect
   B. Strategies for how to approach the test
   C. To identify the content topics for which I need the most practice
   D. I'm not sure yet.

YOUR GUIDE TO USING THIS BOOK

This book is organized to provide as much—or as little—support as you need, so you can use this book in whatever way will be most helpful for improving your score on the AP U.S. Government and Politics Exam.

- The remainder of **Part I** will provide
  - guidance on how to use this book.
  - a diagnostic practice test, with answers and explanations, to help you determine your strengths and weaknesses.

- **Part II** of this book will
  - provide information about the structure, scoring, and content of the AP U.S. Government and Politics Exam.
  - help you to make a study plan.
  - point you toward additional resources.

- **Part III** of this book will explore various strategies:
  - how to attack multiple choice questions
  - how to write a high scoring free-response answer

- **Part IV** of this book contains drills organized according to the topics tested on the exam.

- **Part V** of this book contains a second practice test, with answers and explanations.

You may choose to use some parts of this book over others, or you may work through the entire book. This will depend on your needs and how much time you have. Let's now look how to make this determination.

HOW TO BEGIN

1. **Take a Test**

   Before you can decide how to use this book, you need to take a practice test. Doing so will give you insight into your strengths and weaknesses, and the test will also help you make an effective study plan. If you're feeling test-phobic, remind yourself that a practice test is a tool for diagnosing yourself—it's not how well you do that matters but how you use information gleaned from your performance to guide your preparation.

   So before you read further, take the full-length Diagnostic Test starting at page 7 of this book. Be sure to do so in one sitting, following the instructions that appear before the test.

2. **Check Your Answers**

   Using the answer key on page 28, count how many multiple-choice questions you got right and how many you missed. Don't worry about the explanations for now, and don't worry about why you missed questions. We'll get to that soon.

3. **Reflect on the Test**

   After you take your first test, respond to the following questions:

   - How much time did you spend on the multiple-choice questions?

   - How much time did you spend on each free-response question?

   - How many multiple-choice questions did you miss?

   - Do you feel you had the knowledge to address the subject matter of the essays?

   - Do you feel you wrote well-organized, thoughtful essays?

- Circle the content areas that were most challenging for you and draw a line through the ones in which you felt confident/did well.

  o **Constitutional Underpinnings:** Principles of democratic government, framers, federalism, checks and balances, separation of powers, etc.

  o **Political Beliefs and Behaviors:** Ideological beliefs about government, political socialization, voting, mass movements, etc.

  o **Political Parties, Interest Groups, and Mass Media:** Organization and communication of citizens' interests and concerns, elections, PACs, etc.

  o **Institutions of National Government:** Organization and powers of major political institutions, ties between branches of government, etc.

  o **Public Policy:** Formation, enactment, implementation, and interpretation of policy; impact of federalism, interest groups, parties, elections, etc.

  o **Civil Rights and Civil Liberties:** U.S. Supreme Court decisions, judicial interpretations, impact of the Fourteenth Amendment, etc.

4. **Read Part II and Complete the Self-Evaluation**

   As discussed in the Guide section above, Part II will provide information on how the test is structured and scored. It will also explain the areas of content that are tested.

   As you read Part II, re-evaluate your answers to the questions above. At the end of Part II, you will revisit and refine the questions you answer above. You will then be able to make a study plan, based on your needs and time available, that will allow you to use this book most effectively.

5. **Engage with Parts III and IV as Needed**

   Notice the word *engage*. You'll get more out of this book if you use it intentionally than if you read it passively, hoping for an improved score through osmosis.

   Strategy chapters will help you think about your approach to the question types on this exam. Part III will open with a reminder to think about how you approach questions now and then close with a reflection section asking you to think about how/whether you will change your approach in the future.

Drill chapters are organized according to the content topics tested on the exam. This allows you to focus on and gain mastery of the areas in which you need the most practice.

6.   **Take the Second Practice Test and Assess Your Performance**

Once you feel you have developed the strategies you need and gained the confidence you may have lacked, you should take the Practice Test in Part V. You should do so in one sitting, following the instructions at the beginning of the test.

When you are done, check your answers to the multiple-choice section with the correct responses beginning on page 322 of this book. Then, see if a teacher will read your essays and provide feedback for your improvement.

Once you have taken the test, reflect on what areas you still need to work on, and revisit the chapters in this book that address those topics. Through this type of reflection and engagement, you will continue to improve.

7.   **Keep Working**

As we will discuss in Part II, there are other resources available to you, including a wealth of information on AP Central. You can continue to explore areas that can stand to improve and engage in those areas right up to the day of the test.

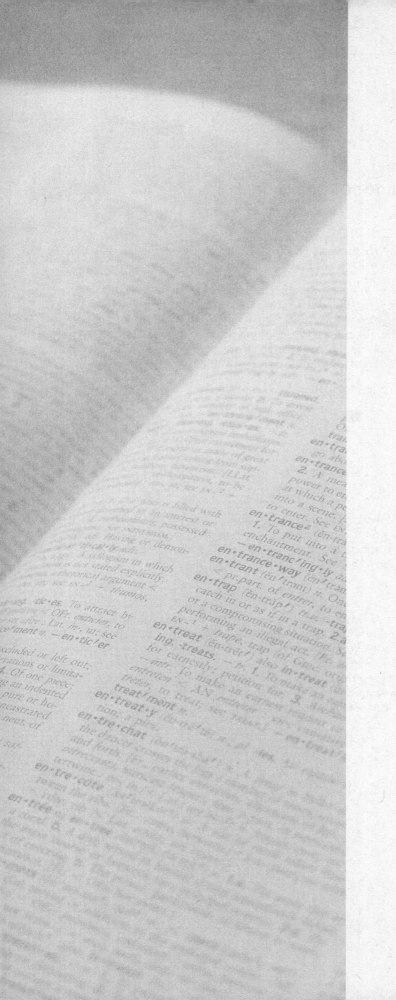

Diagnostic Test

AP® U.S. Government and Politics Exam

SECTION I: Multiple-Choice Questions

DO NOT OPEN THIS BOOKLET UNTIL YOU ARE TOLD TO DO SO.

At a Glance

Total Time
45 minutes
Number of Questions
60
Percent of Total Grade
50%
Writing Instrument
Pencil required

Instructions

Section I of this examination contains 60 multiple-choice questions. Fill in only the ovals for numbers 1 through 60 on your answer sheet.

Indicate all of your answers to the multiple-choice questions on the answer sheet. No credit will be given for anything written in this exam booklet, but you may use the booklet for notes or scratch work. After you have decided which of the suggested answers is best, completely fill in the corresponding oval on the answer sheet. Give only one answer to each question. If you change an answer, be sure that the previous mark is erased completely. Here is a sample question and answer.

Sample Question   Sample Answer

Chicago is a   
(A) state
(B) city
(C) country
(D) continent
(E) village

Use your time effectively, working as quickly as you can without losing accuracy. Do not spend too much time on any one question. Go on to other questions and come back to the ones you have not answered if you have time. It is not expected that everyone will know the answers to all the multiple-choice questions.

About Guessing

Many candidates wonder whether or not to guess the answers to questions about which they are not certain. Multiple choice scores are based on the number of questions answered correctly. Points are not deducted for incorrect answers, and no points are awarded for unanswered questions. Because points are not deducted for incorrect answer, you are encouraged to answer all multiple-choice questions. On any questions you do not know the answer to, you should eliminate as many choices as you can, and then select the best answer among the remaining choices.

This page intentionally left blank.

UNITED STATES GOVERNMENT AND POLITICS

Section I

Time—45 minutes

60 Questions

Directions: Each of the questions of incomplete statements below is followed by five suggested answers or completions. Select the one that is best in each case and then fill in the corresponding oval on the answer sheet.

1. Which of the following statements is LEAST true of voters in federal, state, and local elections?

   (A) Voter turnout is lower in midterm elections than it is in presidential elections.
   (B) Voters lacking party affiliation tend to vote less regularly than those with strong party affiliation.
   (C) Young adults are less likely to vote than senior citizens.
   (D) College educated individuals tend to vote more often than those with less than a high school education.
   (E) Individuals are more likely to vote when they believe they know which candidate will win an election.

2. A presidential veto would most likely be overturned in which of the following situations?

   (A) Approximately 30% of the senators and representatives are members of the President's political party.
   (B) The majority of American citizens support the proposed legislation.
   (C) The chief justice of the Supreme Court was appointed by the president.
   (D) The president's successful reelection campaign advocated bipartisanship.
   (E) Before being sent to the president, the bill was adopted by narrow margins in both houses of Congress.

GO ON TO THE NEXT PAGE.

Questions 3-4 are based on the table below.

General Election Exit Poll Data
(by percentage)

	2000			2004			2008		
	D	R	I	D	R	I	D	R	I
Gender									
Male	39	48	13	47	43	10	42	48	10
Female	54	38	8	58	38	4	60	32	8
Race									
White	34	48	18	38	48	14	42	48	10
Black	62	25	13	63	20	17	66	24	10
Hispanic	74	20	6	72	21	7	66	28	6
Asian	48	45	7	45	48	7	49	49	2
Other	59	36	5	52	40	8	51	48	1
Education									
High school	58	40	2	60	39	1	63	35	2
Trade school	48	40	12	52	42	6	55	40	5
College	44	50	6	50	45	5	50	43	7
Post-Baccalaureate	38	62	0	40	59	1	41	57	4
Age									
18-24	66	24	10	70	26	4	73	23	4
25-44	63	29	8	68	25	7	71	19	10
45-64	49	43	7	55	44	1	58	40	2
65 and older	42	55	3	45	54	1	40	59	1
Region									
East	45	42	13	48	48	4	49	48	3
Midwest	52	35	13	50	42	8	51	39	10
South	39	55	6	35	60	5	32	62	6
West	70	24	6	72	20	8	75	18	7

3. Which of the following conclusions is most supported by the table above?

(A) Hispanic voters were more likely to vote Republican than they were Democratic.

(B) The majority of voters in the West voted Republican in all three elections.

(C) Half as many females voted independently in 2000 than they did in 2004.

(D) In all years, voters age 18-24 were more likely to vote Democratic than Republican.

(E) The majority of voters who attended trade school were more likely to vote Republican in 2008.

4. Which of the following can be inferred from the table above?

(A) White voters were most supportive of independent candidates in 2004.

(B) In all elections, the majority of voters age 45-64 voted Republican.

(C) The Democratic base in the West grew consistently from 2000 to 2008.

(D) Voters age 65 and older were less likely to vote for an independent candidate in 2008 than they were in 2004.

(E) Male voters typically voted Democratic in the period 2000-2008.

5. Which of the following is generally understood to be the purpose of the Tenth Amendment to the Constitution?

(A) It allows for trial by jury in common-law cases.

(B) It grants voting rights to all American women.

(C) It lowers the legal voting age from 21 to 18.

(D) It prohibits excessive bail in federal cases.

(E) It reserves powers to the states.

GO ON TO THE NEXT PAGE.

Federal Domestic Assistance Programs (FDAP)

Year	Total FDAP Grants (Billions of $)	FDAP Grants as a Percentage of State & Municipal Budgets	Department of Health & Human Services Grants (Part of FDAP)	
			Grants (Billions of $)	As a Percentage of FDAP Grants
1972	195.3	14.6	35.1	18.0
1982	182.1	22.0	30.0	16.5
1992	175.8	30.8	37.1	21.1
2002	380.7	19.8	108.3	28.4
2012	512.4	25.0	156.2	30.5

6. Which of the following conclusions can be drawn from the table above?

    I. The share of FDAP grants allocated to the Department of Health & Human Services increased between 1982 and 2002.

    II. FDAP grants comprised a larger share of state & municipal budgets in 1992 than in 1972.

    III. The amount of money allocated for FDAP grants increased from 1972 to 1992.

    (A) I only
    (B) II only
    (C) I and II only
    (D) II and III only
    (E) I, II, and III

7. When an appeal is made to the Supreme Court, the Court usually

    (A) refuses to hear the appeal
    (B) declares a mistrial
    (C) orders the lower court to retry the case
    (D) rules in favor of the defendant
    (E) overturns the decision of lower court

8. Which of the following may file an *amicus curiae* brief?

    (A) A defendant who wants to know what witnesses the plaintiff plans to call.
    (B) Former presidents who wish to send instructions to the justices who they appointed.
    (C) A senator who wants to impeach a Supreme Court justice.
    (D) A plaintiff who demands that the defendant turn over evidence.
    (E) Companies that are not involved in a court case but wish to affect the outcome.

9. Which of the following principles is realized when the federal government provides most of the funding to a project in which multiple levels of government work together?

    (A) Confederation
    (B) Fiscal federalism
    (C) Grant-based funding
    (D) Dual federalism
    (E) Executive agreement

10. Given the structure of the electoral college system, presidential candidates tend to

    (A) avoid battleground states and focus their campaigns on "safe" states
    (B) campaign more heavily in states with large populations
    (C) spend more television advertising money in the Plains States
    (D) campaign extensively in states that heavily favor one party over the other
    (E) focus on winning the popular vote

11. In the House of Representatives, the Rules Committee

    (A) determines both the rules of the House and conditions for legislative process
    (B) plays a pivotal role in the management of the Library of Congress
    (C) has jurisdiction over fisheries and wildlife
    (D) determines what behavior is deemed ethical in the House
    (E) is responsible for overseeing the federal budget process

GO ON TO THE NEXT PAGE.

12. The Commerce Clause of the Constitution has been used to

    (A) release detainees from prison following unlawful arrest
    (B) maintain the navy
    (C) increase the power of the national government
    (D) veto legislative bills of attainder
    (E) declare war

13. Each of the two main political parties of the United States is organized

    (A) as a single party with a presence at the national level only
    (B) into a federal structure in which state and local parties have no power
    (C) as a relatively independent organization that exists at all levels of government
    (D) in a top-down fashion, so that instructions are dispersed from the national level to the state and local levels
    (E) as a coalition of entirely local parties

14. The Dred Scott decision of 1857 was overturned by the

    (A) *Plessy v. Ferguson* decision
    (B) Missouri Compromise
    (C) Jim Crow laws
    (D) Fourteenth Amendment
    (E) Fifteenth Amendment

15. Which of the following is the main point of the cartoon above?

    (A) The vice president does not get to have his or her name on the ballot.
    (B) The role of the vice president is a limited one.
    (C) Gun rights will be put in jeopardy if Theodore Roosevelt becomes vice president.
    (D) Theodore Roosevelt disagrees with his party's platform.
    (E) Vice presidential nominees do not get to later run for president after being on a ballot once.

GO ON TO THE NEXT PAGE.

Questions 16-17 are based on the table below.

Popular Vote Summary for the 2000 & 2004 Presidential Elections
(Number of Recorded Votes)

State	2000 George W. Bush (R)	Al Gore (D)	2004 George W. Bush (R)	John Kerry (D)
Alabama	941,173	692,611	1,176,394	693,933
California	4,567,429	5,861,203	5,509,826	6,745,485
Delaware	137,288	180,068	171,660	200,152
Georgia	1,419,720	1,116,230	1,914,254	1,366,149
Hawaii	137,845	205,286	194,191	231,708
Iowa	634,373	638,517	751,957	741,898
Louisiana	927,871	792,344	1,102,169	820,299
Missouri	1,189,924	1,111,128	1,455,713	1,259,171
New York	2,403,374	4,107,697	2,962,567	4,314,280
Texas	3,799,639	2,433,746	4,526,917	2,832,704

16. Which of the following conclusions regarding voting behavior can be inferred from the table above?

 (A) Voters in states that favored the Republican candidate in 2000 did not support the Republican candidate in 2004.
 (B) Voters in states that have large populations were more likely to vote Democratic than Republican.
 (C) Voters were unsatisfied with George W. Bush's first term in office.
 (D) Individual voting patterns were inconsistent from 2000 to 2004.
 (E) Voters in states that favored the Democratic candidate in 2000 also supported the Democratic candidate in 2004.

17. Which of the following conclusions about the 2000 and 2004 election results in the states identified above CANNOT be drawn from the table?

 (A) In 2004, George W. Bush won the popular vote in all the states where he won in 2000.
 (B) The Democratic popular vote in Delaware increased from 2000 to 2004.
 (C) States with less than a million recorded votes in 2004 were more likely to vote Democratic.
 (D) In 2004, John Kerry won the popular vote in all the states where Al Gore won in 2000.
 (E) More individuals voted in 2004 than they did in 2000.

18. The Reorganization Plan 1 of 1939 and Executive Order 8248 allow the President to select the staff for the

 (A) Peace Corps
 (B) White House Office
 (C) Senate Committee on Appropriations
 (D) Cabinet
 (E) House Committee on Foreign Affairs

19. Which of the following processes best exemplifies the federal structure of the United States government?

 (A) Amending the United States Constitution
 (B) Imposing export taxes
 (C) Spending treasury money without the passage of an appropriations bill
 (D) Granting titles of nobility
 (E) Issuing bills of attainder

20. Which of the following statements about voting populations is most accurate?

 (A) Individuals are less likely to vote in a closely contested race.
 (B) Voters are more likely to vote at age 18 than they are at age 65.
 (C) An individual with a graduate degree is more likely to vote than an individual who has only a high school diploma.
 (D) Affluent individuals are less likely to vote than impoverished individuals.
 (E) Voter turnout is affected by neither education nor age.

21. Every ten years, the majority of state legislatures are responsible for

 (A) redrawing congressional district boundaries
 (B) electing a new state governor
 (C) evaluating the physical accessibility of polling venues
 (D) deciding where to construct new elementary schools
 (E) proposing revisions to current school curricula

GO ON TO THE NEXT PAGE.

22. Members of Congress are allowed to mail letters to their constituents at the government's expense because of

    (A) gerrymandering
    (B) pork-barrel legislation
    (C) the Sixteenth Amendment
    (D) cloture
    (E) the franking privilege

23. A presidential plurality victory occurs when

    (A) the winning candidate receives less than 50% of the popular vote
    (B) candidates receive an equal number of electoral votes and the popular vote determines the winner
    (C) the Senate declares the formal winner
    (D) the winning candidate receives more than 50% of the popular vote
    (E) the House of Representatives declares the formal winner

24. The practice of drawing congressional district lines in an attempt to give one party a benefit over another is referred to as

    (A) front-loading
    (B) prior restraint
    (C) reapportionment
    (D) gerrymandering
    (E) extradition

25. The right of American citizens to petition the government for a redress of grievances is protected under the

    (A) First Amendment
    (B) Second Amendment
    (C) Third Amendment
    (D) Eighth Amendment
    (E) Tenth Amendment

26. The separation of church and state is articulated in the

    (A) establishment clause
    (B) Nineteenth Amendment
    (C) inevitable discovery rule
    (D) Seventh Amendment
    (E) full faith and credit clause

27. All of the following are ways in which lobbyists attempt to persuade legislators EXCEPT

    (A) distributing propaganda to media
    (B) endorsing candidates for office
    (C) socializing with government officials
    (D) providing expert testimony before Congress
    (E) acquiring corporate campaign donations for candidates

Party Identification in Texas, 1992-2008
(% of Registered Voters)

	1992	1996	2000	2004	2008
Republican	29	30	38	34	36
Democrat	30	28	24	26	35
Independent	41	42	38	40	29

28. Which of the following statements can be supported by the table above?

    I. From 1992-2008, the majority of registered voters in Texas identified as Independents.
    II. The percent of registered voters in Texas who identified as Republican was greater in 2000 than in any other year from 1992-2008.
    III. A larger share of the electorate in Texas identified as Democrats in 2008 than in 2000.

    (A) I only
    (B) II only
    (C) III only
    (D) I and III only
    (E) II and III only

29. Which of the following best describes a block grant?

    (A) Money provided to individuals to fund research projects
    (B) Funds with few restrictions that are provided to state or local governments for general purpose use
    (C) Funds distributed among states according to a set formula
    (D) Money that can only be used for a specific purpose
    (E) Grants allocated by individual members of Congress for special projects for their constituents

GO ON TO THE NEXT PAGE.

30. The Voting Rights Act of 1965

    (A) granted women the right to vote
    (B) banned race-based discrimination
    (C) granted African-Americans the right to vote
    (D) allowed states to alter voting procedures without federal permission
    (E) suspended the use of literacy tests at voting centers

Public Approval Ratings, 2001-2005

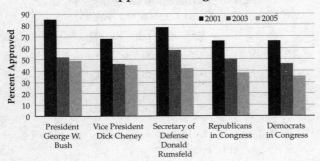

Individual or Group

31. Which of the following statements regarding approval ratings can be concluded from the table above?

    (A) Vice President Dick Cheney consistently received higher approval ratings than did President George W. Bush.
    (B) Donald Rumsfeld's approval rating dropped by approximately 75 percent between 2001 and 2005.
    (C) Democrats in Congress had a higher approval rating in 2005 than they did in 2001.
    (D) George W. Bush received a higher approval rating in 2001 than Donald Rumsfeld received in any of his years in office.
    (E) Unlike the approval ratings received by Democrats in Congress, the approval ratings of Republicans in Congress increased between 2001 and 2005.

32. Which of the following cases established the precedent that a defendant must be informed of the right to remain silent, the right to a lawyer, and protection from self-incrimination?

    (A) *Weeks v. United States*
    (B) *Betts v. Brady*
    (C) *Mapp v. Ohio*
    (D) *Escobedo v. Illinois*
    (E) *Miranda v. Arizona*

33. All of the following are constitutionally mandated presidential powers EXCEPT the power to

    (A) negotiate treaties
    (B) veto legislation
    (C) grant reprieves and pardons
    (D) declare war
    (E) serve as the head of state

34. Which of the following statements does NOT accurately describe voting behavior in the United States?

    (A) Registered voters between the ages of 35 and 45 are more likely to vote than are those under the age of 21.
    (B) A registered voter who has attained his or her General Educational Development (GED) is less likely to vote than a high school dropout.
    (C) Registered voters are more likely to vote in general elections than they are in primary elections.
    (D) More women than men have voted in every presidential election since 1980.
    (E) In the 2012 election, the majority of the Hispanic vote went to Barack Obama.

35. Which of the following is a direct result of an electoral system that features single-member districts?

    (A) Only two major parties can successfully be supported.
    (B) National campaigns can be conducted without incurring great expense.
    (C) Third parties can be as successful as the two major political parties can.
    (D) Each political party tends to focus its campaign on a single issue.
    (E) Voter turnout is higher than in other systems.

36. Under the system of checks and balances, all of the following statements are true EXCEPT:

    (A) The president's nominees must be approved by the Senate before taking office.
    (B) Two-thirds of the Senate must approve presidentially negotiated treaties.
    (C) The president can override a congressional veto and pass laws.
    (D) Congress can override a presidential veto.
    (E) Different branches of government share power and must cooperate in order to pass legislation.

GO ON TO THE NEXT PAGE.

37. The majority of Supreme Court justices

    (A) are appointed by presidents of the same political party
    (B) have no prior judicial experience
    (C) switch party affiliation during their term
    (D) stay on the court for only a decade
    (E) have no party affiliation

38. Ruled unconstitutional in 1983, the legislative veto had allowed

    (A) the executive branch to veto legislation approved by Congress
    (B) federal district courts to overturn legislation
    (C) the president to veto state laws
    (D) Congress to nullify resolutions approved by the executive branch
    (E) the president to overturn Supreme Court decisions

39. Which of the following actions can the President take without congressional approval?

    (A) Grant reprieves and pardons
    (B) Appoint Supreme Court justices
    (C) Negotiate and ratify treaties
    (D) Declare war
    (E) Appoint the Secretary of the Treasury

40. The line-item veto was ruled unconstitutional because it

    (A) violated the legislative process by which bills become laws
    (B) allowed Congress to eliminate sections of legislation without a two-thirds majority
    (C) gave states the ability to override federal legislation
    (D) empowered Congress to nullify executive actions
    (E) allowed the president to pass legislation without congressional approval

41. Which of the following best states an argument made by James Madison in *The Federalist* number 10?

    (A) Honest politicians can prevent factions from developing.
    (B) Factions are more likely to occur in large republics than in small ones.
    (C) The negative effects of factionalism can be reduced by a republican government.
    (D) Free elections are the people's best defense against factionalism.
    (E) Factions cannot emerge in a republic when decisions are made by the majority.

42. An "unfunded mandate" is created when the federal government requires state and municipal governments to

    (A) collect a sales tax in their areas without instructions on how to spend the revenues
    (B) comply with federal laws, even if those laws conflict with state and municipal laws
    (C) issue short-term bonds without specifying the interest rate for those bonds
    (D) fulfill a particular duty but does not provide the finances for doing so
    (E) attract new businesses to their areas by lowering tax rates

43. Which of the following is an example of "horse-race journalism"?

    (A) A news story focuses on a politician's scandals rather than achievements.
    (B) A television news anchor reports an event before the station's rivals.
    (C) A reporter announces which candidate leads in a public opinion poll.
    (D) A newspaper editor prints stories about long-term political developments.
    (E) A radio broadcaster interviews a senator about recent policy decisions.

GO ON TO THE NEXT PAGE.

44. Federal election laws require that, in

 (A) an area that has a substantial community of non-English speakers, voters be provided with ballots in their native language
 (B) an electoral district that has historically low voter turn-out, polling places be open for longer than the typical work day
 (C) a state with a budget deficit, a tax be collected from each voter to pay for the cost of the election
 (D) a region with racial diversity, congressional district lines be drawn to guarantee that at least one elected congressperson be of a racial minority
 (E) an area that lacks adequate public transportation, all voters with drivers licenses be automatically registered to vote

45. Which of the following is the largest source of "automatic spending" for the federal government?

 (A) Salaries to employees of the U.S. Post Office
 (B) Interest payments made to U.S. bondholders
 (C) Entitlement programs
 (D) National defense
 (E) Infrastructure investments in roads and bridges

46. Which of the following best describes the Supreme Court's doctrine of incorporation?

 (A) Although the Constitution empowers the federal government to regulate international trade, states may establish boycotts of goods imported from countries that use child labor.
 (B) While the Congress creates laws, and the executive branch enacts and enforces those laws, only the Supreme Court may decide which laws and executive actions are unconstitutional.
 (C) The Fifth Amendment guarantees that an individual may not be deprived of life, liberty, or property without due process, and this protection provides a legal justification for those who do not wish to serve on a jury.
 (D) Although the Securities and Exchange Commission has the power to establish regulations for the financial markets, it does not have the authority to levy fines against or otherwise punish those who do not comply.
 (E) The Bill of Rights articulates certain rights in order to protect individuals from the federal government, and the Fourteenth Amendment extends most of those rights to protect individuals from the state governments as well.

47. Which of the following plays the most significant role in forming a child's political views?

 (A) The geographical area in which the child grows up
 (B) The child's family
 (C) The media to which the child is exposed
 (D) The child's religion
 (E) The child's teacher

48. Which of the following was the legal basis for the 1973 *Roe v. Wade* majority opinion, in which the Supreme Court struck down a state ban on abortion?

 (A) The Nineteenth Amendment secures for women the right to vote.
 (B) The Civil Rights Act of 1964 prohibits discrimination based on gender.
 (C) The Bill of Rights implies a right to privacy.
 (D) The Ninth Amendment reserves powers to the people.
 (E) The First Amendment guarantees freedom of religion.

49. When the Founders met in 1787 to write the Constitution, their primary objective was to

 (A) establish a bill of rights that would protect citizens from the government
 (B) create a national court system for hearing disputes between citizens of different states
 (C) return to the states those powers that the Articles of Confederation had given to the central government
 (D) create a government in which small states had equal influence as large states
 (E) replace the weak central government created by the Articles of Confederation with a stronger one

50. Which of the following best articulates the doctrine of original intent?

 (A) When a law is unclear, the Supreme Court may consider the intent of a law or the letter of the law, but not both.
 (B) Copyright laws exist to protect the rights of those who create original works.
 (C) Appellate judges should respect the original decisions of trial judges.
 (D) The Constitution should be interpreted in light of the intent of those who wrote it.
 (E) The Supreme Court should not hear a case unless the Court intends to issue an original decision that is different from past decisions.

GO ON TO THE NEXT PAGE.

51. Which of the following is a significant difference between the Senate and the House of Representatives?

    (A) Only the House has the power to issue subpoenas.
    (B) Only the Senate may introduce revenue bills.
    (C) States are equally represented in the House, while representation in the Senate is proportional to population.
    (D) The Senate allows unlimited debate, while the House does not.
    (E) The House has the power to confirm presidential appointments, while the Senate does not.

52. Appointments to which of the following positions must be confirmed by the Senate before taking effect?

    I. Director of Homeland Security
    II. Secretary of the Treasury
    III. National Security Advisor
    IV. U.S. Ambassador to the United Nations

    (A) II only
    (B) I and III only
    (C) II and IV only
    (D) I, II, and IV only
    (E) I, II, III, and IV

53. Which of the following CANNOT limit the influence of the federal courts?

    (A) A constitutional amendment to the contrary of a court decision
    (B) The impeachment of a federal judge
    (C) A governor's failure to enforce a court decision
    (D) A national election recalling an unpopular judge
    (E) Appointment of new judges

54. Which of the following is true of the House Committee on Ways and Means?

    (A) Its primary role is to appropriate spending for infrastructure projects.
    (B) It is the primary author of congressional banking reform legislation.
    (C) It allocates funding for canals and waterways.
    (D) It serves the same function as the Senate Committee on Appropriations.
    (E) Its jurisdiction includes the tax system.

55. Of the following interest groups, which has created the largest number of political action committees (PACs) since the 1970s?

    (A) Environmental activists
    (B) Labor unions
    (C) For-profit business
    (D) Religious institutions
    (E) Senior citizens

56. Which of the following is NOT true of executive orders?

    (A) Presidents avoid using executive orders for controversial actions.
    (B) Executive orders have the same effect as laws passed by Congress.
    (C) Presidents have made increased use of executive orders since the 1970s.
    (D) Executive orders bypass congressional approval.
    (E) The courts have jurisdiction over executive orders.

57. All of the following are core values of American political culture EXCEPT

    (A) income equality
    (B) democracy
    (C) individual liberty
    (D) due process
    (E) equality before the law

58. Why do political scientists identify the presidential elections of Franklin Roosevelt in 1932 and Richard Nixon in 1968 as well as the midterm election of 1994 as "critical elections"?

    (A) The issues at stake in those elections were more important than in most elections.
    (B) Those elections saw major shifts in party alignment that would last for decades.
    (C) Minority voters played a key role in deciding the winners of those elections.
    (D) Those elections took place during wartime.
    (E) The personalities of the candidates were more important to voters than issues in those elections.

GO ON TO THE NEXT PAGE.

Presidential Appointments of Article III (Lifetime) Judges by Gender, Ethnicity, and Disability
(As of Jan. 2012)

President	Total	Male	Female	White	African American	Hispanic	Asian American	Native American	People with Disabilities
James Carter	262	221 (84.3%)	41 (15.7%)	205 (78.2%)	37 (14.1%)	16 (6.1%)	3 (1.1%)	1 (0.3%)	1
Ronald Reagan	383	351 (96.1%)	32 (8.8%)	360 (93.9%)	7 (1.8%)	14 (3.6%)	2 (0.5%)	0	1
George H. W. Bush	193	157 (81.3%)	36 (18.7%)	172 (89.1%)	13 (6.7%)	8 (4.1%)	0	0	1
William Clinton	378	267 (70.6%)	111 (29.4%)	285 (75.3%)	62 (16.4%)	25 (6.6%)	5 (1.3%)	1 (0.2%)	3
George W. Bush	327	256 (78.2%)	71 (21.8%)	269 (82.2.%)	24 (7.3%)	30 (9.1%)	4 (1.2%)	0	2
Barack Obama	173	102 (59.0%)	71 (41.0%)	111 (64.2%)	30 (17.3%)	21 (12.1%)	12 (6.9%)	0	1

Source: Alliance for Justice

59. Which of the following conclusions can be drawn from the data above?

   (A) Republican presidents appointed a higher percentage of minorities to the judiciary than Democratic presidents.
   (B) Democratic presidents appointed a higher percentage of males to the judiciary than Republican presidents.
   (C) President Clinton made more judicial appointments than President Reagan.
   (D) President Obama appointed the highest percentage of women to the judiciary.
   (E) President Reagan appointed the highest percentage of African Americans to the judiciary.

60. Which of the following accurately describes individual entitlements?

   (A) Congress provides funds to the states, and the states decide how best to spend the money.
   (B) Congress is allowed to fund these programs only when the federal government has a budget surplus.
   (C) Congress must pay benefits to anyone who qualifies to receive them.
   (D) Congress grants money to states, provided that certain criteria are met.
   (E) Congress must pass a law each year to determine how to allocate these funds.

END OF SECTION I

This page intentionally left blank.

UNITED STATES GOVERNMENT AND POLITICS

Section II

Time—1 hour and 40 minutes

Directions: You have 100 minutes to answer all four of the following questions. Unless the directions indicate otherwise, respond to all parts of all four questions. It is suggested that you take a few minutes to plan and outline each answer. <u>Spend approximately one-fourth of your time (25 minutes) on each question.</u> Illustrate your essay with substantive examples where appropriate. Make certain to number each of your answers as the question is numbered below.

1. One purpose of the U.S. Constitution's system of checks and balances is to keep one faction or political party from gaining complete control of government. The result in a two-party system is that sometimes one party controls the executive branch while the other party controls the legislative branch.

   (a) Describe two obstacles to Congress in passing legislation when the other party controls the presidency.

   (b) Identify and explain two ways Congress attempts to overcome the obstacles described in (a).

GO ON TO THE NEXT PAGE.

Percentage of National Budget Spent by Government Agencies, 1976-2002

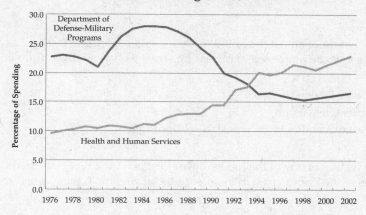

Source: Office of Management and Budget, *The President's Budget for Fiscal Year 2014: Historical Tables*, Table 5.3, April 2013.

2. Use the graph above and your knowledge of U.S. politics to do the following:

(a) Describe the major trend illustrated in the graph.

(b) Identify two political factors that significantly contributed to the trends in the graph.

(c) Explain how each of the two factors you identified in (B) affected the percentage of spending by government agencies between 1976 and 2002.

GO ON TO THE NEXT PAGE.

3. For people and groups interested in social welfare policy, the structure and substance of the three branches of the federal government's political institutions provide opportunities and impediments to exercising political influence.

    (a)   Identify one feature of one of the following and explain how that feature has presented opportunities to those interested in increasing social welfare in their efforts to gain political influence.

- The Supreme Court
- The bicameral legislature
- The president's ability to influence the national agenda

    (b)   Identify one feature of one of the following and explain how that feature has presented impediments to those interested in increasing social welfare in their efforts to gain political influence.

- The Supreme Court
- The bicameral legislature
- The president's ability to influence the national agenda

GO ON TO THE NEXT PAGE.

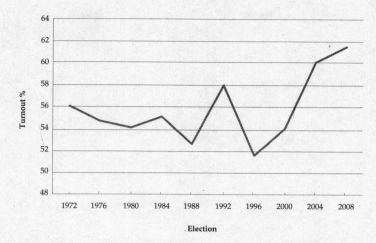

Source: Cook, R. (2012, June). "Voter Turnout: Heading Downward in 2012?"
University of Virginia Center for Politics: Sabato's Crystal Ball.

4. Use the graph above and your own knowledge of U.S. politics to answer parts (a), (b), and (c).

(a)   Identify one four-year shift on the graph in which the percentage of voter turnout increased and explain one cause of the shift.

(b)   Identify one four-year shift on the graph in which the percentage of voter turnout decreased and explain one cause of the shift.

(c)   Whether voter turnout increases or decreases in presidential election years, midterm elections receive lower levels of turnout than presidential elections. Identify two reasons turnout for midterm elections is lower than turnout for presidential elections and explain why each reason leads to that result.

END OF EXAMINATION

Diagnostic Test:
Answers and
Explanations

ANSWER KEY

Section I

1.	E		31.	D
2.	A		32.	E
3.	D		33.	D
4.	C		34.	B
5.	E		35.	A
6.	C		36.	C
7.	A		37.	A
8.	E		38.	D
9.	B		39.	A
10.	B		40.	A
11.	A		41.	C
12.	C		42.	D
13.	C		43.	C
14.	D		44.	A
15.	B		45.	C
16.	E		46.	E
17.	D		47.	B
18.	B		48.	C
19.	A		49.	E
20.	C		50.	D
21.	A		51.	D
22.	E		52.	D
23.	A		53.	D
24.	D		54.	E
25.	A		55.	C
26.	A		56.	A
27.	E		57.	A
28.	E		58.	B
29.	B		59.	D
30.	E		60.	C

Once you have checked your answers, remember to return to page 3 and respond to the Reflect questions.

EXPLANATIONS

Section I

1. **E** Individuals are actually *less* likely to vote when they believe they know who will win an election, so (E) is the best choice. The other choices accurately reflect voting behavior in the United States and, therefore, can be eliminated.

2. **A** Proposed legislation that has been vetoed by the president will become law if two-thirds of the members in each house of Congress vote to override the veto. If 30 percent of the members of Congress are of the president's party, then approximately 70 percent are not. In that scenario, the opposition party is more likely to attain the two-thirds majority needed to override a veto, so (A) is the best choice. If the scenario in choice (B) were to occur, Congress might be more likely to override a veto than if the public were opposed to the bill; however, reaching a two-thirds majority in Congress is usually very difficult and likely to occur only when a single party has a strong majority in each house. Choices (C) and (D) are irrelevant to overriding a presidential veto. Choice (E) is incorrect, for if the proposed legislation had been adopted by a narrow margin (51 percent, for example), it would be very unlikely that two-thirds of each house would vote to overturn a veto. In order for that to happen, members of Congress who had originally voted against the bill would now support the bill and oppose the president.

3. **D** Choice (A) is incorrect because 74 percent, 72 percent, and 66 percent of Hispanic voters supported the Democratic candidate in 2000, 2004, and 2008, respectively. Choice (B) is false because the majority of voters in the West voted Democratic in all three elections, holding 70 percent, 72 percent, and 75 percent of the vote, respectively. Choice (C) is incorrect as 8 percent of females voted independently in 2000 and 4 percent of females voted independently in 2004. Choice (E) is incorrect because 55 percent of voters who attended trade school voted Democratic in 2008. Accordingly, the correct answer is (D) because voters age 18–24 supported the Democratic candidate at a rate of 66 percent, 70 percent, and 73 percent.

4. **C** Choice (A) is incorrect because white voters were most supportive of the Republican candidate (48 percent) in 2004. Choice (B) is incorrect because voters age 45–64 generally voted Democratic (49 percent, 55 percent, and 58 percent in each election, respectively). Choice (D) is incorrect since 1 percent of voters age 65 and older voted for the independent candidate in 2004 and 2008. Choice (E) is incorrect because male voters supported the Republican candidate in 2000 and 2008 (48 percent in each year) and the Democratic candidate in 2004 (47 percent). Accordingly, the correct answer is (C) because voters in the West supported the Democratic candidates in each of the three elections at a rate of 70 percent, 72 percent, and 75 percent, respectively.

5. **E** The Seventh Amendment allows for trial by jury in common-law cases, so eliminate (A). Choice (B) is the result of the Nineteenth Amendment, (C) the Twenty-sixth Amendment, and (D) the

Eighth Amendment, so eliminate those as well. The Tenth Amendment states that any powers not given to the federal government by the Constitution are reserved to the states, so the best answer is (E).

6. **C** Roman Numeral I is correct because grants to the Department of Health and Human Services (HHS) increased from 16.5 percent of FDAP grants to 30.5 percent of FDAP grants between 1982 and 2002. Eliminate choices (B) and (D) since they don't include Numeral I. Numeral II is correct because FDAP grants comprised 30.8 percent of state and municipal budgets in 1992, compared with 14.6 percent in 1972. Eliminate choice (A) because it doesn't include Numeral II. Numeral III is incorrect because FDAP grants decreased from $195.3 million in 1972 to $175.8 million in 1992. Eliminate choice (E) because it includes Numeral III.

7. **A** Choice (A) is correct for two main reasons: the Supreme Court will not grant appeal until all legal options in the lower appellate courts have been attempted, and the Supreme Court usually agrees with the lower court decision. Choices (C) and (E) are incorrect because of this agreement. Choice (B) can be eliminated because the Supreme Court rarely declares a mistrial. Choice (D) is incorrect because the Supreme Court hears the arguments of both sides without favoring either one.

8. **E** An *amicus curiae*, or "Friend of the Court," brief can be filed by any qualified individual or organization not directly involved in a lawsuit but with a vested interest in the outcome. Accordingly, the correct answer is (E). Choices (A) and (D) are incorrect because they describe situations other than the filing of an amicus curiae brief. Choice (B) is incorrect because a president is not allowed to send instructions to a justice. Choice (C) is incorrect because a senator would not file a brief with the Court to impeach one of its justices.

9. **B** Federalism is the principle that the federal government shares power with state and local governments. "Fiscal federalism," or "cooperative federalism," occurs when all three levels of government work together on a project and the funds come from the federal government. Choice (A) is incorrect because a confederation is a loose association of relatively independent states; in such a system, most power is left to the states and the cooperation described in the question is unlikely. Eliminate choice (C) because grants do not necessarily require collaboration with the federal government. The theory of dual federalism is that the national and state governments operate largely independent from one another; this theory was popular in the early history of the United States. Since this is not described in the question, eliminate (D). Eliminate choice (E) since executive agreements refer to presidential agreements made with foreign nations.

10. **B** The number of electoral votes a state has is equal to the number of senators and representatives from that state. Accordingly, states with larger populations, such as New York, have more electoral votes than states with smaller populations, such as Hawaii. Furthermore, most states have "winner take all" rules regarding electoral votes: this means that the candidate who wins the popular vote in a state receives all of that state's electoral votes. Therefore, during the general election, candidates tend to campaign in states with large populations in an attempt to garner a windfall of electoral votes. Choices (A) and (D) are incorrect because candidates campaign more heavily in

battleground states (those that do not favor either candidate) in an effort to win their electoral votes, rather than in states the candidates think they'll surely win ("safe" states that strongly support them) or lose (states that strongly support the opponent). Eliminate (C) because television advertising is not more valuable to candidates in the Plains States than elsewhere. Choice (E) is incorrect because the popular vote does not determine the winner of the electoral vote.

11. **A** In the House of Representatives, the Rules Committee sets the conditions for debate and amendment of most legislation. Accordingly, the Rules Committee determines the rules of the House and conditions for legislative process. Choice (B) can be eliminated because the House Administration Committee is responsible for managing the Library of Congress. Eliminate choice (C) because the Natural Resources Committee has jurisdiction over fisheries and wildlife. Choice (D) can be eliminated because the Ethics Committee is responsible for determining what behavior is deemed ethical in the house. Eliminate choice (E) because the Budget Committee is responsible for overseeing the federal budget process.

12. **C** The Commerce Clause (Article 1, Section 8, Clause 3) of the Constitution gives the federal government the power to regulate interstate commerce and has been used to increase the power of the national government. The Supreme Court has broadened this power to include activities that *affect* interstate commerce. In *Wickard v. Filburn* (1942), the Court found that a farmer who grew wheat for his or her own consumption was subject to federal regulation because the wheat he or she grew affected the interstate market for wheat. In *Heart of Atlanta Motel v. United States* (1964), the Court found that the Civil Rights Act of 1964, which prohibited many forms of discrimination and segregation, was within the federal government's authority under the commerce clause because accommodations affected interstate commerce. Choice (A) is incorrect because the judicial branch is responsible for releasing detainees following unlawful arrest. Choices (B) and (E) are incorrect because these are powers granted to Congress by other clauses in Article 1, Section 8. Choice (D) is incorrect because Article 1, Section 9 prohibits Congress from passing bills of attainder.

13. **C** Political parties have organizations at the national, state, and local levels, so eliminate choices (A) and (E). They are not, however, organized in a way in which all power is enshrined in the national level, whose decisions are issued to the state and local levels, so eliminate choices (B) and (D). Instead, a political party is something of a hodgepodge of organizations at the national, state, and local levels. These organizations operate largely independent of each other, so choice (C) is the best.

14. **D** Prior to the Civil War, the Supreme Court ruled in *Dred Scott* that African Americans could not become U.S. citizens and that Congress could not prohibit slavery in the territories. The decision overturned the Missouri Compromise, which prohibited slavery in certain territories, so eliminate choice (B). Choice (A) is correct because the Fourteenth Amendment grants African Americans citizenship. *Plessy* allowed state and local Jim Crow segregation laws, so eliminate choices (A) and (C). Eliminate choice (E) because the Fifteenth Amendment prohibits laws that would deny anyone the vote based on "race, color, or previous condition of servitude."

15. **B** The office of vice president, which contains only two constitutional duties, can be viewed as a limited, particularly by somebody as politically ambitious as Theodore Roosevelt. The cartoon shows Roosevelt as restricted in the role of vice presidential nominee: in the cartoon, he is literally tied up. According to the Twelfth Amendment, the vice presidential candidate's name must be included on the ballot, so choice (A) is incorrect. The issue of gun rights was not particularly relevant in the 1900 election. The gun is only present because it was a staple for cartoonists when they drew Roosevelt, who was an avid hunter. Eliminate choice (C). Theodore Roosevelt was a vocal supporter of the Republican Party and did not oppose the party until the 1912 election, when he ran for president as a third party candidate. Eliminate choices (D) and (E).

16. **E** Eliminate choice (A) because voters in states that favored the Republican candidate in 2000 also supported the Republican candidate in 2004. Choice (B) can be eliminated because Texas, a state having a large population and a large popular vote, favored the Republican candidate in both 2000 and 2004. Eliminate choice (C) because, regardless of party leanings, the popular vote for George W. Bush increased from 2000 to 2004. Choice (D) can be eliminated because the table provides information about voting patterns on a statewide basis, not on an individual basis. Also, the voting patterns in the states remained consistent from 2000 to 2004; i.e., states with a popular vote that favored the Republican candidate in 2000 also favored the Republican candidate in 2004. Choice (E) is correct because voters in states that supported Al Gore in 2000 also supported John Kerry in 2004.

17. **D** The table supports all of the statements except for choice (D): Al Gore won Iowa in 2000, but George W. Bush won Iowa in 2004. This makes choice (D) the best answer because the question asks for the choice that CANNOT be drawn from the table. Choice (A) is supported by the table because George W. Bush won Alabama, Georgia, Louisiana, Missouri, and Texas in 2000 and again in 2004. Choice (B) is supported by the table because the Democratic vote in Delaware increased from 180,068 in 2000 to 200,152 in 2004. Choice (C) is supported by the table because two states had less than a million recorded votes each (Delaware and Hawaii) and both voted for the Democratic candidate in 2004. Choice (E) is supported by the table because each state recorded more votes in 2004 for the Republican candidate and for the Democratic candidate than the state recorded in 2000 for the Republican candidate and the Democratic candidate.

18. **B** The Reorganization Plan 1 of 1939 and Executive Order 8248 allow the president to select the staff for the White House Office; this makes choice (B) the best answer. The president has the ability to both organize and staff the White House Office according to the way he or she desires. Choices (A) and (D) can be eliminated because both the director of the Peace Corps and cabinet members are nominated by the president but must be confirmed by the Senate. Eliminate (C) since party conference members select Senate committee members prior to the start of a new Congress. Eliminate choice (E) because the House is responsible for staffing its congressional committees.

19. **A** Under federalism, national and local governments both hold power; certain powers are exclusive to the national government, others exist solely for use by the states, and still others are shared by

the two. The process of amending the Constitution illustrates this sharing of power, making choice (A) the best answer. A proposed amendment to the Constitution requires a two-thirds majority in both the House and Senate and ratification (approval) from at least three-fourths of the states. (There is a second method of proposing an amendment to the Constitution that bypasses Congress: a constitutional convention can be called by two-thirds of the states and amendments could be proposed there. However, this method has never been used.) Choices (B), (C), (D), and (E) can be eliminated because the Constitution prohibits the federal government from engaging in each of these acts.

20. C Education plays a significant role in voter turnout: the more educated an individual, the more likely he or she will vote in an election. Choice (A) can be eliminated because individuals are more likely to vote in a tight race. Eliminate choice (B) because younger voters are less likely to vote than older voters. Choice (D) can be eliminated because wealthy individuals are more likely to vote than economically disadvantaged individuals. Eliminate (E) because both education and age impact voter turnout.

21. A Following the release of census data every ten years, the congressional district are redrawn. In most states, the legislature performs this task. Choice (B) can be eliminated because eligible voters in each state are responsible for electing state governor. Eliminate (C) because the U.S. Department of Justice, authorized under the Americans with Disabilities Act, is responsible for evaluating the physical accessibility of polling venues. Choice (D) can be eliminated because school districts are to decide whether or not to construct new schools. Eliminate choice (E) since the state boards of education are responsible for proposing revisions to current school curricula.

22. E Members of Congress are allowed to mail letters to their constituents free of charge because of the franking privilege. Accordingly, choice (E) is correct. Eliminate choice (A) can be eliminated because gerrymandering refers to the practice of drawing congressional district lines in an attempt to give one party a benefit over another. Choice (B) can be eliminated because pork-barrel legislation refers to proposed legislation that provides real benefits to constituents in hopes of garnering constituent votes. Eliminate choice (C) because the Sixteenth Amendment gives Congress the power to lay and collect takes on incomes. Choice (D) can be eliminated because cloture is a motion used in the Senate to end a debate.

23. A A presidential plurality victory occurs when a winning candidate receives less than 50 percent of the popular vote. While the popular vote has been counted since 1824, it has no effect on the outcome of a presidential election. Article II of the U.S. Constitution establishes that presidential elections are decided by the Electoral College. If no candidate wins a majority of the vote in the Electoral College, then the House selects the winner among the top three candidates. Accordingly, the remaining choices can be eliminated.

24. D The practice of drawing congressional district lines in an attempt to give one party a benefit over another is referred to as gerrymandering. Choice (A) can be eliminated because front-loading refers to the strategy of states pushing forward the date of their primary elections. Eliminate choice

(B) since prior restraint refers to the censorship of news material before it is made public. Choice (C) can be eliminated because reapportionment refers to the process by which census data is used to redraw congressional districts and redistribute seats among states in the House of Representatives. Eliminate (E) because extradition refers to the process by which governments return fugitives to the jurisdiction from which they have fled.

25.   **A**   According to the Constitution, the First Amendment states that "Congress shall make no law respecting an establishment of religion, or prohibiting the free exercise thereof; or abridging the freedom of speech, or of the press; or the right of the people peaceably to assemble, and to petition the government for a redress of grievances." Eliminate choice (B) because the Second Amendment states that a "well regulated militia, being necessary to the security of a free state, the right of the people to keep and bear arms, shall not be infringed." Choice (C) can be eliminated because the Third Amendment states that "no soldier shall, in time of peace be quartered in any house, without the consent of the owner, nor in time of war, but in a manner to be prescribed by law." Eliminate choice (D) because the Eighth Amendment states that "excessive bail shall not be required, nor excessive fines imposed, nor cruel and unusual punishments inflicted." Choice (E) is incorrect because the Tenth Amendment states that "the powers not delegated to the United States by the Constitution, nor prohibited by it to the states, are reserved to the states respectively, or to the people."

26.   **A**   The Establishment Clause prevents the government from establishing a state religion. Choice (B) can be eliminated because the Nineteenth Amendment granted women the right to vote. Eliminate choice (C) because the inevitable discovery rule allows the use of illegally acquired evidence if the court agrees the evidence would have eventually been gathered by legal means. Choice (D) can be eliminated because the Seventh Amendment provides individuals with the right to a jury trial in civil cases. Eliminate (E) because the full faith and credit clause mandates that states accept court judgments, contracts, and civil acts of all the other states.

27.   **E**   While lobbyists and interest groups are allowed to provide financial support for a candidate, corporations, trade groups, and unions are forbidden by law to do so; instead, a corporation must form a political action committee (PAC) in order to make donations. Choices (A), (B), (C), and (D) are all ways in which lobbyists attempt to further their interests.

28.   **E**   Roman Numeral I is incorrect because only 29–41 percent of registered voters identified as Independents; more than 50 percent would be required in order to qualify as a majority. Therefore, eliminate choices (A) and (D). Roman Numeral II is correct because the table shows that 38 percent of registered voters identified as Republican in 2000, more than in any other year from 1992–2008. Therefore, choice (C) can be eliminated. Roman Numeral III is correct because the table shows that the percentage of voters in Texas who identified as Democrats increased from 24 percent to 35 percent from 2000–2008. Therefore, eliminate choice (B) and select choice (E).

29.   **B**   A block grant is a large amount of money provided by the federal government to state or local governments with only general guidelines regarding its use. Aside from the overall guidelines, state

and local governments have the power to decide the best way in which to spend the grant money. Eliminate choices (A), (C), (D), and (E) because those answers represent project, formula, categorical, and earmark grants, respectively.

30. E The Voting Rights Act of 1965 gave federal officials the power to register voters, suspended literacy tests, and prohibited states from altering voting procedures without federal permission. Eliminate choices (A), (B), and (C) because those changes occurred with the passage of the Nineteenth Amendment, the Civil Rights Act, and the Fifteenth Amendment, respectively. Eliminate choice (D) because The Voting Rights Act of 1965 banned certain states from altering voting procedures without federal permission (known as the preclearance requirement). The Voting Rights Act (VRA) has been renewed four times since 1965, but the Supreme Court's ruling in *Shelby County v. Holder* (2013) has left the future of the VRA in doubt. The Court struck down Section 4(b) of the VRA, which determines which states are subject to the preclearance requirement. Until Congress revises Section 4(b), no states are subject to the preclearance requirement.

31. D George W. Bush received an approximate approval rating of 85 percent in 2001 and the highest approval rating Donald Rumsfeld received was approximately 78 percent in 2001. Eliminate choice (A) because Vice President Dick Cheney consistently received lower approval ratings than George W. Bush. Choice (B) can be eliminated because Donald Rumsfeld's approval rating dropped by approximately 50 percent between 2001 and 2005. Eliminate choice (C) because Democrats in Congress had a lower approval rating in 2005 than they did in 2001. Choice (E) can be eliminated because the approval rating of Republicans in Congress decreased between 2001 and 2005.

32. E *Miranda v. Arizona* established that all defendants must be informed of their legal rights prior to arrest. Eliminate choice (A) because *Weeks v. United States* established that illegally obtained evidence is not admissible in federal court. Choice (B) can be eliminated because *Betts v. Brady* established that state governments were not required to provide lawyers to impoverished defendants in capital cases. Eliminate choice (C) because *Mapp v. Ohio* increased protection for defendants by extending the exclusionary rule to the states. Choice (D) can be eliminated because *Escobedo v. Illinois* only established that, upon request, a lawyer must be provided to a defendant.

33. D While the president is the commander-in-chief of the armed forces and can deploy troops, only Congress has the power to declare war. Since the president has the power to negotiate treaties, which must be ratified by the two-thirds of the Senate, veto legislation, and grant reprieves and pardons, choices (A), (B), and (C) can be eliminated. Choice (E) can be eliminated because the president is the chief executive, which is the same as the head of state.

34. B There is a direct correlation between educational attainment and the likelihood that an individual will vote in an election; i.e., individuals with greater educational attainment are more likely to participate in the voting process. Eliminate choice (A) because older voters are more likely to vote than younger voters. Choice (C) can be eliminated because voter turnout is greater in general elections than it is in primary elections. Eliminate choice (D) because, since the 1980 presidential election, the percentage of female voters has surpassed the percentage of male voters in each presidential

election. Choice (E) can be eliminated because more than 70 percent of the Hispanic vote went to Barack Obama in the 2012 election.

35.   **A**   In an electoral system with single-member districts, the candidate who wins a plurality (more votes than any other candidate) wins the seat. The party whose candidate receives the second-largest number of votes does not win any representation in the government. The House of Representatives and many state legislatures are based on a system of single-member districts. This system leads to the creation of large parties that try to appeal to a wide voting base in order to win as many votes as possible; therefore, eliminate choice (D). Choice (C) can be eliminated because a third party that receives 10 percent of the votes in every district, for example, does not receive 10 percent of the seats in the legislature; such a party would receive no representation. In an electoral system based on single-member districts, there is no reward for coming in second (or third) place. Choice (B) is incorrect because national campaigns require a great deal of money to plan and implement, regardless of the electoral system. Choice (E) can be eliminated because voters in a two-party system often feel that they have a very limited choice of candidates on election day; therefore, votes are less motivated to vote.

36.   **C**   Only Congress can pass laws, and the legislative veto was found by the Supreme Court to be unconstitutional; therefore, choice (C) is the best. Choices (A) and (B) are a true statements: these are included in the Senate's "advice and consent" power, found in Article II, Section 2 of the Constitution. Choices (D) and (E) are correct statements: Article I, Section 7 of the Constitution describes the process by which a bill becomes a law, including the presidential veto and Congress's power to override a presidential veto with a two-thirds majority in each body.

37.   **A**   Presidents appoint Supreme Court justices with political views similar to their own; therefore, choice (A) is the best and choice (E) is incorrect. Choice (B) is incorrect because approximately two-thirds of all Supreme Court justices (as well as eight of the nine justices as of 2013) have prior judicial experience. Choice (D) is incorrect because the average tenure of a Supreme Court justice is 16 years. While some Supreme Court justices do switch party affiliation during their term, most justices remain loyal to their original parties: eliminate choice (C).

38.   **D**   The legislative veto power was written into legislation from the 1930s until 1983, when the Supreme Court it unconstitutional (*Immigration and Naturalization Service v. Chadha*). The legislative veto had allowed Congress to nullify actions of the executive branch, which makes choice (D) the best. The Supreme Court ruled that the legislative veto violated the law-making process outlined in the Article I, Section 7 of the Constitution. Choice (A) is incorrect because the president is granted a veto power by Article I, Section 7; however, this power does not extend to state laws, so eliminate choice (C). Judicial review, established by the Court decision in *Marbury v. Madison*, empowers the courts to strike down legislation but does not empower the president to overturn Court decisions; therefore, choices (B) and (E) are incorrect.

39.   **A**   Article II, Section 2 of the Constitution empowers the president to grant reprieves and pardons. Since this power is not subject to congressional approval, choice (A) is the best. Article II, Section 2

also describes the Senate's "advice and consent" power: the president may nominate justices and agency leaders, subject to Senate confirmation, and negotiate treaties, subject to Senate ratification. Eliminate choices (B), (C), and (E) because these actions require congressional approval. Although the president is the commander-in-chief of the armed forces (Article II, Section 2), only Congress can formally declare war (Article I, Section 8); therefore, eliminate choice (D).

40.   **A**   The Line Item Veto Act of 1996 gave the president the power to veto individual sections of a bill without vetoing the entire bill. Shortly thereafter, the Supreme Court ruled the line-item veto unconstitutional because it violated the Presentment Clause (Article I, Section 7) of the Constitution by providing the president too much legislative authority. Choice (B) is incorrect because Congress generally requires only a simple majority to pass legislation. Choice (C) is incorrect because it describes the theory of nullification. Choice (D) is incorrect because it describes the legislative veto (which was determined by the Supreme Court in 1983 to be unconstitutional). Choice (E) is incorrect because only Congress may pass legislation according to Article I, Section 1 of the Constitution.

41.   **C**   In *The Federalist* Papers, Alexander Hamilton, James Madison, and John Jay argued in favor of states' ratification of the Constitution. Choice (B) would be an argument against the Constitution, so eliminate it. In *The Federalist* number 10, James Madison addresses the concerns of those who fear that the Constitution grants too much power to the federal government: Madison argues that the federal government would protect individual liberties better than states and that a republican system of government would prevent a majority from oppressing a minority. While the founders felt that free elections were beneficial, choice (D) is incorrect because it is not the argument made in *Federalist* number 10. Eliminate choices (A) and (E) because factions can emerge even when politicians are honest and the majority makes decisions.

42.   **D**   A *mandate* is issued when the federal government orders state or municipal governments to provide a particular service to their citizens. A mandate is *unfunded* when the federal government has not provided the money necessary for the state or municipal governments to provide those services. Therefore, choice (D) is the best answer. Choice (A) is incorrect because sales taxes are determined by state and local governments. Choice (B) is incorrect because it describes the supremacy clause of the Constitution. Choice (C) is incorrect because the issuance of municipal bonds is a decision made by state and local governments. Choice (E) is incorrect because states and municipal governments can lower the state and local tax rates (not federal tax rates) without federal involvement.

43.   **C**   "Horse-race journalism" refers to the media practice of focusing its reports on how candidates fare relative to each other in public opinion polls rather than on substantive issues in the campaigns. This makes choice (C) the best answer. The other choices are incorrect because they are not about campaigns. Even if these other choices took place during a campaign, they would still be incorrect because they do not draw attention to the relative position of the candidates in the polls.

44.   **A**   Subsequent amendments to the Voting Rights Act of 1965 have aimed to protect "language minority groups." To protect minority groups from being denied the right to vote based solely on

language, federal election laws require that, in areas where more than five percent of the voting population belongs to a single language minority, election materials be provided in that minority's preferred language.

45. C   The federal government's discretionary spending is determined each year by Congress through its regular budgeting process. These expenditures include (D) and (E). Non-discretionary spending is sometimes referred to as "automatic" or "uncontrollable" because those expenditures are required by law, outside of the usual budgeting process. Congress enacts laws to set the eligibility requirements for entitlement programs, such as Social Security and Medicare, and unless Congress changes the eligibility requirements, each year's expenditures are usually the result of how many people participate in these programs. (B) is another form of automatic, or uncontrollable spending, but (C) makes up a greater amount of spending. The post office (A) is generally a self-sufficient entity, so its employees' salaries are paid by the post office, not Congress.

46. E   Choice (E) best describes the doctrine of incorporation. Choice (A) is incorrect because states may not regulate international trade. Choice (B) is incorrect because it describes judicial review. Choices (C) and (D) begin correctly but end with incorrect conclusions: the Fifth Amendment does not allow people to avoid jury duty, and the SEC can levy fines and bring lawsuits against those who violate its regulations.

47. B   Political socialization is the process by which children and adolescents learn about politics, and it affects their political views for the rest of their lives. A child's family plays the greatest role in shaping his or her understanding of politics, so choice (B) is the best. Although choices (A), (C), (D), and (E) influence a child's political views, they do not play the *most significant* role in doing so; therefore, those choices are incorrect.

48. C   In the *Roe v. Wade* decision, the Supreme Court found that the Bill of Rights implies a right to privacy, and the due process clause of the Fourteenth Amendment extends that right to the state level. Therefore, states cannot invade women's privacy by banning abortions, and choice (C) is the best. The other choices correctly connect laws with their effects, but these choices were not used in crafting the *Roe* decision.

49. E   The founders met in 1787 to write the Constitution in response to the failures of the Articles of Confederation. The primary failure of the government created by the Articles of Confederation was that it was too weak to deal with the problems faced by the young country; therefore, choice (E) is the best. Although the Bill of Rights was eventually added to the Constitution, it was in reaction to the stronger federal government that the Constitution created; therefore, you should eliminate choice (A). Choice (B) describes the Supreme Court, which was created by the Constitution but was not the primary objective of the Founders. Choice (C) is incorrect because states had more power under the Articles of Confederation than under the Constitution. Choice (D) is incorrect because states were equally represented in Congress under the Articles of Confederation.

50. **D** The doctrine of original intent holds that the Constitution should be understood to mean only what the framers who wrote it intended for it to mean. This doctrine is at odds with those who see a "living Constitution" whose meaning changes as the times change. Therefore, choice (D) is the best. Choices (A) and (E) are incorrect because they do not accurately describe how the Supreme Court hears cases. Choice (B) is true but does not describe the doctrine of original intent. Choice (C) is incorrect because, although judges respect others' opinions, appellate judges are not bound to the decisions of trial judges.

51. **D** The filibuster allows senators to engage in unlimited debate; no such rule exists in the House. Therefore, the best choice is (D). Choice (A) is incorrect because both houses can issue subpoenas. Choice (B) is incorrect because the Constitution dictates that revenue (tax) bills originate in the House. Choice (C) gets it backwards: each state has two senators, and representation in the House is proportional to population. Choice (E) is incorrect because only the Senate may confirm presidential appointments.

52. **D** Start with the positions you know the most about. Maybe you recall that the Secretary of the Treasury is a member of the cabinet, and therefore requires Senate confirmation. Eliminate choice (B) because it does not include II. All U.S. Ambassadors must be confirmed by the Senate; therefore, you may eliminate choice (A) because it does not include IV. The Director of Homeland Security is also a member of the cabinet, so eliminate choice (C) because it does not include I. The National Security Advisor is a member of the White House staff, not the cabinet, and is not subject to Senate confirmation. Eliminate choice (E) because it includes III, and choose choice (D).

53. **D** Choice (D) is the best answer because federal judges are appointed and therefore not subject to recall elections. The other choices are valid recourses for those who disagree with a court's ruling. Constitutional amendments are not subject to judicial review, so eliminate choice (A). Judges can be impeached for their crimes, so eliminate (B). If a governor (or any government executive, such as the president or a mayor) disagrees with a ruling, he or she might choose not to enforce the court's decision. This is not a long-term solution, as the issue would likely be taken up by the court again, but the executive would be able to limit the reach of the courts for a while, so eliminate (C). The appointment of new judges sympathetic to Congress and/or the president would make it more likely that laws would be upheld, thus reducing the courts' checks on congressional and presidential power; therefore, you may eliminate (E).

54. **E** The primary role of the House Committee on Ways and Means is to write laws dealing with revenue (taxes), so choice (E) is the best. It does not oversee infrastructure, banking, or canals and waterways, so eliminate choices (A), (B), and (C). Choice (E) is incorrect because the Senate Committee on Finance is the analog of the House Committee on Ways and Means; even so, the two committees are not exactly the same. The Constitution states that all revenue bills must begin in the House, not the Senate.

55. **C** Of the interest groups in the answer choices, business and labor unions make the most use of PACs, so eliminate choices (A), (D), and (E). More PACs have been created to support business interests than labor unions, so the best choice is (C).

56. **A** Choices (B), (C), (D), and (E) correctly describe executive orders, while choice (A) does not. Presidents have made increased use of executive orders (C) in large part because they are not subject to congressional approval (D). This allows presidents to take unilateral action, especially on controversial issues, so choice (A) is best. Because executive orders have the same effect as laws passed by Congress (B), they too are subject to judicial review (E).

57. **A** Choices (B), (C), (D), and (E) correctly identify core values of American political culture; therefore, choice (A) is the best. Americans generally agree on the concept of equal opportunity but generally oppose the idea of equality of outcome. Equal opportunity means that everyone is given the same chance to achieve: some will succeed, and some will fail. Equality of outcome means that the government guarantees that everyone receives the same results: no matter how hard someone works or how talented someone is, no one receives more than anyone else. *Equality before the law* is an example of equal opportunity. *Income equality*, in which everyone receives the same amount of money, is an example of equality of outcome.

58. **B** "Critical elections" mark dramatic party realignments, as happened in the 1932, 1968, and 1994 elections; therefore, choice (B) is the best. The issues discussed during the elections of 1932, 1968, and 1994 were important, so eliminate choice (E). However, choice (A) is incorrect because it is highly subjective and would not be a point of agreement among political scientists. Many minority voters were disenfranchised during the 1930s, so eliminate choice (C). Choice (D) is incorrect because the U.S. was not at war in 1932 or 1994.

59. **D** In assessing choices (A) and (B), recall that the Republicans presidents are Ronald Reagan, George H.W. Bush, and George W. Bush; the Democratic presidents are James Carter, William Clinton, and Barack Obama. Choice (A) is incorrect because white judges comprised 93.9 percent, 89.1 percent, and 82.2 percent of the Republican presidents' appointments, respectively; this means that minorities constituted 6.1 percent, 10.9 percent, and 17.8 percent of their appointments, respectively. On the other hand, white judges comprised 78.2 percent, 75.3 percent, and 64.2 percent of the Democratic presidents' appointments, respectively; this means that minorities constituted 21.8 percent, 24.7 percent, and 35.8 percent of their appointments, respectively. Choice (B) is incorrect because 84.3 percent, 70.6 percent, and 59.0 percent of Democratic appointments were male judges, compared with 91.6 percent, 81.3 percent, and 78.2 percent of Republican appointments. Choice (C) is incorrect because President Clinton made 378 appointments, and President Reagan made 383 appointments. Choice (D) is correct because 41.0 percent of President Obama's appointments were women, the highest of any other president shown. Choice (E) is incorrect because 1.8 percent of President Reagan's appointments were African Americans, the lowest of any president shown.

60.   **C**   Choice (C) accurately defines an entitlement program, such as Social Security or Medicare. Choice (A) is incorrect because it describes a block grant. Choice (B) is incorrect because entitlement programs pay benefits regardless of whether the federal government has a budget surplus or deficit. Choice (D) is incorrect because it describes a categorical grant. Choice (E) is incorrect because individual entitlement revenues are collected and benefits are paid outside the normal budgeting process: this means that, once created, entitlement programs continue, year in and year out, until Congress changes them by law.

Section II

Question 1

This question offers the opportunity to earn six points, two for part (a) and four for part (b).

To earn two points for part (a), describe two ways the president can stymie the power of the legislature. Possible answers include:

- Veto power
- Marshalling public support against legislation
- Nominating Supreme Court justices who would strike down Congress's legislation

Two points in part (b) are gained by identifying two ways Congress can fight the president's power to shape and control legislation. Once you've identified a way that Congress can overcome a president's power you can then get an additional point for each way you've identified by explaining how the method works. You can only get credit for the explanation points for each method *after* you've made the identification.

For example, you would get one point in part (b) for identifying that Congress can override the president's veto. You would then get a second point for writing that Congress needs at least two-thirds of the votes in the House and the Senate in order to override a presidential veto. If your presidential obstacle is "nominating Supreme Court Justices who would strike down congressional legislation," you would get a point for writing that the Senate has the option to deny confirmation of a Supreme Court nominee. The second point could be gained by noting that the Senate holds confirmation hearings for all Supreme Court nominees and the Senate can deny the president's nominee a seat on the Supreme Court if they have a simple majority (51 votes) to defeat the nomination. This scenario happened in 1987, when conservative Robert Bork's Supreme Court nomination was defeated in the Democratic controlled Senate, 58–42.

Question 2

This question is worth five possible points, one for part (a), two for part (b), and two for part (c).

You earn the point in part (a) for noting that the percentage of Department of Defense spending dropped significantly between 1976 and 2002 (from about 23 percent of the total budget to about 16 percent), while spending by Health and Human Services increased dramatically during the same period (from about 9 percent of the budget to about 23 percent). Even though the Department of Defense percentage bumps up between about 1980 and 1984, the more significant, long-term trend is downward.

There are more than two relevant political factors that affect the two trends, but you have to identify just two to get the points for part (b). One factor you could cite is that the Cold War came to an end in the late 1980s and early 1990s, leading to a significant decrease in military spending. Another is that the senior population increased during the period, leading to increased spending by Health and Human Services.

The key to gaining two points in part (c) is in expressing *how* the factors identified in part (b) led to spending increases and decreases in the respective departments. You could describe how Americans viewed military programs to be less of a high priority at the end of the Cold War, leading to a drawdown of some military resources. Fewer military programs meant that the Department of Defense used a lower percentage of the national budget. As for the other example, the increased senior population led to higher enrollment in the Medicare program, which provides government medical insurance for seniors. Since Medicare is a social insurance program funded by the U.S. Government, higher enrollment in the program resulted in a rise in the cost of the program and the agency's budget ate up a higher percentage of the national budget.

Question 3

This question offers a total of six points, three in part (a) and three in part (b).

The point structure for parts (a) and (b) are very similar: 1 point for identifying a feature that leads to opportunities/impediments for those interested in increasing social welfare and 2 points for explaining how the feature presents opportunities/impediments to increasing social welfare. A one-point explanation identifies an understanding that the identified feature is an opportunity/impediment. A two-point explanation explains how the feature is an opportunity/impediment and makes a clear link between the opportunity/impediment and the identified feature. You are allowed to use the same feature in parts (a) and (b) or you can use two different features in the two parts.

To get the identification point in part (a), name a feature of one of the listed institutions that helps those interested in increasing social welfare. For example, the bicameral legislature has two houses, the House of Representatives and the Senate. One feature of the House is that representation is proportional to the population. Proportional representation presents an opportunity to those looking to increase social welfare because a proposed increase in social welfare with strong popular support can have equally strong support by Representatives in the House.

The Supreme Court has the power of judicial review, which also presents an opportunity to those who seek to increase social welfare. The Supreme Court could use judicial review to strike down laws that decrease social welfare or laws that would bar an increase in social welfare laws. Additionally, when the Supreme Court chooses not to strike down a law that increases social welfare, it validates the Constitutionality of that law. An example comes from the Supreme Court decision in *National Federation of Independent Business v. Sebelius* where the Supreme Court largely decided in favor of the constitutionality of the Patient Protection and Affordable Care Act (aka Obamacare). The designers of Obamacare sought to increase social welfare by

1) making it illegal for insurance companies to deny coverage to those with prior medical conditions (called "guaranteed issue"),
2) increasing the number of people with health insurance through the use of government subsidies to pay for insurance for low income Americans, and
3) allowing for the creation of "insurance exchanges" to be run by the states (insurance exchanges provide a system for people and businesses to pool their money and compare insurance rates more easily), among other things.

Obamacare also created an "individual mandate" which required individuals to buy health insurance or pay a fine (the theory behind the "individual mandate" is that all citizens had to pay into the system to help pay for increased benefits). The constitutionality of the "individual mandate" was one issue challenged in the Supreme Court case. The Court ruled that the individual mandate is a tax and constitutional because Congress has the power to tax. In this case, the Supreme Court's upholding of the "individual mandate" helped those who wanted to increase social welfare. While there are many concepts and examples to choose from, your identification should be of a valid, relevant feature of the listed governmental concept.

While there are also many features you can choose from that present impediments to those who would like to increase social welfare, two examples include the Senate feature of our bicameral legislature and judicial review by the Supreme Court (again!). You can choose either two different features for part (a) and part (b) or you can repeat one feature in both parts. If you repeat the feature, you would earn two identification points for knowing one feature (making your life easier, which is our goal).

If you were to choose the Senate as an impediment, you could point out that each state gets two votes worth of representation in that institution whether the state has a high or low population. This can be an impediment to those who'd like to increase social welfare because a proposal with popular support among the nation's citizenry won't necessarily have popular support among the Senate population, since the Senate population is less likely to reflect the views of the U.S. population. Furthermore, Senate rules allow for filibusters and senatorial holds, which means that a simple majority of 100 senators isn't always enough to pass a legislative proposal; under those circumstances, legislators need 60 total votes to pass legislation. These circumstances represent a high hurdle for legislation that would increase social welfare.

Under judicial review, the Supreme Court has the ability to strike down laws, including laws that increase social welfare. A different aspect of the Obamacare example (see above) suffices as an explanation for how judicial review can serve as an impediment to an increase in social welfare. Obamacare initially expanded the Medicaid program (which provides health insurance to low income people) by giving more money to states provided that states allow more people to enroll in Medicaid (Medicaid is run at the state level and funded by federal block grants). States that didn't comply with the expansion faced the possibility of losing all Medicare funding. The Supreme Court used the principle of judicial review to overrule the possibility of states losing all Medicaid funding for failing to expand the program in line with Obamacare. In this case, judicial review acted as an impediment to increasing social welfare. Making clear connections between the feature and the explanation is the key to earning four of the six points available in this question.

Question 4

Students may earn a total of eight points on this question. Two points are available for part (a), two for part (b), and four for part (c).

Part (a) asks you two identify a four-year shift on the graph in which the percentage of voter turnout increased. You get one point for identifying any of: 1980–1984, 1988–1992, 1996–2000, 2000–2004, and 2004–2008. You get another point for identifying a cause that explains either 1) why the turnout may have been lower in the earlier year or 2) why the turnout may have been higher in the later year. Answers will vary depending on which time period you chose. The following are some appropriate reasons.

1) The 1992 turnout was high because it was a three-way race with a third party candidate, Ross Perot of the Reform Party, who attracted the votes of many (nearly 20 million) who may not have voted in a two-party race.

2) The 2004 turnout was high because of significant events that occurred between 2001 and 2004, including the September 11, 2001 terrorist attacks, the American invasion of Afghanistan, and the American invasion of Iraq.

3) In 2008, record numbers of young and minority voters went to the polls in support of Barack Obama

Keep in mind that it will usually be easier to explain a big increase like 2000–2004 (about 6 percentage points), than a small increase like 1980–1984 (about 1 percentage point).

Part (b) asks you two identify a four-year shift on the graph in which the percentage of voter turnout increased. You get one point for identifying any of: 1972–1976, 1976–1980, 1984–1988, and 1992–1996. You get another point for identifying a cause that explains either 1) why the turnout may have been higher in the earlier year or 2) why the turnout may have lower in the later year. Again, the answers will vary depending on which time period you choose. Some appropriate reasons are

1) The Vietnam War ended, Vice President Agnew resigned due to a bribery scandal, and President Nixon resigned due to the Watergate scandal between 1972 and 1976, demoralizing the electorate's confidence in government.

2) The economic "malaise" and long Iranian hostage crisis led to a low level of turnout for incumbent Jimmy Carter in 1980.

3) Though Ross Perot ran in 1996, the Reform Party split and he didn't gain as much popular support, receiving less than half the votes he received in 1992.

Part (c) awards two points for two reasons midterm elections have lower turnout than presidential elections. Some acceptable answers include

- Lower media attention/interest for midterm elections
- Many congressional candidates run unopposed
- Fewer citizens are aware of midterm elections
- Midterm elections are viewed as less important than presidential elections

For each reason you give you get a point for explaining why the reason leads to lower turnout. You must identify a reason before you can get a point for explaining it. If you chose the reason that many congressional candidates run unopposed, then the explanation could be that some citizens wouldn't take the time to vote when the outcome of the race is certain.

DIAGNOSTIC TEST SCORING WORKSHEET

Section I: Multiple-Choice

$$\underline{\hspace{3cm}} \times 1.0000 = \underline{\hspace{4cm}}$$

Number of Correct   Weighted
(out of 60)   Section I Score
(Do not round)

Section II: Free Response

Question 1 $\underline{\hspace{3cm}} \times 2.5000 = \underline{\hspace{3cm}}$
(out of 6)   (Do not round)

Question 2 $\underline{\hspace{3cm}} \times 3.0000 = \underline{\hspace{3cm}}$
(out of 5)   (Do not round)

Question 3 $\underline{\hspace{3cm}} \times 2.5000 = \underline{\hspace{3cm}}$
(out of 6)   (Do not round)

Question 4 $\underline{\hspace{3cm}} \times 1.8750 = \underline{\hspace{3cm}}$
(out of 8)   (Do not round)

AP Score Conversion Chart U.S. Government and Politics	
Composite Score Range	AP Score
96-120	5
82-95	4
66-81	3
42-65	2
0–41	1

Sum $= \underline{\hspace{4cm}}$
Weighted Section II
Score (Do not round)

Composite Score

$$\underline{\hspace{3cm}} + \underline{\hspace{3cm}} = \underline{\hspace{3cm}}$$

Weighted   Weighted   Composite Score
Section I Score   Section II Score   (Round to nearest
whole number)

Part II
About the
AP U.S.
Government
and Politics
Exam

- The Structure of the AP U.S. Government and Politics Exam
- How the AP U.S. Government and Politics Exam is Scored
- How AP Exams Are Used
- Other Resources
- Designing Your Study Plan

THE STRUCTURE OF THE AP U.S. GOVERNMENT AND POLITICS EXAM

The AP U.S. Government and Politics Exam is a two-part test. The chart below illustrates the test's structure.

Section	Question Type	Number of Questions	Time Allowed	Percent of Final Grade
I	Multiple Choice	60	45 minutes	50
II	Free Response	4	100 minutes	50

The test is designed to test an overview of U.S. government. It doesn't give all subjects equal weight, however. Here's how the test questions break down.

Subject	Percent of Questions
Constitutional Underpinnings	5 to 15
Political Beliefs and Behaviors	10 to 20
Political Parties, Interest Groups, and Mass Media	10 to 20
Institutions of Government: Congress, President, Judiciary, and Bureaucracy	35 to 45
Public Policy	5 to 15
Civil Rights and Civil Liberties	5 to 15

While most of the questions deal with the institutions of government, the questions are nearly evenly divided among the four institutions. There are no definition questions, although you need to know the definitions of words to understand the questions. The questions tend to deal with the dynamics of how government operates within a political environment. For example, you may be asked how interest groups attempt to influence policy making in Congress and the bureaucracy or how the president attempts to influence Congress through public opinion. The test writers want to know whether you understand the general principles that guide U.S. government and the making of public policy.

In addition to the multiple-choice questions, there are four mandatory free-response questions. You'll have a total of 100 minutes to answer all of them. You should spend approximately twenty-five minutes per question, but be aware that you must manage your own time. Additional time spent on one question will reduce the time that you have left to answer another. Writing more than is necessary to answer the question will not earn you extra points.

HOW THE AP U.S. GOVERNMENT AND POLITICS EXAM IS SCORED

The graders assign each of your free-response answers a numerical score. Weighing the average on the free-responses and the score on the multiple-choice questions each as 50 percent, the graders create a final score from a low of 1 to a high of 5. The chart below tells you what that final score means.

Score (Meaning)	Percentage of test takers receiving this score	Equivalent grade in a first-year college course	Credit granted for this score?
5 (extremely qualified)	13	A	Most schools (contact admissions department to verify)
4 (well qualified)	17	A-, B+, B	Most schools (contact admissions department to verify)
3 (qualified)	26	B-, C+, C	Some do, but some don't (contact admissions department to verify)
2 (possibly qualified)	24	C-	Very few do (contact admissions department to verify)
1 (no recommendation)	20	D	No

To score the multiple-choice questions on the practice tests in this book, award yourself one point for every correct answer and credit 0 points to your score for every question you left blank. Remember that there is no longer a guessing penalty on the test. This will give you a raw score.

Here's what that score would translate into on the AP U.S. Government and Politics Exam, assuming you performed as well on the essay questions.

Multiple-Choice Raw Score	AP Score
0 to 26	1
27 to 35	2
36 to 43	3
44 to 52	4
53 to 60	5

Of course, if you follow our advice for how to write a good free-response essay, you could score higher on the free-response section than on the multiple-choice section and thus potentially increase your final score by one point.

HOW AP EXAMS ARE USED

Different colleges use AP exams in different ways, so it is important that you visit a particular college's website in order to determine how it accepts AP exam scores. The three items below represent the main ways in which AP exam scores can be used.

- **College Credit.** Some colleges will give you college credit if you score highly on an AP exam. These credits count towards your graduation requirements, meaning that you can take fewer courses while in college. Given the cost of college, this could be quite a benefit, indeed.

- **Satisfy Requirements.** Some colleges will allow you to "place out" of certain requirements if you do well on an AP exam, even if they do not give you actual college credits. For example, you might not need to take an introductory-level course, or perhaps you might not need to take a class in a certain discipline at all.

- **Admissions Plus.** Even if your AP exam will not result in college credit or even allow you to place out of certain courses, most colleges will respect your decision to push yourself by taking an AP course or, even, an AP exam outside of a course. A high score on an AP exam shows mastery of more difficult content than is typically taught in many high school courses, and colleges may take that into account during the admissions process.

OTHER RESOURCES

There are many resources available to help you improve your score on the AP U.S. Government and Politics Exam, not the least of which are your **teachers**. If you are taking an AP course, you may be able to get extra attention from your teacher, such as feedback on your essays. If you are not in an AP course, you can reach out to a teacher who teaches AP U.S. Government and Politics to ask if he or she will review your essays or otherwise help you master the content.

Another wonderful resource is **AP Central**, the official website of the AP exams. The scope of the information available on this site is quite broad and includes the following:

- course description, which includes further details on what content is covered by the exam

- sample questions from the AP U.S. Government and Politics Exam

- free-response question prompts and multiple-choice questions from previous years

The AP Central home page address is: **http://apcentral.collegeboard.com/apc/Controller.jpf.**

For up-to-date information about the ongoing changes to the AP U.S. Government and Politics Exam Course, please visit: **http://apcentral.collegeboard.com/apc/public/courses/teachers_corner/2259.html.**

Finally, **The Princeton Review** offers tutoring and small group instruction. Our expert instructors can help you refine your strategic approach and enhance your content knowledge. For more information, call 1-800-2REVIEW.

DESIGNING YOUR STUDY PLAN

As part of the Introduction, you identified some areas of potential improvement. Let's now delve further into your performance on the Diagnostic Test, with the goal of developing a study plan appropriate to your needs and time commitment.

Read the answers and explanations associated with the multiple-choice questions (starting at page 28). After you have done so, respond to the following questions:

- Review the topic list on page 48. Next to each topic, indicate your rank of the topic as follows: "1" means "I need a lot of work on this," "2" means "I need to beef up my knowledge," and "3" means "I know this topic well." (If you prefer a more detailed breakdown of these topics, see pages 56–57.)

- How many days/weeks/months away is your exam?

- What time of day is your best, most focused study time?

- How much time per day/week/month will you devote to preparing for your exam?

- When will you do this preparation? (Be as specific as possible: Mondays and Wednesdays from 3 to 4 p.m., for example.)

- What are your overall goals for using this book?

Part III
Test-Taking Strategies for the AP U.S. Government and Politics Exam

PREVIEW ACTIVITY

Review your responses to the questions on pages 3 and 4 of Part I and then respond to the following questions:

- How many multiple-choice questions did you miss even though you knew the answer?

- On how many multiple-choice questions did you guess blindly?

- How many multiple-choice questions did you miss after eliminating some answers and guessing based on the remaining answers?

- Did you find any of the free-response questions easier or harder than the others—and, if so, why?

HOW TO USE THE CHAPTERS IN THIS PART

Before reading the following strategy chapters, think about what you are doing now. As you read and engage in the directed practice, be sure to appreciate the ways you can change your approach.

Chapter 1
How to Approach
Multiple-Choice
Questions

THE BASICS

The directions for the multiple-choice section of the AP U.S. Government and Politics Exam are pretty simple. They read

Directions: Each of the questions or incomplete statements below is followed by five suggested answers or completions. Select the one that is best in each case and then fill in the corresponding oval on the answer sheet.

In short, you're being asked to do what you've done on many other multiple-choice exams: Pick the best answer, then fill in the corresponding bubble on a separate sheet of paper. You will *not* be given credit for answers you record in your test booklet (e.g., by circling them) but do not fill in on your answer sheet. The section consists of 60 questions, and you will be given 45 minutes to complete it.

The College Board also provides a breakdown of the general subject matter covered on the exam. This breakdown will not appear in your test booklet; it comes from the preparatory material the College Board publishes. Here again is the chart we showed you in Part II.

Subject	Percent of Questions
Constitutional Underpinnings	5 to 15
Political Beliefs and Behaviors	10 to 20
Political Parties, Interest Groups, and Mass Media	10 to 20
Institutions of Government: Congress, President, Judiciary, and Bureaucracy	35 to 45
Public Policy	5 to 15
Civil Rights and Civil Liberties	5 to 15

Constitutional Underpinnings	• the political and economic circumstances at the time of the framing of the Constitution • the motivations of the framers • the weaknesses of the Articles of Confederation • the strengths of the Constitution • separation of powers • the nature and political impact of Federalism • principles of democratic government • system of checks and balances

Political Beliefs and Behavior	• the ideological beliefs people maintain regarding their government • political socialization • public opinion and its impact on policy • how and why citizens vote as they do • the methods of political participation • the reasons citizens disagree over political beliefs and behavior
Political Parties, Interest Groups, and Mass Media	• what parties do and how they operate • how parties are organized • how parties link citizens to government • how parties help make and use the rules of elections • how electoral laws affect the outcome of elections • what interest groups do and what makes them effective • the role of PACs and their impact on the political process • the types of mass media • the purpose of the media • the impact of the media on the political agenda
Institutions of Government: Congress, President, Judiciary, and Bureaucracy	• the structure and function of the legislature, executive branch, judiciary, and bureaucracy • the structural and political interrelationships of the institutions of government • the connections between the national government, citizens, political parties, public opinion, elections, interest groups, and the states
Public Policy	• the process of making public policy • citizen participation in policy making • the interactions between Congress, the courts, and the bureaucracy on policy making • the impact of elections in policy making • the participants in domestic and economic policy making • the limitations of domestic and economic policy making
Civil Rights and Civil Liberties	• substantive and procedural rights and liberties • the impact of the Fourteenth Amendment on rights and liberties • the consequences of judicial interpretation on rights and liberties

As you can see, the primary focus of the test is the nuts and bolts of the federal government. The test also emphasizes political activity—the factors that influence individual political beliefs, the conditions that determine how and why people vote, and the process by which groups form and attempt to influence the government. All these subjects, you should note, are important. As much as 30 percent (or as little as 10 percent) of your exam may focus on constitutional issues and civil rights.

TYPES OF QUESTIONS

The majority of questions on the multiple-choice section of the test are pretty direct. Here's an example.

1. A "pocket veto" can occur only when

   (A) Congress amends a bill
   (B) the president is out of the country
   (C) a bill passes Congress with a greater than two-thirds majority in each house
   (D) the Supreme Court has ruled that the proposed legislation is unconstitutional
   (E) a bill reaches the president's desk within 10 days of the end of a congressional session

Sometimes, the College Board makes the questions a little trickier. One way it does this is by phrasing a question in such a way that four answers are correct and one is incorrect. We call these questions "NOT/EXCEPT" questions because they usually contain one of those words (in capital letters, so they're difficult to miss). Here's an example.

2. In the twentieth century, the Democratic Party traditionally received majority support from all of the following groups EXCEPT

   (A) the wealthy
   (B) African Americans
   (C) Jews
   (D) union members
   (E) teachers

Another way is the Roman Numeral format question. This type of question can have more than one correct answer. Here's an example.

3. The increased use of the presidential primary since the 1960s has had the following effect(s)

    I. Weakened the influence of the political parties
    II. Increased the power of political activists in the parties
    III. Increased the cost of running for political office
    IV. Increased the drama of the party convention
    V. Decreased the number of persons challenging incumbents

    (A) I only
    (B) I, II, and III only
    (C) II and III only
    (D) II and IV only
    (E) III, IV, and V only

Once or twice during the multiple-choice section, you will be asked to interpret an illustration, often a map or a political cartoon. These are usually rather easy. The key is not to try to read too much between the lines. Here's an example.

"Sorry, but all my power's been turned back to the states."

4. The principle of government most relevant to the cartoon is

    (A) judicial restraint
    (B) checks and balances
    (C) federalism
    (D) executive privilege
    (E) representative democracy

Finally, there will be one or two questions on the test asking you to interpret a graph or chart. Again, these are usually very direct, and the most important thing for you to do is *not* to over-interpret the data. The correct answer will be indisputably supported by the information in the chart. Here's an example.

Average, highest, and lowest approval ratings, by percentage of all eligible voters, for U.S. presidents, 1953 to 1974

	Average	Highest	Lowest
Eisenhower	65	79	48
Kennedy	70	83	56
Johnson	55	79	35
Nixon	49	67	24

Source: Gallup poll

5. Which of the following conclusions can be drawn from the information presented in the chart above?

(A) Eisenhower was the most consistently popular president in the nation's history.

(B) Kennedy received greater congressional support for his programs than did any other president during the period in question.

(C) Nixon's lowest approval rating was the result of the Watergate scandal.

(D) The difference between Johnson's highest and lowest approval ratings was the greatest for any president during the period in question.

(E) Eisenhower and Johnson were equally well liked by all Americans.

Answers to these and other drill questions appear at the end of this chapter.

HOW TO CRACK THE AP U.S. GOVERNMENT AND POLITICS MULTIPLE-CHOICE SECTION

If you've paid attention in class, you should do well on this test. If you haven't paid close attention, you may still be able to master the material if you review intensively. Either way, you will do better if you know what to expect of the test. On the next few pages, we'll discuss some things that all AP U.S. Government and Politics Exam multiple-choice sections have in common.

The Questions Are of Mixed Difficulty

The examination is made up of questions of varying difficulty. It is not unusual to have many questions on the examination that fewer than 50 percent of the students answer correctly. Some are so difficult that fewer than 25 percent of students answer them correctly. There are also some very easy questions, which the vast majority of students answer correctly. But watch out for the really difficult questions that may involve very technical issues, such as committee seniority or campaign finance reform.

There Are No Trivial Pursuit Questions on This Exam

Here's some more good news. The AP U.S. Government and Politics Exam doesn't ask about trivial matters. You will probably never see a question on the exam such as this one.

6. The American equivalent of the British Exchequer
   is the

   (A) House Finance Committee
   (B) Internal Revenue Service
   (C) United States Mint
   (D) Office of Budget and Management
   (E) Federal Reserve Board

To answer this question correctly, you would have to be fairly familiar with the British government. The AP U.S. Government and Politics Exam does not require such knowledge. This question is atypical in another way as well: It does not have a varied selection of possible answers. Even if you had known that the British Exchequer has something to do with money and government, you could not have eliminated any of the incorrect answers on this question. On an actual AP test, at least a couple of these answers would have been completely unrelated to finance, and you could have eliminated them to guess from among the remaining answers.

Process of Elimination

It is more important to focus on eliminating incorrect answers than on finding the correct answers because that is the most efficient way to take a multiple-choice exam. Use Process of Elimination (POE) to whittle down the answer choices to one, because incorrect answers are much easier to identify than is the correct one. When people look for the correct answer among the answer choices, they have a tendency to try to justify how each answer may be correct. They'll adopt a forgiving attitude, but this is a situation in which a savage brutality is needed. Eliminate incorrect answers. Terminate them with extreme prejudice. If you've done your job well, only the correct answer will be left standing at the end.

All of this probably sounds pretty aggressive to you. It is. Good test takers take multiple-choice tests aggressively. They sift through the answer choices, discard incorrect answers without remorse, guess with impunity, and prowl the test searching for questions they can answer, all with the tenacity and ruthlessness of a shark. All right, maybe that's a bit overdramatic, but you get the point. So, eliminate as many answers as you can to increase your odds of answering difficult questions correctly.

Common Sense Can Help

Sometimes answers on the multiple-choice section contradict common sense. Eliminate those answers because common sense works on the AP U.S. Government and Politics Exam.

Think about which of the answer choices to the question below go against common sense.

---

7. Which of the following best explains the way in which federal legislation is implemented?

   (A) Most laws outline general goals and restrictions, which the federal bureaucracy interprets and translates into specific guidelines.
   (B) The manner of implementing federal legislation is negotiated between a joint congressional committee and a presidential advisory committee.
   (C) All of the regulations pertaining to a piece of legislation are contained within the legislation itself.
   (D) After a bill is signed, all disputes pertaining to its implementation are decided by the congressional committee responsible for the bill.
   (E) The details of implementing congressional legislation are worked out in the courts on a case-by-case basis.

Here's How to Crack It

You should have been able to apply common sense to eliminate answers (D) and (E) pretty quickly. Congressional committees work on bills *before* they reach the floor for a vote, and this work takes up all their time. They would hardly have time to hear all disputes concerning bills that have already passed. Furthermore, such a system would violate the system of checks and balances, because the responsibility for interpreting laws belongs to the judiciary. All the same, the details of congressional legislation could never be worked out in the courts. There would simply be too many cases for the courts to be able to process them all. Similarly, answer (B) contradicts the principle of separation of powers. It is the executive branch's responsibility to enforce the law; it is not required to confer with Congress on the manner in which it performs this task. Answer (C) is impractical. You have no doubt seen "photo ops" of politicians standing before the mountains of federal regulations on the books. Those regulations are created by the federal bureaucracy as guidelines for implementing legislation. They are not contained within the legislation itself. The correct answer, by POE, is (A).

Answer Key for Sample Questions in This Chapter

1. E
2. A
3. B
4. C
5. D
6. B
7. A

Summary

o   Rest assured that the AP U.S. Government and Politics Exam tests a relatively small amount of information. Be confident: You can review this material fairly quickly and still get a good grade on this exam.

o   Familiarize yourself with the different types of questions that will appear in the multiple-choice section.

o   Remember that most of the questions on this exam are of medium difficulty. The test does not bother with trivial matters or minute exceptions to general trends. The test writers want to know that you understand the general principles underlying U.S. government.

o   Tailor your studying to suit the test's most common topics. Don't spend a lot of time studying civil rights and civil liberties until you have completely reviewed the workings of the federal government and the basics of political behavior.

o   Use POE on all but the easiest questions. Once you have worked on a question, eliminated some answers, and convinced yourself that you cannot eliminate any other incorrect answers, you should guess and move on to the next question.

o   Use common sense.

o   Remember not to leave any questions blank. There is no "guessing penalty" on this exam!

Chapter 2
How to Approach
Free-Response
Questions

You may be surprised to see the words "free response" at the start of this chapter. No essay? What is a "free response," anyway? The first thing to be aware of is that this response is hardly free. The College Board wants a very specific type of writing, and it is one that you might not be used to. Forget the idea of crafting a fine piece of writing that convinces the reader of your opinion. Instead, think "just the facts, ma'am." Your basic goal here is to read the questions and answer them to the best of your ability.

You will have 100 minutes to answer four questions, so be sure to budget your time well. Give as much detail as necessary to answer the question, but no more! Above all, don't worry. So long as you know the basics of American government, this section should be a breeze.

WHAT ARE THE AP U.S. GOVERNMENT AND POLITICS EXAM FREE-RESPONSE QUESTIONS LIKE?

The AP U.S. Government and Politics Free-Response Section contains four free-response questions. Each counts equally. The entire free-response section counts as 50 percent of your examination grade. Even though the free responses are all mandatory, you may have some choices within a free-response question. For example, a question may look like this:

1. Procedural due process rights have been expanded a great deal over the last half-century.

   (a) Define procedural due process and explain why it is important to the American legal system.

   (b) Explain the difference between procedural due process and substantive due process.

   (c) Choose two of the following cases and explain how they expanded procedural due process rights.
   - *Mapp v. Ohio*
   - *Gideon v. Wainwright*
   - *Escobedo v. Illinois*
   - *Miranda v. Arizona*

Choices within questions allow you to showcase what you know best, instead of having to write about many subjects, some of which you might not remember as well. Again, depth-not-breadth is the focus here. Think of this as a "data dump" where you can show off your knowledge and "wow" the grader. Note that you will not get a higher score for writing more than what the question requires. You cannot make up points lost in a previous free-response question, so be sure to focus on only the topic that the question asks about. If there is a choice within a question, make certain you choose the subject you know the most about. Be explicit. Also remember that if the question deals with a Supreme Court case, you shouldn't worry about the background of the case. It is the ruling and the consequences that are important.

If you are confronted with a free-response question that you feel unprepared to answer, don't panic. Skip it and come back to it later. Writing another free-response essay may get your juices flowing and prompt you to recall your knowledge of the first subject. Just remember to keep track of your time so that you have time to return to the question that you skipped.

You cannot be penalized for just *attempting* to write an answer. Therefore, never leave a free-response question blank. Write something about the subject, even if it is just basic knowledge you picked up from a magazine or a website.

The free-response essays are graded using an answer standard, to which only the graders have access. A certain number of points is given for each piece of information supplied correctly. The numerical grade of the essay is determined by adding the points earned for each part of the response.

Each free-response essay uses a different scoring standard. One essay could be graded using a total of five points, another a total of seven points, and another a total of ten points. While the total score for each question may differ, the value of each question is equal in determining the final score on the free-response section. Each of the four free-response questions is worth one-eighth of the total exam, or 12.5 percent. The highest possible score on the free-response section is 60 points.

A simple way for you to get an idea of the kinds of questions that might be asked, and the structure of an answer standard, is to visit the College Board website at **www.collegeboard.com**. In the section devoted to Advanced Placement, you will find AP U.S. Government and Politics free-response questions from the last five years, with the grading standard for each question. These are extremely helpful. They allow you to acquaint yourself with how the points break down and what the graders are seeking. Be sure to check them out.

Another way to understand the types of questions that may be asked is to look in the table of contents of an AP U.S. Government and Politics textbook. Test writers essentially take the concepts found in a few individual chapters and combine them into a question. For example, they may ask about the ways in which interest groups attempt to influence policy. Information about such a question will be found in the chapters on interest group politics, elections, and the branches of government. The test writers are trying to force you to synthesize (combine, analyze, and evaluate) many separate pieces of information into a coherent point of view. Therefore, the question may be written as follows:

1. Interest groups can have both a positive and negative impact on American politics.

    (a)   Describe one positive effect that interest groups have on politics.

    (b)   Describe one negative effect that interest groups have on politics.

    (c)   Choose one of the groups below and identify two methods it uses to affect public policy.
- NRA
- AARP
- AMA
- NOW

In the free-response section you will not be required to write a complete essay with a thesis statement, evidence, and conclusion: There simply isn't time. This response is an opportunity to showcase your knowledge of U.S. government and politics, not a time to highlight your understanding of proper syntax and your hatred of dangling modifiers. You won't be graded down if you *do* write a thesis statement, evidence, and conclusion, but this practice will waste precious time that you could have spent writing a more complete answer for what they *do* ask of you. **Do exactly the tasks that the question asks of you.** This may seem obvious, but many students get off track and neglect to address all facets of the questions with clear responses. If the question asks you to analyze data by explaining trends shown in a graph, do so. Make sure your analysis can be backed up by the data in the graph. If the graph question contains a Part B (it often does), it will probably ask for an explanation of the data in the graph. This part of the answer will come from your knowledge of the subject. Because time is a factor, and you will be awarded no more points for extras, do nothing more than what the question asks.

An example of a stimulus-type free-response question may look as follows:

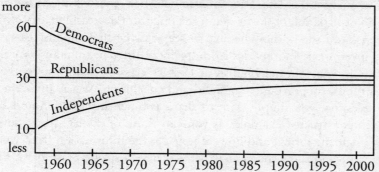

Percentage of U.S. Population Affiliated with a Political Party

2. Using the information in the figure and your knowledge of United States politics, complete the following tasks:

    (a)   From the data in the chart, identify two trends that have occurred in the membership of the political parties in the past forty years.

    (b)   Based on your knowledge of American politics, explain what impact the two trends that you identified in part (a) have had on those running for political office.

Part (a): Answer (Keep in mind that this is just an outline.)

- The data shows that the number of Republicans has remained constant.
- The data shows that the number of Democrats has declined.
- The data shows that the number of Independents has increased.
- The data shows that the two political parties are approximately equal in number.
- The data shows that the Independents have come from the Democratic Party.
- The data shows that there are now almost as many Independents as members of the two major parties.

Part (b): Answer

- Independents are people who belong to no party. They vote for the candidate they like best regardless of the party with whom the candidate is affiliated. Independents are usually upset with one of the parties because of the positions they have taken on particular issues. Independents tend to be centrists. Therefore candidates will try to appeal to Independents by taking centrist positions, because Independents will probably decide the outcome of an election. This often makes it difficult to differentiate the policy positions of candidates. Perhaps this is one reason voters say it doesn't matter who they vote for, which in turn can cause depressed voter turnout.

Note that the question in Part (a) does not ask for a thesis statement. It simply asks you to analyze the data. Part (b) also does not require a thesis statement. It contains an explanation of the data and the impact of decreasing party affiliations on elections. You should now be able to see that the free-response essay on the AP U.S. Government and Politics Exam really is different from an essay that you might write in your normal English or History class: It doesn't stress the importance of a thesis, supporting paragraphs, and conclusion. When answering a free-response question, you simply want to share as much information and as many strong, well-constructed examples as you can think of. Don't stress yourself out worrying about the format and flow. Simply get the information from your brain onto the paper and show the grader that you have a strong grasp of U.S. governmental policies and precedents.

Be Optimistic

Both the exam writers and the graders realize that 25 minutes is not very much time to respond to a question. They understand that it will take about five minutes for you to understand the question and begin to organize your answer. Obviously, there is not enough time to give a very in-depth answer. Because of the time constraint, you will have to choose only those parts of your answer that give the strongest response to the question. The graders are not looking for the final word on the subject. Instead, they are checking to see whether you can

- address the question

- clearly explain the issues involved

These should be your goals in writing your AP U.S. Government and Politics Exam free-response essays.

PLANNING AND WRITING YOUR FREE RESPONSE

There are two essential components to writing a successful timed free response. The first is to plan what you are going to write before you start writing. The second is to use a number of tried-and-true writing techniques that will make your essay better organized, better thought out, and better written.

Before You Start Writing

Read the question carefully and figure out what you are being asked. Then, brainstorm for a minute or two. In your test booklet, write down everything that comes to mind about the subject; there is room on the back pages of the booklet and in the blank space at the bottom of the question pages. Look at your notes and consider the results of your brainstorming session as you decide which points you will argue in your response. Tailor your argument to the information, but don't make an argument that you know is wrong or with which you disagree. If you do either of these things, your response will probably be awful. Finally, go through the results of your brainstorming. Some of what you wrote down will be "big picture" conclusions, some will be facts that can be used as evidence to support your conclusions, and some will be interesting material that, nonetheless, will not fit into a well-organized free-response essay and should be discarded.

Next, make an outline. The outline should be brief—just a few words for each paragraph. You should plan to write as many paragraphs as are appropriate for answering the question. For example, some free responses will require two paragraphs on relevant issues; others will need five. Sometimes the question or part of the question can be answered with a couple of paragraphs and a bulleted list. If the question does not require a full essay, you should not write one.

As You Are Writing

Observe the following guidelines:

- **Keep sentences as simple as possible.** Long sentences get convoluted very quickly and will give your graders a headache.

- **Use appropriate political science terminology.** Don't overdo it, however, because it will look as if you're trying to show off. Remember that good writing doesn't have to be complicated; most great ideas can be stated simply. Never use a word if you are unsure of its meaning or proper usage. A malapropism may give your graders a good laugh, but it won't earn you any points and will probably cost you a higher score.

- **Write clearly and neatly.** Here's an easy way to put graders in a good mood. Graders look at a lot of chicken scratches; it strains their eyes and makes them grumpy. Also keep in mind that they have as little as two minutes to read each response. Neatly written essays make them happy. When you cross out, do it neatly. Write in blue or black ink. If you're making any major changes—e.g., if you want to insert a paragraph in the middle of your response—make sure you indicate them clearly.

- **Define your terms.** Most questions require you to use terms that mean different things to different people. One person's "liberal" is another person's "conservative" and yet another person's "radical." The folks who grade the test want to know what you think these terms mean. When you use them, define them. Take particular care to define any such terms that appear in the question. Almost all official College Board materials stress this point, so don't forget: Define any term that you suspect can be defined in more than one way.

- **Use structural indicators to organize your paragraphs.** Another way to clarify your intentions is to organize your response around structural indicators. For example, if you are making a number of related points, number them ("First...Second...Finally..."). If you are attempting to compare and contrast two viewpoints, use the indicators "on the one hand" and "on the other hand" or "whereas."

- **Stick to your outline.** Unless you get an absolutely brilliant idea while you're writing, don't deviate from your outline. If you do, you'll risk winding up with an incoherent response.

- **Back up your ideas with examples.** Yes, we've said it already, but it bears repeating. Don't just throw ideas out there and hope that you're right. You will score big points if you substantiate your claims with facts. If you cannot recall real, specific examples, use hypothetical situations to illustrate your point.

- **Try not to write just one or two paragraphs.** A too-short response will hurt you more than will one that is too long.

How to Crack the Free-Response Questions

Answering the free-response questions on the AP U.S. Government and Politics Exam is not very different from answering the essay questions you have been answering all your life. The following are the keys to success:

- **Read the question carefully.** Tailor your answer to the question. When you have written all your notes and your outline, and you are prepared to begin writing your response, reread the question to ensure your answer is right on target.

- **Answer each part of the question directly.** If one part of the question asks how Jefferson's concern about term limitations is relevant today, you should probably have a sentence in your essay—and in a fairly prominent place such as the first paragraph or the first line in a subsequent paragraph—that reads "Jefferson's concern is relevant (or irrelevant) today." Don't be coy.

- **Don't panic.** As you scan the four questions, you may well come to rest on the one that deals with a subject your teacher didn't cover or you didn't get around to studying. Don't worry: Everyone finds some questions harder than others. To build your confidence, answer the question you find easiest before turning to the intimidating one.

- **Watch your time.** You need to average no more than 25 minutes per question. The biggest mistake you can make, with the exception of failing to respond to the question, is failing to leave yourself enough time to answer all four questions. It's okay to spend as much as 30 minutes on a given question, but you'd better make it worthwhile. You also probably don't want to spend that much time on the first essay or you'll feel rushed while writing the remaining three.

- **If you draw a total blank on a question, take a deep breath and ask yourself what you do know about the topic.** You may realize that you know more than you think. Try to figure out what the question is trying to ask and/or how you can approach it.

- **If you are running out of time on your fourth free-response question, abbreviate and write partial sentences.** The graders know that you may have to rush to finish the last question. Although, under ideal circumstances, you would write in complete, well-considered sentences, you may not have time to do so. Don't panic: Do the best you can and know that the graders will give you some leeway at the end of your response—especially if you are clear and coherent at the beginning and throughout the middle.

Summary

o   Read questions carefully. Look for the multiple parts of each question. Make sure you respond to each of these parts of the question—the graders will be looking for your response to each part.

o   Mark up the question. You may bracket the core of the question, underline the operative words such as identify, discuss, describe, and analyze, or circle limiters like, "since 1992," "give one example," and "list three."

o   Look out for questions that require a definition of a term. If they ask for a definition, write one.

o   Although you are not writing a history essay, making chronological points can strengthen your writing in certain areas (e.g., the development of civil rights law). Do not write a mere list of historical data points in chronological order. Political science relies on analytical writing to substantiate claims, so back up your statements with proof.

o   Don't start writing until you have brainstormed, chosen a thesis if required, and written a brief outline.

o   Follow your outline. Stick to one main idea per paragraph. Support your ideas with facts.

o   Write clearly and neatly. Don't use sentences that are too long. Toss in a couple of political science terms that you know you won't misuse. When in doubt, stick to simple syntax and vocabulary.

o   Bring a watch to the exam and spend 25 minutes on each response. Write explicitly and without equivocation.

o   Every piece of data that supports your argument should be linked to it. Do not just list information without relating it to the point you are trying to make.

Part IV
Drills

Chapter 3
Constitutional Underpinnings

DRILL 1

1. The supremacy clause of the Constitution does which of the following?

   (A) Favors federal laws when conflict arises between federal and state laws
   (B) Overturns federal laws that conflict with state laws
   (C) Gives precedence to state laws when disagreement occurs between federal and state laws
   (D) Provides the president with the supreme power to overturn state laws that conflict with federal laws
   (E) Grants the Supreme Court the authority to decide whether or not to nullify federal laws

2. The requirement that treaties negotiated by the president must be approved by two-thirds of the Senate before going into effect is an example of

   (A) judicial review
   (B) the system of checks and balances
   (C) judicial restraint
   (D) the process of ratifying an amendment
   (E) judicial activism

3. Which of the following is a purpose of providing Supreme Court justices with tenure?

   (A) Tenure forces justices to remain loyal to political affiliations.
   (B) It is difficult to find qualified individuals to become Supreme Court justices.
   (C) Tenure removes direct political pressures.
   (D) Tenure ensures lifelong cooperation between the executive, legislative, and judicial branches.
   (E) Tenure ensures that justices will make decisions that reflect the will of the American people.

4. Which of the following events showed that a strong, constitutionally designed national government was necessary to safeguard property and maintain order?

   (A) The U.S. joining the North American Free Trade Agreement (NAFTA)
   (B) *Wesberry v. Sanders*
   (C) The Great Compromise
   (D) Shays's Rebellion
   (E) The Virginia Plan

5. Which of the following powers is granted to the president by the Constitution?

   (A) The capacity to make war
   (B) The ability to influence policy
   (C) The power to remove Supreme Court justices
   (D) The authority to communicate with both Congress and the American people
   (E) The ability to declare war

6. All of the following are concurrent powers under the federalist system of the Constitution EXCEPT the power to

   (A) collect taxes
   (B) build roads
   (C) operate courts of law
   (D) borrow money
   (E) coin money

7. All of the following statements about the Commerce Clause are true EXCEPT:

   (A) The Commerce Clause does not give Congress the power to regulate guns near state-operated schools.
   (B) The Commerce Clause is one of the most fundamental powers the founders provided to Congress.
   (C) The Constitution states that Congress shall have power to regulate commerce with foreign nations, states, and Indian tribes.
   (D) The Commerce clause provides wide-ranging power to the United States over navigable waters.
   (E) The Court has held, since *Gibbons v. Ogden*, that Congress can regulate both commercial and non-commercial transactions that involve interstate commerce.

8. The congressional power to regulate interstate commerce

   (A) was decreased with the ruling in *Gibbons v. Ogden* (1824)
   (B) does not include the power to regulate interstate navigation
   (C) never included the ability to regulate recreational facilities
   (D) includes the power to regulate non-commercial transactions
   (E) is the power most often challenged in federal courts

9. The line-item veto

  (A) grants senators the right to veto individual sections of state legislation
  (B) was declared unconstitutional as it violated the separation of powers
  (C) occurs if the president does nothing with a bill for 10 days
  (D) was last used by President Obama in the Patient Protection and Affordable Care Act
  (E) grants the president the power to veto state legislation

10. The section of the Constitution that prohibits the government from designating an official religion of the United States is referred to as the

  (A) establishment clause
  (B) exclusionary rule
  (C) dealignment
  (D) realignment
  (E) Thirteenth Amendment

11. A key characteristic of a federalist government is

  (A) the ability to grant titles of nobility
  (B) shared power amongst national and local governments
  (C) that decisions are made by an external member-state legislature
  (D) the state's authority to act with absolute power in foreign affairs
  (E) the power to use money from the treasury without passage of an appropriations bill

12. The Constitution and its amendments mandate all of the following EXCEPT:

  (A) Congress shall have power to lay and collect taxes on incomes.
  (B) A well-regulated militia and the right of the people to bear arms shall not be infringed.
  (C) The right of the people to be secure in their persons, houses, papers, and effects, against unreasonable search and seizures, shall not be violated.
  (D) The right of U.S. citizens to vote shall not be denied based on gender.
  (E) In times of heightened national security, soldiers may be quartered in any house without the consent of the owner.

13. All of the following statements about the national government under the Articles of Confederation are true EXCEPT:

  (A) There was no national currency.
  (B) There was no effective control over interstate trade.
  (C) No Supreme Court existed to interpret law.
  (D) A majority rule was needed to amend the Articles of Confederation.
  (E) The government could not draft soldiers.

14. Which of the following statements regarding voting is false?

  (A) The Fifteenth Amendment banned laws that would prevent African Americans from voting based on race.
  (B) Jim Crow laws were passed in the post-Reconstruction Era South to enforce racial segregation and restrict the rights of African Americans.
  (C) The Twenty-fourth Amendment imposed poll taxes to prevent blacks and poor whites from voting.
  (D) The Voting Rights Act of 1965 allowed the federal government to register voters in states in which less than 50% of the population was registered to vote.
  (E) The Nineteenth Amendment granted women the right to vote.

15. The document that advocates for a large republic and warns of the dangers of democracy is the

  (A) *Federalist* No. 10
  (B) Necessary and Proper Clause
  (C) Bill of Rights
  (D) Great Compromise
  (E) New Jersey Plan

16. The section of the Constitution that allows Congress to pass laws that are "necessary and proper" is referred to as

  (A) the exclusionary rule
  (B) the privileges and immunities clause
  (C) the elastic clause
  (D) prior restraint
  (E) eminent domain

DRILL 2

1. Which of the following events can occur during the amendment process?

   (A) Two-thirds of the state legislatures must ratify an amendment.
   (B) Three-fourths of the state legislatures can petition Congress to call a constitutional convention.
   (C) The president can amend the constitution in times of war without congressional approval.
   (D) A proposed amendment can be approved by two-thirds of both houses of Congress.
   (E) Two-thirds of special state ratifying conventions can approve an amendment.

2. Which of the following statements about the "wall of separation" is FALSE?

   (A) The "wall of separation" relates to the separation of Church and State.
   (B) Thomas Jefferson used the phrase to describe the First Amendment's restriction on the legislative branch federal government.
   (C) The "wall of separation" is explicitly stated in the Constitution.
   (D) The phrase played a major role in the ruling of *Everson v. Board of Education* (1947).
   (E) In *Engel v. Vitale*, the Court ruled prayer in public school unconstitutional as it breaches the "wall of separation."

3. Which of the following amendments did not impact voting rights in the United States?

   (A) Ninth Amendment
   (B) Fifteenth Amendment
   (C) Nineteenth Amendment
   (D) Twenty-fourth Amendment
   (E) Twenty-sixth Amendment

4. Which of the following statements is true regarding *The Federalist Papers*?

   (A) They were a series of newspaper articles supporting the Articles of Confederation.
   (B) They are not the primary source for understanding the original intent of the Framers.
   (C) Alexander Hamilton, John Jay, and Benjamin Franklin wrote *The Federalist Papers*.
   (D) They advocate for a large confederation.
   (E) They warn against the dangers of democracy.

5. When the Supreme Court applies the Bill of Rights to state laws on a case-by-case basis, this is

   (A) use of the preferred position doctrine
   (B) referred to as selective incorporation
   (C) an example of a shield law
   (D) referred to as judicial review
   (E) an example of separation of powers

6. Which of the following was not an accomplishment of the United States government under the Articles of Confederation?

   (A) The negotiation of the treaty that ended the Revolutionary War
   (B) Establishing the precedent of federalism
   (C) Establishing the Northwest Ordinance
   (D) Satisfactory resolution of Shays's Rebellion.
   (E) Victory in the Revolutionary War

7. Which amendment mandates that American citizens cannot be denied the right to vote based on race, color, or prior servitude?

   (A) Sixth Amendment
   (B) Eleventh Amendment
   (C) Thirteenth Amendment
   (D) Fifteenth Amendment
   (E) Nineteenth Amendment

8. When an individual tries to interpret the meaning of a constitutional Amendment, he or she is

   (A) attempting to understand the original intent of the framers of the Constitution
   (B) enacting the power of judicial review
   (C) enacting the power of original jurisdiction
   (D) using the power of eminent domain
   (E) practicing due process

Free Response

Time—25 minutes

1. Both the Constitution and the Bill of Rights contain provisions that limit the power of the federal government. In addition, these documents have been amended, either formally or informally, over the years to restrict the power of state governments as well.

   (a) Explain the limitations that each of the following place on the authority of state governments.

   - The doctrine of selective incorporation
   - The Naturalization Clause of the Fourteenth Amendment

   (b) Explain the limitations that each of the following places on the authority of the federal government.

   - Free exercise clause
   - Civil trial by jury

   (c) Describe one limitation that the Constitution places on the authority of the executive branch.

DRILL 3

1. The full faith and credit clause refers to the

   (A) ability of Congress to pass laws "necessary and proper" to the performance of its duties
   (B) requirement that marriages, licenses, and other acts of state courts in one state are honored in all states
   (C) prohibition of the government from designating an official religion of America
   (D) system that prevents any branch of government from becoming too powerful
   (E) concept that a state may not refuse police protection or access to its courts to American citizens because they live in a different state

2. Reserved powers refer to constitutional powers that

   (A) are shared by both state and national governments
   (B) are granted solely to the federal government
   (C) are specifically enumerated in the Tenth Amendment
   (D) belong solely to the states
   (E) are provided to the states when deemed necessary by the Supreme Court

3. What was the primary point of contention between the Federalists and Anti-Federalists?

   (A) The power of the state governments relative to the federal government
   (B) Women's suffrage
   (C) The power of the president relative to Congress
   (D) Free speech and the exercise thereof
   (E) The continuation of slavery

4. A system of government in which political power is mainly divided between the central government and regional governments is called

   (A) a confederation
   (B) a system of separation of powers
   (C) an autocracy
   (D) a democracy
   (E) a federalist system

5. Which of the following is an important principle of the United States Constitution?

   (A) Free health care
   (B) A president with the power of a monarch
   (C) Separation of powers
   (D) Truth in advertising
   (E) The establishment of the Internal Revenue Service

6. The United States Constitution leaves creation of voter eligibility requirements to which of the following?

   (A) The president
   (B) Individual states
   (C) The chief justice of the Supreme Court
   (D) Civil rights organizations
   (E) The Speaker of the House

7. Federalism is best explained as the relationship between

   (A) the Army and the Navy
   (B) the president and the Supreme Court
   (C) freedom of speech and freedom of the press
   (D) states and the national government
   (E) the House and the Senate

8. Which of the following describes a difference between the Constitution and the Articles of Confederation?

   (A) The Constitution prevents Congress from creating laws.
   (B) The Constitution promotes the sovereignty of states more than the Articles of Confederation did.
   (C) The Constitution created a system of federal courts while the Articles of Confederation did not.
   (D) The approval of all states is required in order to amend the Constitution, but the Articles of Confederation could be amended by three-fourths of the states.
   (E) The Constitution distributes money equally to all states.

Free Response

Time—25 minutes

1. Article I of the Constitution establishes a Congress that consists of two separate houses. Those houses differ not only in the ways in which members are elected to those houses, but also in the powers that are apportioned to each house.

    (a) Describe one of the powers held solely by the Senate. Explain why that power was apportioned to the Senate.

    (b) Describe one of the powers held solely by the House of Representatives. Explain why that power was apportioned to the House of Representatives.

    (c) Discuss two advantages of a legislative system that is composed of two separate houses.

DRILL 4

1. The Constitution does NOT grant to the federal government the power to

   (A) levy taxes
   (B) coin money
   (C) negotiate treaties
   (D) declare war
   (E) create political parties

2. Shays's Rebellion exposed the weaknesses of the

   (A) Articles of Confederation
   (B) Constitution
   (C) Bill of Rights
   (D) Great Compromise
   (E) Three-fifths Compromise

3. Which of the following is a power of the presidency that does NOT require congressional approval?

   (A) The appointment and installment of Supreme Court justices
   (B) The power to force Congress into session
   (C) The ability to use money from the Treasury to wage war
   (D) The power to make and declare war
   (E) The capacity to negotiate treaties and establish treaties

4. Which of the following would lead to the end of a Supreme Court justice's tenure?

   I.   Removal following impeachment
   II. Presidential removal
   III. Voluntary retirement
   IV. Resignation

   (A) I only
   (B) I and III only
   (C) II and IV only
   (D) II, III, and IV only
   (E) I, III, and IV only

5. Which of the following was NOT a weakness of the federal government under the Articles of Confederation?

   (A) The lack of a national currency
   (B) The lack of a Supreme Court to interpret the laws
   (C) The requirement that all 13 states approve new legislation
   (D) Dependence on state legislatures for revenue
   (E) The inability to control import and export taxes imposed between states

6. Which of the following is NOT true of the First Amendment's establishment clause?

   (A) It forbids the government to establish a national religion.
   (B) It bars the use of secular governmental programs that impede the observance of a religion.
   (C) It is one of the least contentious of all clauses found in the Constitution.
   (D) In conjunction with the free exercise clause, it bans government involvement in religious matters.
   (E) It prohibits the government from taking actions that favor one religion over another.

7. In the United States, voting rights cannot not be denied or abridged EXCEPT

   (A) on account of gender
   (B) to a citizen who is eighteen years of age or older
   (C) to a citizen who is an imprisoned, or released, felon
   (D) to an individual born or naturalized in the United States
   (E) to a citizen on account of race, color, or previous condition of servitude

8. All of the following are prohibited by United States legislation EXCEPT

   (A) gender discrimination by institutions of higher education that receive federal funds
   (B) the execution of individuals who are mentally retarded
   (C) basing an employee's salary on race, gender, religion, or national origin
   (D) the formation of political action committees by unions
   (E) the use of a line-item veto

Free Response

Time—25 minutes

1. Since 1789, the United States Constitution has defined the organization and function of the government. Despite this continuity, there have been changes in the way the scope and purpose of the Constitution is interpreted.

   (a) Describe two ways in which formal amendments can be made to the Constitution.

   (b) Explain why formal amendments are rarely made.

   (c) Explain two other ways through which the scope and purpose of the Constitution have been changed. Describe one specific example of each method.

Chapter 4
Constitutional Underpinnings: Answers and Explanations

ANSWER KEY

Multiple-Choice Questions

Drill 1
1. A
2. B
3. C
4. D
5. A
6. E
7. E
8. E
9. B
10. A
11. B
12. E
13. D
14. C
15. A
16. C

Drill 2
1. D
2. C
3. A
4. E
5. B
6. D
7. D
8. A

Drill 3
1. B
2. D
3. A
4. E
5. C
6. B
7. D
8. C

Drill 4
1. E
2. A
3. B
4. E
5. C
6. C
7. C
8. D

EXPLANATIONS

Drill 1

1. **A** The supremacy clause of the Constitution requires conflicts between federal and state law to be resolved in favor of federal law. Furthermore, state constitutions or laws that violate the U.S. Constitution, federal treaties, or international treaties can be nullified through the supremacy clause.

2. **B** The requirement that treaties negotiated by the president must be approved by two-thirds of the Senate before going into effect is an example of the system of checks and balances. While the president has the power to negotiate, no treaty will go into effect until two-thirds of the Senate approves of the treaty. Choice (A) can be eliminated because judicial review is the power of the Supreme Court to declare laws and executive actions unconstitutional. Choice (C) can be eliminated because judicial restraint refers to the actions of a court that show an unwillingness to break precedent or to overturn legislative or executive acts. Choice (D) can be eliminated because the process of ratifying an amendment requires that both houses of Congress approve the legislation by a two-thirds vote. Finally, eliminate choice (E) because judicial activism refers to a court that often strikes down, alters, or overturns the acts of the legislative and/or executive branch.

3. **C** Subject to good behavior, Supreme Court justices were given tenure by the framers of the Constitution in order to ensure that justices are free from direct political pressures. Eliminate choices (A) and (E) because justices can change party affiliation and are not forced to make popular decisions. While choice (B) may be true, it is not the purpose of providing tenure to Supreme Court justices. Finally, choice (D) can be eliminated because tenure does not ensure lifelong cooperation between the Supreme Court and the branches of government.

4. **D** Shays's Rebellion was a six-month rebellion in which over 1,000 armed farmers attacked a federal arsenal to protest the foreclosure of farms. Shays's Rebellion alarmed the statesmen and exposed the inadequacies of the Articles of Confederation. Thus, the importance of Shays's Rebellion to the development of the Constitution was that it indicated that a strong, constitutionally designed national government was needed to protect property and maintain order.

5. **A** Only Congress has the power to declare war, even though the president, as commander-in-chief of the armed forces, can deploy troops; thus, choice (E) is incorrect. While the president does have the power to influence policy and communicate with both Congress and the American people, these power are informal and not enumerated by the Constitution; accordingly, eliminate choices (B) and (D). Eliminate choice (C) because the president cannot remove a Supreme Court justice from his or her position. Rather, if the need arises, a justice can be impeached by the House and then tried in the Senate.

6. **E** Federalism is a system of government under which the national, state, and local governments share power. Concurrent powers are those shared by federal and state governments. The powers to collect taxes, build roads, operate courts of law, and borrow money are all concurrent powers; thus, choices (A), (B), (C), and (D) are incorrect. Choice (E) is correct because Congress alone has the power to coin money.

7. **E** Choices (A), (B), (C), and (D) are all accurate statements regarding the Commerce Clause. However, choice (E) is false and therefore the best response. Since *Gibbons v. Ogden*, the Court has held that Congress can solely regulate commercial transactions that significantly affect interstate travel.

8. **E** The congressional power to regulate interstate commerce is the most frequently challenged power in federal courts. Eliminate choice (A) because congressional power to regulate interstate commerce increased with the ruling in *Gibbons v. Ogden* (1824). Eliminate choice (B) because the ruling in *Gibbons v. Ogden* stated that the power to regulate interstate commerce also included the power to regulate interstate navigation. Eliminate choice (C) because in *Daniel v. Paul* (1969) the court ruled that the federal government could regulate recreational facilities. Finally, eliminate (D) because in *Garcia v. San Antonio Metropolitan Transit Authority* (1985) the court ruled that Congress can only regulate activities that are linked with commercial transactions.

9. **B** The line-item veto, passed by Congress in 1996, granted the president the power to veto individual parts of a bill. However, in *Clinton v. New York City* (1996), the Supreme Court declared the line-item veto an unconstitutional delegation of legislative authority to the president. Eliminate choice (A) because the line-item veto was never intended for, or used by, senators. Eliminate choice (D) because Obama has never used the line-item veto. Eliminate choice (C) because if a president fails to do anything with a bill for 10 days, the bill is pocket-vetoed. Finally, choice (E) can be eliminated because the line-item veto was never intended for presidential use over state legislation.

10. **A** The establishment clause is a section in the First Amendment that prohibits the government from designating one faith as the official religion of the United States. Eliminate choice (B) because the exclusionary rule prohibits the use of illegally obtained evidence at trial. Choice (C) can be eliminated because dealignment refers to a recent trend in which voters act increasingly independent of a party affiliation. Eliminate choice (D) because realignment occurs when a party undergoes a significant shift in its electoral base and/or political agenda. Finally, eliminate choice (E) because the Thirteenth Amendment abolished slavery.

11. **B** A federalist government is a system of government under which the national, state, and local governments share powers. Eliminate choices (A) and (E) because the federal government neither has the power to grant titles of nobility nor the power to use money from the treasury without passage and approval of an appropriations bill. Eliminate choice (C) because a confederation is a system of government in which decisions are made by an external member-state legislation. Finally,

eliminate choice (D) because a federalist government does not grant states the absolute authority in foreign affairs.

12.   E   According to the Third Amendment, no soldier shall, in time of peace be quartered in any house, without the consent of the owner, nor in time of war, but in a manner prescribed by law. Accordingly, choice (E) is not mandated by the Constitution. Eliminate choice (A) because the Sixteenth Amendment states that Congress shall have power to lay and collect taxes on incomes, from whatever source derived, without apportionment among the several states, and without regard to any census of enumeration. Choice (B) can be eliminated because the Second Amendment states that a well-regulated militia, being necessary to the security of a free state, the right of the people to keep and bear arms, shall not be infringed. Eliminate choice (C) because the Fourth Amendment ensures the right of the people to be secure in their persons, houses, papers, and effects, against unreasonable search and seizures, shall not be violated.

13.   D   Under the Articles of Confederation, the national government had no national currency, could not effectively control interstate trade, did not have a Supreme Court to interpret law, and was unable to draft soldiers. Thus, eliminate choices (A), (B), (C), and (E). However, under the Articles of Confederation, the national government needed unanimity, not majority rule, to amend the Articles.

14.   C   All of the statements regarding voting are true except for choice (C). The Twenty-fourth Amendment outlawed poll taxes that had been used to prevent blacks and poor whites from voting.

15.   A   Alexander Hamilton, James Madison, and John Jay wrote a series of articles supporting the Constitution; these papers were deemed *The Federalist Papers* and are the primary source for understanding the intent of the framers of the Constitution. *The Federalist* No. 10 advocates for a large republic and warns of the dangers of democracy. Eliminate choice (B) because the necessary and proper clause allows Congress to "make all laws" that appear "necessary and proper" to implement its delegated powers. Eliminate the Bill of Rights because these rights protect the rights of individuals from government infringement. Eliminate choice (D) because the Great Compromise created a bicameral legislature. Finally, eliminate choice (E) because the New Jersey Plan proposed that each state would be represented equally in the legislature.

16.   C   As stated in the Constitution, the elastic clause allows Congress to pass laws that are "necessary and proper" to the performance of its duties. The clause is deemed "elastic" since it allows Congress to stretch its powers beyond those enumerated in the Constitution. Eliminate choice (A) because the exclusionary rule prohibits the use of illegally obtained evidence at trial. Eliminate choice (B) because the privileges and immunities clause dictates that a state cannot refuse police protection or access to its courts to U.S. citizens because they live in a different state. Choice (D) can be eliminated because prior restraint refers to the censorship of news material before it is made public. Finally, choice (E) can be eliminated because eminent domain refers to the power of the government to take away property for public use as long as there is just compensation.

Drill 2

1. **D**   One way to amend the Constitution is to propose the amendment to both houses of Congress and receive two-thirds approval in each. Eliminate choice (A) because three-fourths of the state legislatures must ratify an amendment. Choice (B) is incorrect because a constitutional convention is called by two-thirds of state legislatures. Eliminate choice (C) because the president can never amend the constitution without congressional approval. Finally, choice (E) can be eliminated because three-fourths of special state ratifying conventions can approve an amendment.

2. **C**   While many individuals believe that the First Amendment mandates a "wall of separation" between Church and State, the concept is neither stated in the Constitution nor the Amendments. All of the remaining answer choices are true with regards to the 'wall of separation.'

3. **A**   The Ninth Amendment states that rights enumerated in the Constitution can not be manipulated to lessen or nullify other rights. The Fifteenth Amendment banned laws that would prevent African Americans or previous slaves from voting; eliminate choice (B). Choice (C) can be eliminated because the Nineteenth Amendment granted women the right to vote. Eliminate choice (D) because the Twenty-fourth Amendment outlawed poll taxes, which had prevented blacks and poor whites from voting. Choice (E) can be eliminated because the Twenty-sixth Amendment extended the right to vote to 18-year-olds.

4. **E**   *The Federalist Papers* were a series of newspaper articles, written by Alexander Hamilton, James Madison, and John Jay, that were designed to persuade the states of the wisdom of a strong central government coupled with autonomous political power retained by the states. *The Federalist* No. 10, perhaps the most famous of *The Federalist Papers*, warns against the dangers of democracy and advocates for a large confederation. *The Federalist Papers* are the primary source for understanding the original intent of the framers of the Constitution. Accordingly, eliminate choices (A), (B), (C), and (D).

5. **B**   Selective incorporation refers to the Supreme Court's process of applying the Bill of Rights to state laws on a case-by-case basis. Eliminate choice (A) because the preferred position doctrine refers to the Court's belief that freedom of speech is fundamental to liberty and any limits on free speech must address severe threats to the nation. Eliminate choice (C) because shield laws are intended to protect reporters in state cases. Judicial review refers to the power of the Supreme Court to declare laws and executive actions unconstitutional. Choice (E) can be eliminated because separation of powers does not relate to this topic.

6. **D**   All of the accomplishments except for answer choice (D) were accomplishments of the U.S. government under the Articles of Confederation. However, the government was unable to effectively

deal with Shays's Rebellion, a six-month rebellion in which farmers attacked a federal arsenal in Massachusetts and which was a major point of contention at the Constitutional Convention.

7. **D** The Fifteenth Amendment states that the right of citizens of the United States to vote shall not be denied or abridged by the United States or by any state on account of race, color, or previous condition of servitude. The Sixth Amendment guarantees the right to a speedy and public trial by an impartial jury in the state wherein the crime was committed; eliminate choice (A). Choice (B) can be eliminated because the Eleventh Amendment lays the foundation for sovereign immunity. The Thirteenth Amendment abolishes both slavery and involuntary servitude; eliminate choice (C). Eliminate choice (E) because the Nineteenth Amendment grants women the right to vote.

8. **A** The doctrine of original intent is that the Supreme Court justices must consider, and emphasize, the original thinking of the framers of the Constitution when considering constitutional matters. Eliminate choice (B) because the power of judicial review is the power of the Supreme Court to declare laws and executive actions unconstitutional. The power of original jurisdiction refers to a Court's power to initially try a case; eliminate choice (C). Choice (D) can be eliminated because eminent domain refers to the power of the government to take away property for public use as long as compensation is provided to the property owners. Due process refers to established legal procedures for the arrest and trial of accused criminals; eliminate choice (E).

Free-Response Question 1

Students may earn a total of five points on this question. Two points are available for part (a), two for part (b), and one for part (c).

Part (a) asks you to describe two limitations to the authority of state governments. You will receive 1 point for each part of the answer. Here are the points you need to make.

- Doctrine of selective incorporation: Elaborates on which of the limitations on power explained in the Bill of Rights apply to states, not just to the national government. Through various Supreme Court cases, many, though not all, of the provisions in the Bill of Rights have been explicitly applied to states.
- Naturalization Clause: States cannot make laws that deny privileges, constitutional rights, or legal protection to any citizen, born or naturalized, within their borders.

Part (b) asks you to describe two limitations to the authority of the federal government. You will receive 1 point for each part of the answer. Here are the points you need to make.

- Free exercise clause: Prevents the government from passing laws restricting the practice of a religion.
- Civil trial by jury: Guarantees the right to a trial by jury in civil matters. The government, or federally appointment judges, cannot unilaterally decide to imprison someone, thereby taking away the right to freedom, without this due process.

Part (c) asks you to describe any one limitation on the authority of the executive branch. To earn credit, some limitations you can discuss include the requirement for congressional approval of presidential appointees and treaties, the power of congress to override a presidential veto, or the power of Congress to impeach the president.

Drill 3

1. **B**   The full faith and credit clause is a section of the Constitution that required states to honor one another's licenses, marriages, and other acts of state courts. Eliminate choice (A) because it refers to the elastic clause. Choice (C) can be eliminated because it refers to the establishment clause. The system that prevents any branch of government from becoming too powerful by dividing important tasks among the three governmental branches is the system of checks and balances; eliminate choice (D). Choice (E) can be eliminated because it refers to the privileges and immunity clause.

2. **D**   Reserved powers are constitutional powers that belong solely to the states. According to the Tenth Amendment, reserved powers include those not specifically granted to the national government or denied to state governments in the Constitution. Thus, choices (A), (B), and (E) are incorrect. Further, since the details of such powers are not given in the Constitution, eliminate (C).

3. **A**   A subject of intense debate among the Founders was in regards to how strong the federal government should be, relative to the states. The Federalists wanted a strong central government and the Anti-Federalists were afraid the states would lose too much of their powers to the federal government. Choice (B) is incorrect because women's suffrage was not an issue of major debate between the Federalists and Anti-Federalists. Choice (C) is incorrect because Federalists and Anti-Federalists believed most of the power in the federal government would be exercised by Congress. Choice (D) is incorrect because the Federalists and Anti-Federalists agreed upon the importance of freedom of speech. Although slavery was debated at the time of the founding of the United States, it was not the primary point of contention between Federalists and Anti-Federalists.

4. **E**   Federalism describes a system of government under which the national government and local governments share powers. Eliminate choice (A) because a confederation is a loose alliance of independent states with a weak central government. Eliminate choice (B) because the separation of powers prevents a single branch of government from becoming too powerful. Choice (C) can be eliminated because an autocratic government has a single ruler whose decisions are not subject to review. Eliminate choice (D) because a democracy is rule by a government chosen by election.

5. **C**   One of the basic tenets of the Constitution is the separation of powers among the three branches of government: legislative, judicial, and executive. Therefore, choice (B) is incorrect. Choice (A) is incorrect because free health care was not included in the Constitution. Choice (D) is incorrect because "truth in advertising" laws came about in 1914 with the establishment of the Federal Trade Commission. Similarly, choice (E) is incorrect because the Internal Revenue Service was created in 1862, well after the ratification of the Constitution.

6. **B** Article I, Section 4, of the U.S. Constitution leaves decisions regarding voter eligibility to the state legislatures. Choices (A), (C), and (E) are incorrect because the federal government does not determine voter eligibility requirements, even though the Supreme Court has issued decisions regarding eligible voters' access to the ballot box. Choice (D) is incorrect because, although civil rights organizations may want certain eligibility requirements eliminated, the organizations do not make the decisions themselves.

7. **D** Federalism is the power relationship between the United States government and the governments of the fifty states. Choice (A) is incorrect because the Army and Navy are two branches of the armed forces of the federal government, unrelated to federalism. Choice (B) is incorrect because the relationship between the president and Supreme Court is an example of separation of powers within the federal government. Choice (C) is incorrect because free speech and free press are First Amendment guarantees. Choice (E) is incorrect because the relationship between the House and Senate is an example of a bicameral legislature, within the federal government, not of federalism.

8. **C** The Constitution created a stronger federal government than did the Articles of Confederation. One sign of this is the federal court system created by the Constitution. Choice (A) is incorrect because Article I, Section 1 of the Constitution explicitly gives Congress the power to make laws. Choice (B) is incorrect because the Articles of Confederation promoted the sovereignty of the states by creating a weak central government. Choice (D) is incorrect because an amendment to the Articles of Confederation required the approval of all states while an amendment to the Constitution requires the approval of only three-fourths of the states. Choice (E) is incorrect because neither the Constitution nor the Articles of Confederation distribute money equally to all states.

Free-Response Question 1

Students may earn a total of six points on this question. Two points are available for part (a), two for part (b), and two for part (c).

Part (a) asks you to describe a power held solely by the Senate and explain why the Senate alone holds that power. You will receive 1 point for each part of the answer.

Some of the powers you might discuss include

- Approving presidential appointments of federal officials and judges
- Ratifying treaties
- Trying impeached officials

Some of the explanations you might discuss include

- Members tend to have more experience
- Members are better able to reflect state interests because they are elected every six years (initially they were appointed by state legislatures)
- Member terms are staggered, which prevents a takeover of the Senate by one popular faction

Part (b) asks you to describe a power held solely by the House of Representatives and explain why the House alone holds that power. You will receive 1 point for each part of the answer.

Some of the powers you might discuss include

- Proposing new tax bills
- Selecting the new president in the case of an electoral college deadlock
- Impeaching government officials

Some of the explanations you might discuss include

- Members are closer to the people because they represent smaller and more equally-sized constituency
- Members cannot be appointed by the governor in case of a vacancy
- Members are elected every two years, so they are more responsive to public opinion

Part (c) asks you to describe the advantages of a legislature that has two parties. You will receive 1 point for each advantage you describe. Here are some of the points you can make.

- Slowing the democratic process through checks to ensure laws are necessary and proper
- Equal representation in the Senate for states with small populations (compromise reached among the framers at the Constitutional Convention)
- Forcing compromise among competing state and minority interests since bills must be passed by both houses
- Enforcement of the federalist system

Drill 4

1. **E** Political parties are not mentioned in the Constitution; in fact, some Founders hoped that political parties would not emerge. Choices (A), (B), and (D) are incorrect because they are powers granted to Congress by Article I, Section 8. Choice (C) is incorrect because Article II, Section 2 grants the president the power to make treaties with the "advice and consent" of the Senate.

2. **A** Prior to the creation of the Constitution, the first government of the United States was formed under the Articles of Confederation. Unfortunately, the Articles of Confederation had numerous weaknesses that placed the newly independent states at risk. During Shays's Rebellion, such weakness was exposed when over 1,000 armed farmers attacked a federal arsenal to protest the foreclosure of farms in western Massachusetts. Due to the inability of the state to handle the rebellion, a Constitutional Convention was called, during which the Articles of Confederation were abandoned and the Constitution was created.

3. **B** One of the formal powers of the president is the power to force Congress into session. Choices (A) and (E) can be eliminated because both the installment of Supreme Court justices and the establishment of treaties require Senate approval. Choice (C) can be eliminated because if war is

declared, the president is at the mercy of Congress for money to fund the war. Finally, eliminate choice (D) because the president can make war, but only Congress has the power to declare war.

4.   **E**   After presidential nomination and Senate confirmation of a Supreme Court justice, the justices have lifelong tenure unless they are removed following impeachment, retire, or resign. The president does not have the power to remove a Supreme Court justice once appointed. Accordingly, the correct answer is choice (E).

5.   **C**   There were a number of weaknesses of the federal government under the Articles of Confederation including, but not limited to, the lack of a national currency, the absence of a Supreme Court to interpret laws, the dependence on state legislatures for revenue, and the inability to control import and export taxes imposed between states. However, under the Articles of Confederation, unanimous approval among the states was not necessary to pass legislation. Rather, the government only needed approval from 9 out of the 13 states to pass legislation.

6.   **C**   The establishment clause states that Congress shall not establish a national religion and, in conjunction with the free exercise clause, bars governmental involvement in religious matters. The establishment clause prohibits the government from establishing of a national religion, favoring one religion over another, and implementing secular programs that hinder the observance of a religion. However, due to the nature of religious beliefs and practices, the establishment clause is one of the more contentious Constitutional clauses.

7.   **C**   Felony disenfranchisement is the practice of forbidding citizens from voting because they have been convicted of a felony. Contrary to the numerous laws that negatively impact a citizen's right to vote, felony disenfranchisement laws continue to be held constitutional in the United States. Accordingly, the correct answer is choice (C). The Nineteenth Amendment guarantees women's suffrage, the Twenty-sixth Amendment guarantees the right to vote for people 18 years of age and older, and the Fifteenth Amendment guarantees the right to vote for all citizens regardless of race, color, or previous condition of servitude.

8.   **D**   The 1974 Federal Election Campaign Act allows corporations, unions, and trade associations to form political action committees in order to raise campaign funds. Eliminate choice (A) because the Title IX, Higher Education Act (1972) prohibits gender discrimination in institutions that receive federal funds. Choice (B) can be eliminated because the case *Atkins v. Virginia* ruled that executing the mentally retarded violated the ban on cruel and unusual punishment, as stated in the Eighth Amendment. Eliminate choice (C) because the Equal Pay Act of 1963 made it illegal to base employee pay on race, religion, gender, or nation of origin. Choice (E) can be eliminated because the case of *Clinton v. New York* ruled that the use of a line-item veto violates the presentment clause of the Constitution.

Free Response Question 1

Students may earn a total of eight points on this question. Two points are available for part (a), two for part (b), and four for part (c).

Part (a) asks you to explain how formal amendments are made to the Constitution. You'll earn one point for each of the two you explain. Although the question does not state so, one must be about the proposal and one must be about ratification.

Proposal may include

- Two-thirds vote (extraordinary, not simple, majority) in the Senate and the House of Representatives
- National convention called by Congress but initiated by the request of two-thirds of the state legislatures

Ratification may include

- Approval of three-fourths of the state legislatures
- Special conventions in three-fourths of the states

Part (b) asks you to explain why formal amendments are rarely made. You will earn one point for stating a reason and other another point for elaborating on that reason. Some of the possible reasons you may choose to discuss include the difficulty of obtaining the number of votes needed, the cost incurred by having a convention, or time limits imposed for a bill to be approved as an amendment.

Part (c) asks you to describe two additional ways that the interpretation of the Constitution can be changed. You will earn one point each for identifying two possible ways and one point each for giving a specific example of those ways. Some of the ways you might discuss include the following:

- Judicial Review
  - Possible Examples: *Dred Scott v. Sanford, Brown v. Board of Education,* or *Miranda v. Arizona*
- Elastic (Necessary and Proper) Clause
  - Possible Examples: formation of a national bank or Roosevelt's New Deal
- New Political Norms
  - Possible Examples: the presidential cabinet, members of the House of Representatives living in the districts they represent, or the president delivering an annual State of the Union address in front of Congress

Chapter 5
Political Beliefs
and Behaviors

DRILL 1

Liberal Identification by Education

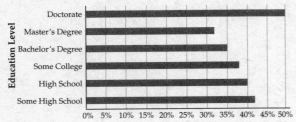

Percent Identified as Liberal

1. Which of the following conclusions can be drawn from the data above?

   (A) As educational attainment increases, so does conservative identification.
   (B) Individuals holding master's degrees are more likely to identify as liberal than are those with some college education.
   (C) The majority of high school dropouts identify as liberal.
   (D) Individuals with bachelor's or master's degrees are less likely to identify as liberal as are those who only finished high school.
   (E) Individuals holding a high school diploma are less likely to vote for a liberal candidate than are those who attended some college.

2. A closed primary refers to

   (A) a primary election in which voters may vote in whichever party primary they choose
   (B) a primary election in which voting is restricted to registered members of a political party
   (C) a primary election in which voters may select a candidate from any party for each office
   (D) an election held between the top two vote earners in a primary election, neither of whom received the legal minimum percentage of votes required to win the election
   (E) choosing candidates from different parties for offices listed on the same ballot

3. When a family's political views pass from older generations to younger generations, the process is called

   (A) socialism
   (B) bolter parties
   (C) capitalism
   (D) saliency
   (E) political socialization

Dissemination of Medicare Benefits by Region (Millions of $)

	2000	2004	2008	2012
North	12.4	13.2	14.0	16.4
Northeast	8.2	9.0	9.6	10.1
Midwest	12.0	13.2	14.2	15.0
West	14.8	16.2	15.8	17.0
East	9.8	10.4	10.4	11.0
South	11.8	13.6	16.2	18.4

4. Which of the following statements can be inferred from the table above?

   (A) The dissemination of Medicare funding has continually increased across all regions between 2000-2012.
   (B) The West received the most Medicare funding in 2012.
   (C) In 2008, the Northeast received approximately one and a half times the amount of Medicare funding as the North.
   (D) The South experienced the greatest increase in Medicare funding from 2000-2012.
   (E) In 2004, the Midwest and the East received the same amount of Medicare funding.

5. Historical voting data support which of the following statements?

   (A) Cuban-Americans tend to vote for Democrats.
   (B) Men are more likely than women to self-identify as Republicans.
   (C) African-Americans tend to support economically conservative candidates.
   (D) Urban voters are more likely to support Republicans than are rural voters.
   (E) A majority of highly educated voters identify with Republicans.

6. House incumbents who run for reelection win about 90 percent of the time because of

   I. fundraising limits set by the Federal Election Commission (FEC)
   II. greater name recognition for incumbents
   III. gerrymandered districts

   (A) I only
   (B) II only
   (C) I and III only
   (D) II and III only
   (E) I, II, and III

7. A citizen in which of the following age groups is least likely to vote?

   (A) 18 to 21 years old
   (B) 28 to 31 years old
   (C) 38 to 41 years old
   (D) 48 to 51 years old
   (E) 65 and older

8. Which of the following shows the greatest correlation to higher education levels?

   (A) Political activism
   (B) Political apathy
   (C) Support for conservative candidates
   (D) Support for liberal candidates
   (E) Support for moderate candidates

9. The biggest influence on children's political beliefs are the opinions of

   (A) their school friends or other close peers
   (B) their religious leaders
   (C) their family members
   (D) dominant television personalities
   (E) influential people of the same race or socioeconomic status

10. The principal values in American political culture include all of the following EXCEPT

    (A) equal protection under the law
    (B) popular sovereignty
    (C) equal opportunity
    (D) multiculturalism
    (E) equal economic outcome

Political Affiliation in California, 1960-2000
(As a percentage of registered voters)

	1960	1970	1980	1990	2000
Democrats	60	54	49	52	51
Republicans	30	27	38	32	38
Independents	10	19	13	16	11

11. Which of the following statements is supported by the data above?

    I. The number of registered voters in California who identified as Republicans decreased between 1960 and 2000.
    II. A majority of the registered voters in California consistently identified as Democrats between 1960 and 2000.
    III. The percentage of registered voters in California who identified as Democrats decreased from 1960 to 2000.

    (A) I only
    (B) II only
    (C) III only
    (D) I and II only
    (E) II and III only

Congressional Job Approval Ratings

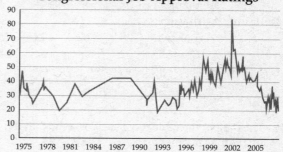

12. Which of the following conclusions about congressional job approval ratings since 1975 is supported by the data in the graph above?

    (A) The approval rating of Congress was higher in the early 1990s than in the late 1990s.
    (B) Congress was more popular in the mid-1990s than in the late 1980s.
    (C) Americans are usually displeased with the performance of Congress.
    (D) A majority of Americans disapproved of the performance of Congress immediately after September 11, 2001.
    (E) The popularity of Congress has been stable since 2000.

Questions 13-14 are based on the table below.

Presidential Candidate Support (in Percentages) by Group

| | 2004 | | 2000 | | | 1996 | | | 1992 | | |
	Kerry (D)	Bush (R)	Gore (D)	Bush (R)	Nader	Clinton (D)	Dole (R)	Perot	Clinton (D)	Bush (R)	Perot
Gender											
Men	44	56	45	52	3	45	44	11	41	37	22
Women	52	48	53	45	2	54	39	7	46	38	16
Race											
White (incl. Hispanic)	44	56	43	55	3	46	45	9	39	41	20
Nonwhite	83	17	87	9	4	82	12	6	77	11	12
Age											
Under 30 years of age	60	40	47	47	6	54	30	16	40	37	23
30 to 49 years	43	57	45	53	2	49	41	10	42	37	21
50 years and older	50	50	53	45	2	50	43	7	46	39	15
Education											
High school or less	54	46	53	45	2	52	35	13	46	35	19
Some college	44	56	44	53	3	46	42	12	40	41	19
College	48	52	46	51	3	47	45	8	4	40	17
Postgraduate	53	47	53	43	4	50	42	8	50	35	15
Setting											
Urban	56	44	62	35	3	58	36	6	50	34	16
Suburban	46	54	47	51	2	47	45	8	37	40	23
Rural	46	54	38	60	3	44	43	13	41	41	18
Political Affiliation											
Republican	5	95	7	92	1	10	85	5	7	77	16
Democrat	93	7	89	10	2	90	6	4	82	8	10
Independent	52	48	44	49	7	48	33	19	39	30	31
Religious Affiliation											
Protestant	38	62	42	55	3	44	50	6	41	41	18
Catholic	52	48	52	46	2	55	35	10	47	35	18

(D) represents Democrat and (R) represents Republican. Party affiliation for other candidates is not given.

Source: The Gallup Organization

13. The data in the table most support which of the following statements?

   (A) A greater portion of college graduates support Republican candidates when there is no major third party candidate than when there is.

   (B) People who live in rural areas are less likely than those in any other setting to support Democratic candidates.

   (C) People are most likely to support a candidate from a party other their own when the candidate is an incumbent.

   (D) The older people are, the more likely they are to support Republican candidates.

   (E) Nonwhites, men, and Catholics are more likely than other groups in their categories to support third party candidates.

14. Based on the information given in the table above, which of the following is true?

   (A) People who live in urban settings have consistently been increasingly likely to support Democrats in presidential elections.

   (B) Catholics are more likely to vote for third party candidates than Protestants are.

   (C) Republican candidates are favored among all groups of people who have more than a high school education.

   (D) Over the time period shown, the level of support among women for Republican candidates has grown.

   (E) When a major third party candidate runs for president, the Republican candidate suffers a greater loss of support from Independents than does the Democratic candidate.

Partisanship by Racial and Ethnic Groups, 2009
(In Percentages)

	Republican	Democrat	Other	No Response
White (non-Hispanic)	35%	26%	38%	1%
Black (non-Hispanic)	5%	64%	29%	2%
Hispanic	13%	32%	50%	5%
Asian	17%	36%	45%	2%
Other	18%	32%	48%	1%

15. The information provided in the table above provides evidence for which of the following statements?

    (A) Whites are the least likely group to be undecided about their political affiliation.
    (B) The Republican Party is more likely to attract more Hispanics than Asians in future elections.
    (C) All non-white groups are more likely than whites are to identify with minor political parties.
    (D) More people abandon their Republican identity than their Democrat identity in order to identify politically with other parties.
    (E) Non-Hispanic blacks are the most homogenous in their political affiliation.

16. All of the following statements concerning the likelihood that a person will vote are true EXCEPT:

    (A) When there is a strong front-runner in a state, people in that state are less likely to vote.
    (B) White-collar workers are more likely to vote than are blue-collar workers, with the exception of blue-collar workers who belong to unions.
    (C) Voters who are registered as independent as less likely to vote than those who are registered Democrats or Republicans.
    (D) Minorities with high incomes are as likely to vote as are whites.
    (E) There is no difference in the likelihood of voting among those with undergraduate degrees and those with postgraduate degrees.

17. Which of the following is least likely to influence an individual's decision to vote for candidates from one party over another?

    (A) Membership in a religious community
    (B) Public statements about controversial issues
    (C) Race
    (D) Presidential endorsement
    (E) Political affiliation

18. Which of the following is most descriptive of the actions of the electorate in the United States?

    (A) Voter turnout is higher in municipal elections than in presidential elections.
    (B) Those with strong party ties are less likely to vote than those who have no party ties.
    (C) Individual votes do not matter in local elections.
    (D) General elections often have higher voter turnout than primary elections.
    (E) Senior citizens do not generally vote.

DRILL 2

Partisanship And Presidential Elections
Percent Voting for Candidates

Candidate's Party	Registered Democrat		Registered Republican		Independent Voters	
	2008	2012	2008	2012	2008	2012
Democrat	90%	93%	10%	3%	46%	46%
Republican	7%	5%	87%	96%	42%	45%

1. Which of the following statements about partisanship and voting decisions in the presidential elections for the two years shown is supported by the data in the table above?

   (A) Fewer independents voted in 2008 than in 2012.
   (B) Registered democrats are more likely to vote within their party's ticket than registered Republicans are.
   (C) Registered party affiliation is a strong indicator of the candidate an individual will vote for.
   (D) Independent voters are more likely to be influenced by a candidate's personality than are voters registered Republican or Democrat.
   (E) More Republicans than Democrats voted in the 2012 election.

2. Delegates to presidential nomination conventions can be best described as

   (A) better off financially than the general population
   (B) representative of a variety of education attainment levels
   (C) more open to opposing political viewpoints than is the general population
   (D) neutral in their formal political affiliations
   (E) uninterested in holding office themselves

3. Which of the following age groups would be most likely to vote in an election?

   (A) 18-29
   (B) 30-34
   (C) 45-54
   (D) 65-74
   (E) 85+

Opinions On Government-Run Health Care
(2011)

Age	Men		Women	
	Supportive	Opposed	Supportive	Opposed
18-30	61%	37%	71%	25%
31-50	60%	37%	62%	37%
51+	57%	40%	55%	42%

4. The information in the table above most clearly provides evidence of

   (A) the likelihood that more men are satisfied with their current health care
   (B) a correlation between age and preference for government intervention
   (C) a greater interest in social issues among women
   (D) a tendency among older people to be undecided about some issues
   (E) a high degree of confidence in the ability of the government to provide social safety nets

5. A major change that resulted from the 1968 presidential nomination process was

   (A) a move away from radio debates to televised debates
   (B) the emergence of party platforms
   (C) an increase in power given to voters
   (D) the development of candidates focused primarily on local issues
   (E) the beginning of an increased reliance on print media for information

6. Which of the following does not play a direct role in political socialization?

   (A) Civic education
   (B) Family
   (C) Diet and nutrition
   (D) Friends
   (E) Religion

Voting Behavior by Gender

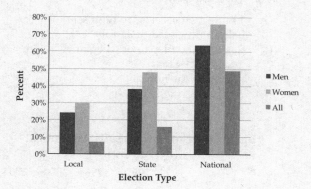

7. Which of the following statements can be inferred from the chart above?

   (A) The majority of all voters participate in national elections.
   (B) The percentage of women who vote in state elections is twice that of men who vote in local elections.
   (C) Less than a quarter of men participate in state elections.
   (D) Voter turnout is lowest for national elections and highest for state elections.
   (E) Less than three-fourths of all women vote in national elections.

8. Which of the following is NOT a characteristic of a closed primary election?

   (A) Only voters registered with a specific party can vote in that party's primary.
   (B) Independent voters are usually left out of the closed primary.
   (C) The party candidates are nominated by party leaders.
   (D) Parties can opt to invite unaffiliated voters to participate in the primary.
   (E) Closed primaries generally strengthen party unity.

9. Which of the following LEAST exemplifies partisan behavior?

   (A) Identifying one's self as a member of a specific party
   (B) Volunteering to help support party candidates
   (C) Supporting social and economic policies endorsed by a specific party
   (D) Engaging in the practice of split-ticket voting
   (E) Registering as a member of a specific party

10. Weekday elections and voter identification requirements have which of the following effects on elections?

    (A) They ensure compliance with the Voting Rights Act.
    (B) They offer equal opportunity for all eligible citizens to vote.
    (C) They make it easier to commit voter fraud.
    (D) They boost party loyalty.
    (E) They lead to lower turnout on Election Day.

11. How does political efficacy demonstrate an important democratic principle?

    (A) It requires that all citizens be educated on the relevant issues before voting.
    (B) It allows for all citizens to affect their society through voting and expression.
    (C) It requires politicians to ensure their constituents are well informed.
    (D) It allows individuals unlimited campaign donations.
    (E) It requires that the media offer balanced information to voters.

12. A state's primary election is considered "closed" if

    (A) the number of eligible candidates is limited
    (B) the results are too close to call
    (C) only the party leaders may select the candidates
    (D) only voters who are members of the party may participate
    (E) voters must participate in a caucus

13. All of the following generalizations about voter behavior are true EXCEPT:

(A) Voters living in the suburbs are more likely to vote Republican than Democrat.
(B) Jewish and Catholic voters tend to vote for Democratic candidates.
(C) Voters in the South are more likely to vote for Republican candidates than for Democratic candidates.
(D) Immigrants are more likely to vote for Republican candidates than for Democratic candidates.
(E) Married voters tend to vote more often than single voters.

14. Which of the following was an unexpected result of the passage of the Twenty-sixth Amendment?

(A) The addition of women to the pool of eligible voters caused an increase in the voter turnout percentage in the 1920 presidential election.
(B) The abolishment of slavery led to a decline in crime rate in the southern United States.
(C) The removal of poll taxes led to a decline in minority voter turnout in the 1964 presidential election.
(D) The sale and transportation of intoxicating liquors within the United States increased.
(E) The influx of eligible voters aged 18-20 caused the voter turnout percentage to fall in the 1972 presidential election.

15. All of the following are founding principles of the United States EXCEPT

(A) limited government
(B) popular sovereignty
(C) human equality
(D) divine right
(E) individual rights

16. Which of the following is an example of formal political socialization?

(A) Taking a civics class in high school
(B) Being influenced by family
(C) Reciting the Pledge of Allegiance before school begins
(D) Watching the news
(E) Attending a religious service

Highest Level of Educational Attainment (By Percent)

	1992	1996	2000	2004
Some high school	13%	10%	11%	9%
High school diploma	27%	25%	20%	24%
Some college	18%	20%	21%	20%
Bachelor's degree	20%	24%	30%	28%
Master's degree	17%	13%	9%	12%
Doctorate	5%	8%	9%	7%

17. Which of the following statements regarding educational attainment during the Bush and Clinton administrations is NOT supported by the table above?

(A) The percent of individuals who received a bachelor's degree in 1992 is less than the percent of those who received a bachelor's degree in 2004.
(B) The percent of individuals who received their bachelor's degree in 1996 is three times that of those who received their doctorate in the same year.
(C) A greater percentage of individuals completed high school in 2004 than in 1996.
(D) The percent of individuals who received a doctorate in 2004 is greater than the percent of those who received a master's degree in 2000.
(E) The percent of individuals who received their high school diploma in 2000 is equal to the percent of those who received their bachelor's degree in 1992.

DRILL 3

Gallup Presidential Approval Rating
Rolling 1-Year Average

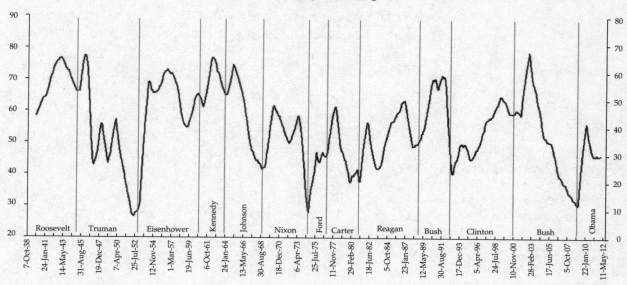

1. What conclusion about presidential approval ratings is supported by the graph above?

   (A) The highest approval ratings occur during Republican administrations.
   (B) President Eisenhower was the most popular president of the last half of the twentieth century.
   (C) President Clinton experienced a net gain in his popularity throughout his presidency
   (D) The Vietnam War had a positive impact on President Johnson's approval ratings.
   (E) President Reagan's approval rating remained static.

2. What best describes the relationship between political efficacy and the controversy that followed the 2000 presidential election?

   (A) Political efficacy remained relatively unchanged following the election.
   (B) Political efficacy increased with the Supreme Court's decision on the election.
   (C) Political efficacy decreased due to President George W. Bush's landslide victory.
   (D) Political efficacy increased with the media coverage that followed the election.
   (E) Political efficacy decreased over the weeks following the election.

3. A primary that is held after no single candidate receives a majority of the votes is known as a

   (A) open primary
   (B) closed primary
   (C) runoff primary
   (D) blanket primary
   (E) nonpartisan primary

4. Which of the following general presidential elections is known for establishing television debates and candidate appearance as important factors in presidential campaigns?

   (A) 1956
   (B) 1960
   (C) 1964
   (D) 1968
   (E) 1972

2008 vs. 2012 Likely Voter Preferences for President

Results re-percentaged to add to 100% after removing undecided/no answer/third-party candidates

| | October 32-Nov 2, 2008 | | Oct 9-15, 2013 | | Net Obama +/- | |
	Obama %	McCain %	Obama %	Romney %	2008 %-pts.	2012 %-pts.
U.S. likely voters	53.5	46.5	48	52	+7	-4
Men	44	56	45	52	3	45
Women	52	48	53	45	2	54
Non-Hisplanic white	44	56	39	61	-12	-22
Nonwhite (incl. Hispanics)	86	14	84	16	+72	+68
Under 30 years	61	39	59	41	+22	+18
30 to 49 years	53	47	45	55	+6	-10
50 to 64 years	54	46	50	50	+8	0
65 years & older	46	54	44	56	-8	-12
Postgraduate	65	35	67	43	+30	+14
College graduate only	51	49	39	61	+2	-22
Some college	52	48	48	52	+4	-4
High school or less	51	49	48	52	+2	-4
East	57	43	52	48	+14	+4
Midwest	53	47	52	48	+6	+4
South	50	50	39	61	0	-22
West	55	45	53	47	+10	+6
Protestants	47	53	41	59	-6	-18
Catholics	53	47	49	51	+6	-2

5. Which of the follow conclusions about the polling leading up to the 2008 and 2012 elections is best supported by the data on the table?

   (A) Level of education played no discernible role in determining a voter's preference.
   (B) Older voters tended to support Obama in both elections.
   (C) Voters from the West preferred Obama to his opponent more so in 2012 than they did in 2008.
   (D) Women were more likely than men to vote for Obama in both elections.
   (E) Catholics largely supported the Republican candidates in both elections.

6. One of the primary reasons for the decrease in voter turnout in the 1996 election was

   (A) that the majority of eligible voters were over fifty years old
   (B) that voters were more likely than in previous recent elections to lack higher education
   (C) that the increased incomes resulting from the 1990s dot-com boom reduced the incentive for people to vote
   (D) the rational ignorance effect
   (E) that it was an off-year election

7. Voters in which of the following categories would be LEAST likely to vote?

   (A) Blue-collar workers who belong to a union
   (B) Professionals
   (C) Voters who are active in their political parties
   (D) Voters aged 18-29
   (E) Voters in swing states

8. All of the following are possible consequences of low voter turnout in the United States EXCEPT

   (A) a perception of the government as illegitimate
   (B) a lack of true democracy
   (C) a lack of minority representation
   (D) a sense of divide among elected officials and their constituents
   (E) an imposition of a fine on non-voters

1. Over the past forty years, Americans have increasingly viewed their government with skepticism and distrust.

   (a) Evaluate the role that campaign finance has had in fostering a skeptical electorate.

   (b) Identify one way in which voters have shown this skepticism in terms of direct participation and one way in terms of indirect participation.

   (c) Define "divided government" and explain one way in which it breeds skepticism towards the political process.

DRILL 4

Right now, which one of the following do you think should be the more important priority for addressing America's energy supply?

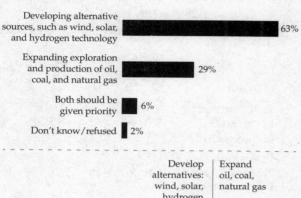

Developing alternative sources, such as wind, solar, and hydrogen technology — 63%

Expanding exploration and production of oil, coal, and natural gas — 29%

Both should be given priority — 6%

Don't know/refused — 2%

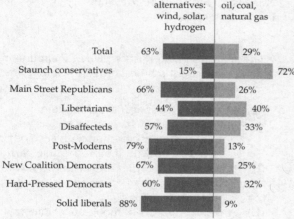

	Develop alternatives: wind, solar, hydrogen	Expand oil, coal, natural gas
Total	63%	29%
Staunch conservatives	15%	72%
Main Street Republicans	66%	26%
Libertarians	44%	40%
Disaffecteds	57%	33%
Post-Moderns	79%	13%
New Coalition Democrats	67%	25%
Hard-Pressed Democrats	60%	32%
Solid liberals	88%	9%

Source: February-March 2011 Pew Research Center for the People and the Press survey. N=3,029.

1. Which statement is best supported by the polling data in the above chart?

(A) Staunch conservatives and Hard-Pressed Democrats share a common viewpoint on the issue of alternative energy.

(B) Libertarians are more likely to support developing alternative energy sources than expanding production of oil, coal, and natural gas.

(C) The typical American is twice as likely to support putting an end to relying on oil, coal, and natural gas than he or she is to support continuing these practices.

(D) New Coalition Democrats make up the largest group of Democrats polled.

(E) Solid liberals are cancelled out by staunch conservatives.

Would you increase, decrease or keep spending the same for...		2009 %	2011 %	Change
Education	Increase	67	62	-5
	Decrease	6	11	+5
Veteran's benefits and services	Increase	63	51	-12
	Decrease	2	6	+4
Health care	Increase	61	41	-20
	Decrease	10	24	+14
Medicare	Increase	53	40	-13
	Decrease	6	12	+6
Combating crime	Increase	45	39	-6
	Decrease	10	18	+8
Energy	Increase	41	36	-5
	Decrease	15	23	+8
Scientific research	Increase	39	36	-3
	Decrease	14	23	+9
Environmental protection	Increase	43	36	-7
	Decrease	16	26	+10
U.S. anti-terrorism defenses	Increase	35	33	-2
	Decrease	17	21	+4
Agriculture	Increase	35	32	-3
	Decrease	12	23	+11
Military defense	Increase	40	1	-9
	Decrease	18	30	+12
Unemployment assistance	Increase	44	27	-17
	Decrease	15	28	+13
Global poverty assistance	Increase	26	21	-5
	Decrease	34	45	+11

Source: Pew Research Center Feb. 2-7, 2011. Percent saying "keep spending the same" not shown.

2. Which of the following conclusions CANNOT be made about respondents to this poll?

(A) Support for funding U.S. anti-terrorism defenses experienced the least amount of change between 2009 and 2011.

(B) Funding for scientific research gained support after 2009.

(C) Respondents are less likely to advocate cutting veterans' benefits than cutting education.

(D) Health care spending became less popular from 2009 to 2011.

(E) Both global poverty assistance and military defense spending lost public support between 2009 and 2011.

Partisan Loyalty In Presidential Elections 1960-1980

Percentage of Partisan Voters Who Decided to Vote for Their Party's Candidate Before and After the Campaign Began

	Democrats		Republicans	
	Before	After	Before	After
1960	82	78	97	76
1964	95	69	80	75
1968	89	71	98	82
1972	59	63	99	74
1976	85	78	94	76
1980	85	64	94	90

3. The table above supports which of the following statements about partisan voting in presidential elections?

   (A) The tendency to engage in partisan voting increased consistently during the time period shown.
   (B) Voters who decide whom to vote for after the campaign began were less likely to be loyal to their party during the time period shown.
   (C) Republicans were less likely to engage in partisan voting than were Democrats during the time period shown.
   (D) In the 1972 election, voters from both parties were more likely to vote for candidates from the opposing party.
   (E) In the 1960 election, a greater percentage of Republicans than Democrats who decided on their candidate before the campaign began voted for the candidate from the opposing party.

4. Which of the following is a consequence of the high financial investment required to be successful in politics?

   (A) Congress passed the Campaign Funding Act, which eliminated campaign contribution limits for presidential elections.
   (B) Delegates to presidential nomination conventions tend to be better off financially than are members of the general population.
   (C) Minorities who cannot afford to vote in presidential elections receive aid from the Federal Election Commission.
   (D) The amount of funding allotted in the annual federal budget for campaign staff for federal elections is increased each year.

Opinions On Immigration (2013)

Percentage of Respondents by Strength of Affiliation to Political Party

Question	Democrats			Republicans		
	Strong	Moderate	Weak	Strong	Moderate	Weak
Favor stronger immigration enforcement	55	88	65	95	88	93
Favor path to citizenship for illegal immigrants	94	61	80	49	58	66

5. The table above supports which of the following statements about political affiliation and opinions on immigration?

   (A) Moderate Republicans and moderate Democrats may have more beliefs on immigration in common with each other than they do with their respective parties.
   (B) Moderates have friendlier attitudes toward immigration than do people from any other group.
   (C) An equal number of moderate Democrats and moderate Republicans favor stronger immigration enforcement.
   (D) If the Republicans control both the House and the Senate, stronger laws on immigration enforcement will be passed.
   (E) Voters who do not support tougher immigration enforcement are likely to support offering a path to citizenship for illegal immigrants.

6. Which of the following best describes why voters been reluctant to vote for third party candidates in modern elections?

(A) Third party candidates do not have the qualifications necessary to compete with Democratic and Republican candidates.

(B) Third party candidates choose platforms that fail to appeal to the general population.

(C) Because Democratic and Republican candidates have greater financial backing and more organizational support, third party candidates are less able to campaign effectively and remain largely unknown.

(D) Third party candidates are not eligible to hold public office and form merely to promote a single stance or principle.

(E) Third party candidates are typically outcasts from either the Democratic or Republican parties and have been simply shunned by their electorate.

7. Which of the following people would be most likely to engage in split ticket voting?

(A) An unaffiliated registered voter
(B) A devout Christian
(C) An African American
(D) Someone whose parents are very active in their political party
(E) A union member

Party Identification Among Registered Voters (In Percentages)

	Solidly Republican	All Republican	Solidly Independent	All Democrat	Solidly Democrat
January 2010	28	43	36	48	34
June 2010	28	42	33	47	36
January 2011	29	45	37	44	31
June 2011	30	47	38	42	29
January 2012	27	44	42	47	30
June 2012	30	42	39	44	30
January 2013	27	40	38	49	33
June 2013	26	43	41	46	31

8. The table above supports which of the following statements about party affiliation over the time period shown?

(A) The tendency to strongly affiliate with any party has consistently decreased over time.

(B) As of June 2013, a higher percentage of people considered themselves solidly independent than identified with any party.

(C) People feel the strongest party identification in election years.

(D) Democrats are able to attract more identification from independent or undecided voters than Republicans are.

(E) People are more likely to identify at least somewhat with a party than to have a strong party identification.

1. Democracy calls for political involvement. While this may consist of regular voting for many people, there are other ways in which the United States can be viewed as a government "of the people."

   (a)   Choose one form of political participation besides voting. Describe one advantage of this form of political participation and one limitation.

   (b)   Choose a second form of political involvement besides voting. Describe one advantage of this form of political participation and one limitation.

DRILL 5

**Distribution Of Total Net Worth
During Bush Administration
(Share Of National Net Worth By Percentile)**

	2001	2004	2007
Top 1%	33.4%	34.3%	34.5%
Next 19%	51.0	50.4	50.5
Bottom 80%	15.6	15.3	15.0

1. Which of the following statements about net worth distribution during the Bush administration is supported by the table above?

   (A) The share of net worth of the Top 1% increased, whereas the share of net worth for the Bottom 80% decreased.
   (B) The share of net worth of the Top 1% decreased, whereas the share of net worth for the Bottom 80% increased.
   (C) The share of net worth of the Top 1% decreased, whereas the share of net worth for the Next 19% increased.
   (D) All income levels observed increases in net worth.
   (E) The increases in share of net worth associated with the Top 1% were due to losses among wealth in the Next 19%.

2. Which of the following factors contributed the most to popular support for passage of the Twenty-sixth Amendment?

   (A) Low voter turnout in previous elections had prompted Congress to expand the electorate to 18 to 20 year olds.
   (B) Members of the armed forces aged 18 to 21 were fighting in World War II, yet they were not eligible to vote.
   (C) Members of the armed forces aged 18 to 21 were fighting in the Korean War, yet they were not eligible to vote.
   (D) Members of the armed forces aged 18 to 21 were fighting in the Vietnam War, yet they were not eligible to vote.
   (E) The Twenty-first Amendment had lowered the drinking age to 18 years old, and the public felt it was fair to lower the voting age as well.

3. Which of the following accurately describes the difference between an open primary and a closed primary election?

   (A) Only party members may vote in an open primary, while voters of any party affiliation may vote in a closed primary.
   (B) Only party members may vote in a closed primary, while voters of any party affiliation may vote in an open primary.
   (C) A voter may select candidates of different political parties on a single ballot in an open primary but not in a closed primary.
   (D) A voter may select candidates of different political parties on a single ballot in a closed primary but not in an open primary.
   (E) A voter may cast multiple ballots in an open primary but only one ballot in a closed primary.

Hispanic Popular Vote in the 2012 Presidential Election

(% who voted for...)

	Obama	Romney
All Hispanics	71	27
Men	65	33
Women	76	23
18-29	74	23
30-44	71	28
45-64	68	31
65 and older	65	35
College grad	62	35
No college degree	75	24
Income less than $50,000	82	17
Income more than $50,000	59	39

Note: Share of the vote that went to third-party candidates not shown.

Source: Pew Hispanic Center analysis of 2012 exit poll results as reported by CNN

4. The data shown above provide clear evidence that in 2012

(A) elderly Hispanic voters were more likely to vote for Romney than for Obama
(B) most Hispanic voters earned less than $50,000 per year
(C) Hispanic women were more likely than Hispanic men to vote for Barack Obama
(D) young Hispanic voters were less likely to vote for Barack Obama than were their older counterparts
(E) level of education makes little to no difference in the likelihood of Hispanic voters supporting Romney

Question: *Religion is known to be a major force in one's political views and affiliation. Which of the following statements most accurately describes your party stance or affiliation?*

Among people of the following religious affiliations…

Judaism	My Political Views Are:	Mormonism
16%	Republican	53%
5%	Lean Republican	12%
9%	Independent	8%
15%	Lean Democratic	8%
51%	Democratic	14%
3%	No Preference	5%

5. The data above does NOT support which of the following conclusions?

(A) Jews are more likely to identify as Democrats than Mormons.
(B) Mormons are more likely to identify as Republicans than Jews.
(C) Mormons are less likely to lean Republican than identify as Republicans.
(D) Jews are more likely to identify as Republicans than to lean Republican.
(E) Jews and Mormons share similar political views.

6. Which of the following conclusions about recent political voting patterns is INCORRECT?

(A) African Americans are more likely to vote for Democratic candidates.
(B) Hispanics are more likely to vote for Democratic candidates.
(C) Women are more likely to vote for liberal candidates than are men.
(D) Southern voters are more likely to vote for a liberal candidate.
(E) Urban populations are more likely to vote for a liberal candidate.

7. Which of the following factors LEAST affects political socialization?

(A) Family
(B) Race
(C) Geography
(D) Mass Media
(E) Religion

Demographics of Likely Voters, Recent Presidential Elections, Gallup Polls

	2004 %	2008 %	2012 %
Male	46	47	48
Female	54	53	52
Non-Hispanic white	82	78	78
Non-white	15	19	20
Black	8	12	11
Hispanic	6	6	7
18 to 29 years	13	14	13
30 to 49 years	38	35	34
50 to 64 years	26	30	31
65+ years	24	21	22
East	23	22	23
Midwest	23	22	23
South	33	33	33
West	22	23	22
High school or less	32	33	31
Some college	33	30	31
College graduate only	15	20	20
Postgraduate	20	16	17
Democrat	37	39	35
Independent	24	31	29
Republican	39	29	36
Democrat/Lean Democratic	48	54	46
Republican/Lean Republican	48	42	49

Note: 2004 and 2008 estimates are based on final Gallup pre-election polls. 2012 estimate is based on Oct. 1-24 Gallup Daily election tracking.

8. Which of the following conclusions is best supported by the data in the table above?

   (A) In the 2008 election, Republican enthusiasm dropped while Democratic enthusiasm rose.
   (B) For all three years given, most voters held a college degree.
   (C) Midwestern voters became more likely to vote during the early years of the twenty-first century.
   (D) The majority of voters in all three elections were under fifty years old.
   (E) There was a drop in enthusiasm with black voters during the 2008 election.

2008 Presidential Election

2012 Presidential Election

■ Obama
■ McCain
■ Electoral votes split

■ Obama
■ Romney

1. The presidential election results from 2008 and 2012 are shown in the figures above. Drawing from your understanding of contemporary voting behavior as well as information from the accompanying maps, respond to the following questions.

(a) Identify one region that has been a Democratic stronghold in the early twenty-first century and describe two reasons for this voting pattern.

(b) Identify one region that has been a Republican stronghold in the early twenty-first century and describe two reasons for this voting pattern.

Chapter 6
Political Beliefs and Behaviors: Answers and Explanations

ANSWER KEY

Multiple-Choice Questions

Drill 1
1. D
2. B
3. E
4. D
5. B
6. D
7. A
8. A
9. C
10. E
11. C
12. C
13. A
14. D
15. E
16. E
17. D
18. D

Drill 2
1. C
2. A
3. D
4. B
5. C
6. C
7. B
8. C
9. D
10. E
11. B
12. D
13. D
14. E
15. D
16. A
17. D

Drill 3
1. C
2. E
3. C
4. B
5. D
6. D
7. D
8. E

Drill 4
1. B
2. D
3. B
4. B
5. A
6. C
7. A
8. E

Drill 5
1. A
2. D
3. B
4. C
5. E
6. D
7. C
8. A

EXPLANATIONS

Drill 1

1. **D** According to the graph, individuals with bachelor's or master's degrees are less likely to identify as liberal as those who only finished high school. Eliminate choices (A) and (E) because the graph does not tell us about conservative identification or about voting trends. Eliminate choice (B) because individuals holding master's degrees are less likely to identify as liberal than those with some college education. Finally, eliminate choice (C) because less than 50 percent of those with "some high school" education identify as liberal.

2. **B** A closed primary refers to a primary election in which voting is restricted to registered members of a political party. Eliminate choices (A), (C), and (D) since they refer to an open primary, a blanket primary, and a runoff primary, respectively. Eliminate choice (E) because that refers to split-ticket rating.

3. **E** Political socialization describes the process in which younger generations of families take on the political views of the older generation. Socialism and capitalism are both economic systems, so eliminate choices (A) and (C). Bolter parties are third parties that split from one of the U.S.'s two major parties, and saliency describes the importance of an issue to an individual or group. Eliminate choices (B) and (D).

4. **D** The graph shows that the South experienced the greatest increase in Medicare funding from 2000–2012, having increased by $6.6 million over the 12-year period. Eliminate choice (A) because the West did not experience a continual increase in funding; funding declined from 2004 to 2008. Choice (B) can be eliminated because the South received the most Medicare funding in 2012. Eliminate choice (C) because, in 2008, the North received approximately one and a half times the amount of Medicare funding as the Northeast. Finally, eliminate choice (E) because the Midwest and the East did not receive the same amount of Medicare funding in 2004.

5. **B** Historical voting data and voting patterns show that a majority of women vote for Democratic candidates while a majority of men vote for Republican candidates. The data doesn't support any of the other choices: Cuban Americans tend to vote Republican, African Americans tend to support economically liberal or moderate candidates, rural voters are more likely than urban voters to vote Republican, and a majority of highly educated voters vote for Democrats. Therefore, eliminate choices (A), (C), (D), and (E).

6. **D** Starting with part I of the answer, there are many loopholes that weaken fundraising limits set by the Federal Election Commission (FEC). To the extent that FEC fundraising limits are effective, they would usually limit an incumbent more that an opposition candidate because incumbents can usually raise more money in the absence of limits. Eliminating part I gets rid of choices (A),

(C), and (E). Notice that both remaining choices, (B) and (D), assert that part II is true, so, if you can eliminate part I, all that is left to do is decide whether part III is true. Part II is definitely true: at the time they are up for reelection, House incumbents have already spent time advertising, campaigning, and networking in their districts and their greater name recognition contributes to their high rate of reelections. Part III is also true because House congressional districts are often drawn with an eye toward making the voting patterns of districts favorable to incumbent members. Political scientists of both parties are very successful at predicting voting patterns and successfully gerrymandering districts, so eliminate choice (B) and select (D).

7. **A** While the Twenty-sixth Amendment lowered the voting age from 21 to 18 in 1971, voting data shows that young people are the least likely age group to vote and the elderly are the most likely to vote. Choice (A) is the youngest group of the five choices and the correct answer.

8. **A** Generally, voters with higher levels of education are more likely to vote and otherwise be politically active. Choice (B) is incorrect because it states the opposite of this correlation. Although there is some correlation between a voter's level of education and his or her political views, the correlation is not nearly as strong as that between education and political activism; therefore, you should eliminate choices (C), (D), and (E).

9. **C** Although all of the factors listed have some influence on the development of political beliefs, research has shown that the beliefs of one's family constitutes the most influential factor.

10. **E** Equal protection under the law and popular sovereignty (majority rule) are guaranteed by the Constitution. Multiculturalism is also an important part of the culture of America, which is a nation of immigrants. Equal opportunity, the notion that all people have the same chances in life if they work hard towards their goals, is embraced but equality of outcome is not. Equality of outcome is the idea that we all earn the same and are rewarded the same, no matter our level of effort. This is counter to American political culture, which embraces the idea that you will get out of life what you put into it. Answer (E) is correct.

11. **C** Notice the shift in language: the chart gives the *percentage* of California voters who identified with each party, but Numeral I refers to the actual *number* of voters. Since the number of registered voters in California increased between 1960 and 2000, and the percentage of California voters who identified as Republicans increased from 1960 to 2000 (according to the table), the number of California voters who identified as Republicans increased: it became a larger piece of a larger pie. Thus, numeral I is supported by the data, and you should eliminate choices (A) and (D). Numeral II is not supported by the table because only 49 percent of voters identified as Democrats in 1980: by definition, a majority is more than 50 percent. Thus, Numeral II is not supported by the data, and you should eliminate choices (B) and (E). Numeral III is supported by the data because the percentage of California voters who identified as Democrats decreased from 60 to 51 percent.

12. **C** Choice (A) is incorrect because the approval rating of Congress was in the 20–40 percent range in the early 1990s and in the 30–50 percent range in the late 1990s. Choice (B) is incorrect because the approval rating of Congress was in the 25–35 percent range in the mid–1990s and between 35 percent and approximately 43 percent in the late 1980s. Choice (C) is supported by the data, as a majority of Americans (i.e., more than 50 percent) approved of Congress's performance only from the late 1990s until about 2004; that's less than 10 years, and the graph shows data for more than 30. Choice (D) is incorrect because approximately 85 percent of Americans approved of Congress's performance immediately following September 11, 2001. Choice (E) is incorrect because the approval rating of Congress was less than 50 percent in 2000, rose to approximately 85 percent, then fell to below 30 percent; in no other period did the popularity of Congress see such dramatic changes.

13. **A** The data for college and postgraduate show 52 and 47 percent, respectively, voting for the Republican in 2004. In every other year shown, there was a major third party candidate and the percentage of votes going to the Republican was less, so choice (A) is correct. Choice (B) is incorrect because in 2004, the percentage of people in rural areas and suburban areas who voted for the Democrat was the same, and in 1992, the percentage in suburban areas was actually lower. In 1996 and 2004 there were incumbents running for president. However, a greater percentage of Democrats voted for Bush in 2000 when he wasn't an incumbent than in 2004 when he was. Choice (C) is incorrect. The 2000 and 2004 elections show that middle-aged people made up the greatest percentage of people who voted for the Republican candidate, so choice (D) is incorrect. The non-white category alone makes choice (E) incorrect because a greater percentage of whites voted for the third party candidate in 1996 and 1992.

14. **D** The percentage of women voting for the Republican candidate rose steadily from 38 to 48 percent during the time shown, so choice (D) is correct. Choice (A) is incorrect because the percentage of urban supporters of Democrats declined from 1996 to 2004. Choice (B) is disproved by both the 2000 and 1992 elections. Choice (C) is incorrect because the data show that Democrats were more popular among those with postgraduate degrees. Finally, choice (E) is incorrect because it cannot be determined from the information provided which party would have received the votes had there not been a major third party candidate.

15. **E** Answer (A) is incorrect because the percentage of those offering "No Response" for whites is the same as those who are classified under the racial group of "other." In addition, "No Response" does not necessarily mean undecided. Choice (B) is incorrect because this table doesn't provide enough information to make predictions. A lower percentage of non-Hispanic blacks than non-Hispanic whites identify with "other" political parties, so choice (C) is incorrect. The table offers no information about previous political affiliations, so choice (D) is not supported. Choice (E) is correct because non-Hispanic blacks have the greatest percentage (64 percent) affiliated with one party.

16. **E** People are less likely to vote if they believe one candidate is too far ahead of the others, so choice (A) is true. White-collar workers do vote more often than blue-collar workers, but people who belong to unions are very likely to vote, so choice (B) is true. A strong party affiliation makes one more likely to vote, so choice (C) is true. Minorities, except those with high incomes, vote less often than whites, so choice (D) is true. Only choice (E) is false because there is a strong correlation between higher education and a tendency to vote. Therefore, individuals with postgraduate degrees are more likely to vote than individuals with only undergraduate degrees, so choice (E) is the right answer.

17. **D** Every answer except (D) has a strong influence over party-based voting decisions. Presidential endorsements often have great influence in intra-party contests, such as primaries, but they aren't as influential as any of the other factors when trying to decide between parties.

18. **D** General elections benefit from higher voter turnout for a number of reasons. One of these reasons is that general elections are considered more exciting, as candidates often run unopposed in primary elections. Also, general elections often receive more media coverage than primary elections. Choice (A) is incorrect because the turnout for elections is usually higher in presidential elections. Choice (B) is incorrect because those with strong political ties are more likely to vote. Choice (C) is incorrect because individual votes have a greater effect in local elections: when only a few hundred people vote in a local election, the outcome could be determined by a single vote. Choice (E) is incorrect because senior citizens have one of the highest turnout rates.

Drill 2

1. **C** The data are given in percentages, so no conclusions about numbers of voters can be made and choices (A) and (E) can be eliminated. Answer (B) is not true because even though a greater percentage of Republicans crossed party lines in the 2008 election, a greater percentage of Democrats crossed party lines in 2012. Answer (D) is incorrect because the table offers no information about the reasons that independent voters select their candidates. A large majority of registered Republicans and Democrats for their own party's candidate in both elections shown, so choice (C) is supported.

2. **A** Delegates to nomination conventions are generally financially well-off, well educated, and strongly involved in politics. Many delegates are current or former party leaders. Therefore, choice (A) is correct because the other answers are contrary to the reality.

3. **D** Generally, older voters are more likely to vote than younger voters: in fact, over 60 percent of 65–74 year olds voted in the 2010 election, while less than 21 percent of those aged 18–29 voted. Therefore, eliminate choices (A), (B), and (C). After one ages past one's seventies, voter likelihood begins to drop off, so choice (E) is incorrect.

4. **B** Among both men and women, the older they are, the less likely they are to support government-run health care, so choice (B) is correct. Less support for government-run health care is not necessarily indicative of satisfaction with the current system, so choice (A) is incorrect. Choice (C) is too broad to be supported by a table, which only contains data about health care preferences. Choice (D) is not supported because the percentage of people not reporting an answer is almost equal in all age and gender groups, with the largest percentage coming from women aged 18–30. Choice (E) is incorrect because "social safety nets" is too broad of a topic to be supported by the information in the table.

5. **C** The controversy surrounding the 1968 Democratic Party nomination process created a need for reform in the process. The Democratic Party instituted primary elections throughout the country that placed nomination power in the hands of voters, rather than with party leaders. The Republicans followed suit with their own primary elections. Choice (A) is wrong because this change happened with the 1960 election. Party platforms have been a part of party conventions since the beginning of the republic, so choice (B) is wrong. Choice (D) is irrelevant to the change resulting from the 1968 election, and choice (E) is wrong, as print media has been on the decline in the modern era.

6. **C** Political socialization refers to the process in which individuals acquire political culture and thereby form views and beliefs. One's civic education, family, friends, and religion all have a direct impact on one's beliefs, views, and attitudes; eliminate choices (A), (B), (D), and (E). One's diet does not directly influence one's political beliefs. Accordingly, choice (C) is the correct answer.

7. **B** According to the chart, the percentage of women who vote in state elections is 48 percent and the percentage of men who vote in local elections is 24 percent. Thus, the percentage of women who vote in state elections is twice that of men who vote in local elections. Choices (A), (C), (D), and (E) are incorrect based on the information provided in the chart. Only 49 percent of all voters participate in national elections, 38 percent of men participate in state elections, voter turnout is highest in national elections, and 76 percent of women vote in national elections.

8. **C** A closed primary is one in which only registered members of a political party can vote. Accordingly, independent voters are usually left out of a closed primary, but can be invited to participate if they are willing to commit to a specific party affiliation. Due to the nature of a closed primary and its participants, closed primaries tend to strengthen party unity as individuals share similar beliefs. The rise of the use of primaries replaced the old system in which party leaders nominated candidates for office; thus, the correct answer is choice (C).

9. **D** Partisan behaviors refer to the behaviors held by strong supporters of a party, cause, or person. Accordingly, it would be extremely unlikely that a partisan would engage in split-ticket voting; rather, most partisans would engage in straight-ticket voting. Thus, choice (D) is the correct answer.

10. **E** Because many people find it difficult to get time off from work to vote, weekday elections ultimately lower voter turnout. Similarly, voter identification requirements lower turnout due to the

presence of eligible voters who do not own identification. Choice (A) is wrong because voter identification laws actually make it more difficult for minorities to vote, which belies the purpose of the Voting Rights Act. Further, this would contradict choice (B). Choice (C) is incorrect because voter identification laws aims to prevent fraud. Choice (D) is incorrect because weekday elections and voter identification requirements are irrelevant to party loyalty.

11. **B** Political efficacy refers to the belief that an individual's actions can influence the government. Choices (A), (C), and (E) are incorrect because citizens are under no obligation to be well informed in order to affect their government. Choice (D) is wrong, as there are laws that place limits on campaign donations.

12. **D** A closed primary election occurs when only members of a particular party may vote for a candidate to represent them. An open primary allows all eligible voters in a state to vote, regardless of party. Primary elections often have many candidates, particularly in the early stages, so choice (A) is incorrect. Choice (C) is incorrect because primary elections give the power to select candidates to the voters rather than party leaders. Caucuses and primary elections, while achieving similar goals, are not the same, so choice (E) is incorrect. Choice (B) is irrelevant: it discusses the results of an election while the concept of a closed election relates to who may vote in an election.

13. **D** All of the generalizations regarding voter behavior are correct as written except for choice (D). Immigrants to the United States are more likely to vote for Democratic candidates than for Republican candidates.

14. **E** The Twenty-sixth Amendment granted eligible individuals aged 18–20 the right to vote. However, the percentage of total voters who turned out in the 1972 presidential elections declined, rather than increased, due to the addition of millions of eligible individuals who did not turn out. All of the other choices can be eliminated because they do not relate to the Twenty-sixth Amendment. Women gained the right to vote with the Nineteenth Amendment, slavery was abolished with the Thirteenth Amendment, poll taxes were abolished with the Twenty-fourth Amendment, and the Twenty-first Amendment repealed the Eighteenth, which had prohibited liquor.

15. **D** The framers of the Constitution were careful to keep a separation between church and state, as many were descendants of pilgrims who escaped religious intolerance. The belief that the government has been ordained by God is known as divine right. Limited government, popular sovereignty, human equality, and individual rights are all found in the major documents of the early republic, such as the Declaration of Independence and the Constitution. Eliminate choices (A), (B), (C), and (E).

16. **A** Most high school students take a civics or government class. This is a common form of political socialization that is considered formal because it explicitly teaches young people how to engage their government. Often the messages people receive that most influence their political identity come

in subtle ways, such as through family or religion. Eliminate choices (B) and (E). Other informal ways that people absorb political messages are through the evening news and even by listening to and reciting the Pledge of Allegiance. Eliminate choices (C) and (D).

17.   D   The percent of individuals who received a doctorate in 2004 is *less* than the percent of individuals who received a master's degree in 2000. All of the other statements are correct as written and, therefore, choice (D) is the correct answer.

Drill 3

1.   C   According to the table, President Clinton's approval rating began at approximately 35 percent, then decreased, increased, and ended at approximately 45 percent: this shows a net gain of approximately 10 points, from 35 to 45 percent, during the Clinton Administration. While Eisenhower, a Republican, had a high approval rating, Democrats such as Roosevelt, Kennedy, and Johnson were even higher. Eliminate choices (A) and (B). The Vietnam War of the mid-1960s to mid-1970s was marked by a sharp decline in presidential approval, so choice (D) is incorrect. President Reagan's presidency is characterized by two significant rises and two significant drops in approval. Since his polling numbers were not consistent, choice (E) must be incorrect.

2.   E   Political efficacy measures the faith that citizens put into government institutions and the belief that an individual citizen can make a difference in politics. Due to the split electorate and the controversial Supreme Court ruling in *Bush v. Gore* that followed the election, many Americans were disenchanted with the political process; therefore, political efficacy decreased, and you should eliminate choices (A), (B), and (D). Choice (C) is incorrect because President George W. Bush narrowly won the electoral vote and lost the electoral vote: he did not win in a landslide.

3.   C   In most states, a plurality of votes is sufficient to win the nomination. However, some states, such as Georgia, Oklahoma, and Texas, require a candidate to receive 50 percent of the votes. If no candidate does, a runoff primary is held between the top two vote-getters. Choice (A) describes a primary in which voters from any party can participate and choice (B) describes a primary in which only voters from the candidates' party can participate. Choices (D) and (E) refer to the same type of primary in which all candidates, regardless of party, run in the same election.

4.   B   The 1960 general election between John F. Kennedy and then Vice President Richard Nixon is remembered for the debate that took place on September 26. Kennedy appeared healthy, charismatic, and strong, while Nixon appeared pale, untrustworthy, and weak. Radio listeners thought Nixon won the debate on the content of his message, but television viewers soundly declared Kennedy the winner. In 1956, Adlai Stevenson had the first televised debate with his opponent in the primaries, Estes Kefauver, but in the general election, Eisenhower refused to debate Stevenson. Eliminate choice (A). Although there were televised debates in the election years given in choices (C), (D),

and (E), none have the recognition for establishing the importance of candidate appearance that the 1960 election does.

5. **D** In 2008 and 2012, 57 and 53 percent of women, respectively, were likely to vote for President Obama, compared with 50 and 43 percent of men, respectively. Choice (A) is incorrect because there are clear differences in likely voting trends from "High school or less" to "postgraduate" in the data. Most voters older than aged 65 favored the Republican in 2008 and 2012, so choice (B) is incorrect. Western voters preferred President Obama by 10 points in 2008, but by only 6 points in 2012, so choice (C) is incorrect. Catholics supported President Obama in 2008, but Mitt Romney in 2012. This discrepancy would invalidate choice (E).

6. **D** The rational ignorance effect occurs when people make a decision that it is not worthwhile to be informed or vote on an issue because they feel their vote will not make a difference. We can arrive at this answer through process of elimination. Choice (A) is wrong because an older electorate would indicate a stronger likelihood to vote. Voters in the 1996 election were more likely than in any previous general election to have a college degree. Eliminate choice (B). Wealthier voters are more likely to vote, so choice (C) is incorrect. An off-year election is one in which members of Congress are elected but a president is not: since 1996 was a presidential election year, you can eliminate choice (E). Since choices (A), (B), (C), and (E) are incorrect, the process of elimination reveals that the best explanation for the decline in voter turnout in 1996 was that voters simply were not as motivated to vote as in previous elections.

7. **D** Younger voters are less likely to vote than older voters. Politically active voters, such as those in unions or those who are active in party politics, are more likely to vote; therefore, you may eliminate choices (A) and (C). Generally, voters with more education and higher incomes are more likely to vote, so eliminate choice (B), since professionals earn more money than those without professional degrees. Voters in swing states are more likely to vote because they are more likely to feel that their votes matter; therefore, eliminate choice (E).

8. **E** Political scientists and pundits lament low voter turnout for a variety of reasons. The United States government is intended to operate with the consent of the governed, but when people don't vote, they aren't consenting to anything and they aren't being represented accurately. Eliminate choices (B) and (D). Other countries, or even United States citizens, can view the government as illegitimate, since it wasn't truly elected by the citizens when voter turnout is low, so eliminate choice (A). Minorities have more barriers to voting, such as identification requirements or difficulty getting to polling places, so low voter turnout generally means fewer minority voters than would be expected. Eliminate choice (C). Some countries, like Australia, impose a fine on people who fail to vote, but there is no such fine in the United States, so choice (E) is correct.

Free-Response Question 1

Students may earn a total of six points on this question. Two points are available for part (a), two points for part (b), and two points for part (c).

(a) For this response, students may earn one point for indicating specific faults associated with the exorbitant costs of elections. For example, you may discuss how fundraising takes government officials away from the business of governing. Furthermore, qualified individuals who lack the skill or will to fundraise are discouraged from running for office.

Other specific points that would make for a strong discussion on this topic include

- PACs
- Interest groups
- Disproportionate influence of wealthy corporations and individuals
- Inefficiency of funds in a large campaign
- Disincentives for small donors to contribute

No matter what examples you choose to discuss, you must connect them back to the central idea of American skepticism towards government in order to earn a second point for part (a).

(b) Students may earn one point for identifying an example of direct participation and one point for identifying an example of indirect participation. With regard to conventional behavior, disenchanted voters tend to

- Stay home on Election Day
- Vote for independent candidates
- Vote for third parties

You can open up the second part of your response to behaviors that do not directly take place on Election Day, such as protest and limiting political action to involvement in local community activity in order to earn a second point for part (b). You should also bring up specific examples of non-conventional participation. Some of these behaviors include boycotts, sit-ins, marches, demonstrations, and violence.

(c) Students may earn one point for defining "divided government" and one point for explaining how it breeds skepticism towards the political process. "Divided government" occurs when one party controls the presidency and another holds a majority in one or both houses of Congress.

In order to earn a second point for part (c), explain how divided government causes skepticism among American voters. Be sure to support your thesis with specific examples that illustrate *how* divided government fosters popular distrust toward the political process. Some of these examples should include

- A polarized and hyper partisan citizenry
- Political stalemates and gridlock
- Moderate voters do not feel their voice is heard
- Overuse of filibusters
- Political barriers to the confirmation of political and judicial appointments

Drill 4

1. **B** Libertarians support alternative energy at a rate of 44 percent and support coal, oil, and natural gas at a rate of 40 percent. "Staunch Conservatives" and "Hard-Pressed Democrats" show significant support for opposite sides of the graph. Eliminate choice (A). According to the chart, 63 percent of Americans support non-oil, coal, and natural gas sources. The percentage of voters who prefer funding these sources of energy or both sources of energy add up to 35 percent. Even if we could extrapolate that the 63 percent want to end funding toward traditional forms of energy (we cannot actually draw this conclusion from the data provided), they would not make up twice the 35 percent. Eliminate choice (C). We have no information on how many people were polled, so choices (D) and (E) are incorrect.

2. **D** The percentage of respondents who supported increasing scientific research fell from 39 percent to 36 percent, while the percentage of respondents who advocated decreasing scientific research grew from 14 to 23 percent. Therefore, choice (B) is an untrue statement and the credited response. In fact, all categories saw a fall in support for increased spending in 2011 and a rise in the percentage of respondents who advocated decreasing spending in 2011. Therefore, choices (D) and (E) are true statements and should be eliminated. Support for increasing anti-terrorism defenses fell by only 2 percent, the smallest decline of any category; thus, choice (A) is a true statement and you should eliminate it. In 2009 and 2011, 2 percent and 6 percent, respectively, of respondents advocated decreasing spending on veterans' benefits, compared with 6 percent and 11 percent, respectively, who advocated decreasing spending on education; therefore, choice (C) is a true statement and should be eliminated.

3. **B** In almost every year shown and in both parties (with the sole exception of Democrats in 1972), the percentage of voters who engaged in partisan voting when making their decision after the campaign began was lower than the percentage of those who made that decision before the campaign began. Eliminate choice (A) because there is no clear pattern over time for the decision to vote for the candidate from one's party. Eliminate choice (C) because the opposite is true; in only 3 out of the 24 data points shown did a lesser percentage of Republicans than Democrats vote for the candidate from their party. Eliminate choice (D) because both Republicans who decided before and after the campaign began were more likely to vote for the Republican candidate. Finally, eliminate choice (E) because party loyalty was higher among the Republicans (97 percent) than among the Democrats (82 percent) for those who decided before the campaign began.

4. **B** Delegates are often party members and elected officials who were themselves successful in politics because they had access to funds to run a winning campaign. The Campaign Funding Act does not exist and contributions limits have been set by the FEC, so eliminate choice (A). There are no direct financial barriers to voting. Some people may have trouble getting to polling places or taking time off work to vote, but the FEC is not involved in eliminating those barriers, so eliminate choice (C). Federal officials cannot use their office staff to work on their campaigns, nor do they receive funding for additional staff for those activities. Eliminate choice (D). Finally, choice (E) is

not true. There are dozens of senators and over 100 representatives currently serving who are under the age of 50.

5. **A** Choice (A) is correct because the percentages of support for the two measures stated are similar among moderates in both groups, whereas both moderate groups vary widely from the opinions of their own parties. Eliminate choice (B) because both strong and weak Democrats are more likely to support a path to citizenship for illegal immigrants than moderate Democrats are. Eliminate choice (C) because the table provides information in percentages, not actual numbers. Eliminate choice (D) because although having control of both chambers of Congress makes passage of Republican-favored laws more likely, the president still has veto power. There is not enough information in table to support this statement. Eliminate choice (E) because the table does not draw a connection between exactly which voters supported which measures.

6. **C** Third parties lack the money and organization to effectively campaign and gain exposure to the public. Many of the top third party candidates have had strong qualifications for public office, such as Theodore Roosevelt, who ran for a third presidential term in 1912 for the Progressive (Bull Moose) Party; therefore, choice (A) is incorrect. Although many third party candidate platforms fail to appeal to the majority of the population, some candidates offer platforms that appeal to the general public; however, the public's lack of awareness of their platforms inhibits their electoral prospects. Therefore, choice (C) is better than choice (B). Choice (D) is incorrect because third party candidates are eligible to hold public, just as Democrats and Republicans are. Although some third party candidates have left the Democratic and Republican parties, their former association with these parties does not inhibit their electoral prospects as much as the lack of party machinery; therefore, choice (E) is incorrect.

7. **A** Someone who chooses not to register with any specific political party is more likely to vote for the candidate whose views he or she agrees with, rather than to vote straight down a party line. Devout Christians overwhelming vote Republican, African Americans overwhelmingly vote Democrat, and unions overwhelmingly vote Democrat, so eliminate choices (B), (C), and (E). Families are the lead influencer over one's political affiliation, so parents who are active in, and therefore loyal to, one party are likely to raise a child who is the same. Eliminate choice (D).

8. **E** Choice (E) is correct because the percentages under the "all" categories are always higher than the percentages under the "solidly" categories. Eliminate choice (A) because both the Republicans and the Democrats saw a spike in strong party identification in January 2013. Eliminate choice (B) because a greater percentage identified as Democrats (46 percent) in June 2013 than independent (41 percent). Eliminate choice (C) because the Democrats had higher percentages of identification in January 2010 and January 2013 than they did in either data point for 2012. Eliminate choice (E) because the opposite is true in January and June 2011. In addition, from the table it is unclear whether the spikes and falls in moderate identification stem from changes of opinion in those who are independent, or those who strongly identify with a party.

Free-Response Question 1

Students may earn six points on this question: three points for part (a) and three points for part (b). Part (a) offers one point for identifying a political behavior, one point for describing an advantage of that form of political participation, and one point for describing a limitation of that form of participation. Part (b) offers the same three points for a second type of political behavior. These political behaviors, advantages, and limitations may include the following.

Political participation besides voting	Advantages	Limitations
File lawsuits, litigation	Does not require a majority of voters or legislative body to effect change	Expensive, legal expertise/representation required
Organize demonstrations/protest	Low cost, gain public awareness of issue	Large numbers of participants needed in order to be effective
Boycott	Low cost, gain public awareness of issue, force target to respond	Large numbers of participants needed in order to be effective
Write letters to elected officials and bureaucrats	Low cost; officials believe opinion is representative of more people than just the author	Officials receive many letters; lack the power of personal, face-to-face contact
Contact media outlets	Increase public awareness, low cost	Subject to media outlet's perspective and willingness to disseminate information
Work for political campaigns	Direct access to voters, increase others' interest in issues and candidates, possible access to candidate	Limited or no opportunity to shape campaign decisions
Run for (or hold) elected office	Gain public awareness of chosen issues, force opponent(s) to respond, opportunity to hold public office and shape policy	Very expensive to campaign
Give financial contribution to a political campaign	Donors may receive access to candidate	Small donations do not yield access to candidate
Register voters	Direct access to voters, increase others' interest in issues and candidates	Reach is limited to meeting voters face-to-face
Participate in town hall meetings	Opportunity to voice opinion directly to others	Need to convince a majority of participants to take action
Join a political organization	Connect to those with similar opinions, learn from their experience	Agenda may be limited to points of consensus
Debate political issues with other citizens	Low cost, personal contact with voters, opportunity to challenge/reconsider opinions	Results are less widespread than with other forms of participation

To best discuss the advantages and limitations of each action, focus on its expediency. Does your chosen action give more or less direct access to the government? Is a majority of voters necessary to affect change? Does it gain public attention? Is this always positive? Is it expensive or cost effective? Let these types of questions direct your analysis.

Drill 5

1. **A**   Based on the data provided in the table, at each year provided, the share of net worth among the Top 1 percent increased (from 33.4 to 34.3 to 34.5 percent) and the share of the Bottom 80 percent decreased (from 15.6 to 15.3 to 15.0 percent); therefore, choices (B) and (C) are incorrect and choice (A) is correct. Choice (D) is incorrect because the data show the share of total net worth held by each group, not the actual net worth; therefore, we cannot conclude whether actual net worth increased or decreased. Choice (E) is incorrect because the data does not provide an explanation for the changes in the share of net worth. Furthermore, the share of net worth held by the Top 1 percent increased 0.9 percent from 2001 to 2004, while the share held by the Next 19 percent decreased only 0.6 percent; therefore, a decrease in the share of net worth among the Next 19 percent could not be the complete explanation for the increase in the share of net worth among the Top 1 percent.

2. **D**   A large proportion of the men drafted to fight in the Vietnam War were 18 to 20 year olds who were ineligible to vote for or against the politicians sending them into combat. Although the push for a lower voting age began with Franklin Roosevelt's lowering of the military draft age during World War II, there was no widespread push for lowering the voting age until the Vietnam War; therefore, choices (B) and (C) are incorrect, and choice (D) is correct. Choice (E) is incorrect because the Twenty-first Amendment did not lower the drinking age: it simply repealed the Eighteenth Amendment, which had banned the manufacture and sale of alcohol. While voter turnout had decreased since 1960, this was not a major factor in lowering the voting age; therefore, choice (A) is incorrect.

3. **B**   Political parties use primary elections to narrow the field of candidates before a general election. In an open primary, the party allows voters of any party affiliation to vote for its candidates. In a closed primary, the party allows only party members to vote for its candidates. Therefore, choice (B) is correct and choice (A) is incorrect. Choices (C) and (D) are incorrect because may vote only for candidates of different parties in a blanket primary, not in an open or closed primary. Choice (E) is incorrect because voters are limited to a single ballot in open and closed primaries.

4. **C**   This graph shows a gender gap, as 76 percent of Hispanic women voted for Obama, while only 65 percent of Hispanic men did so. While elderly Hispanic voters were more likely to vote for Romney than were their younger counterparts (35 to 23 percent), they were still far more likely to vote for Obama than Romney (65 to 35 percent); therefore, you may eliminate choices (A) and (D). Although 82 percent of Hispanic voters who earn less than $50,000 per year voted for Obama, the data does not indicate what percent of Hispanic voters earn less than $50,000 per year; therefore, you may eliminate choice (B). Choice (E) is incorrect because Hispanic voters with a college degree were less likely to vote for Obama than were Hispanic voters without college degrees (62 to 75 percent).

5. **E** The data suggest that most Jews identify as Democrats (51 percent) and most Mormons identify as Republicans (53 percent). Therefore, choices (A) and (B) are correct statements and should be eliminated, while choice (E) is an incorrect statement and is the credited response. Choice (C) is a correct statement because 12 percent of Mormons lean Republican while 53 percent identify as Republicans; therefore, you may eliminate choice (C). Choice (D) is a correct statement because 16 percent of Jews identify as Republicans while 5 percent lean Republican; therefore, you may eliminate choice (D).

6. **D** In general, the South has been a staunch supporter of conservative views and the Republican Party. Minorities tend to vote liberal and support Democratic candidates, so eliminate choices (A) and (B). Women tend to be more liberal in voting than men, so eliminate choice (C). Urban populations, which also tend to have a higher percentage of minorities, also lean more liberal and are more likely to vote for Democrats, so eliminate choice (E).

7. **C** Political socialization is the learning process by which individuals develop an attitude, behavior, or opinion regarding a political stance. Family, race, religion, and mass media play key roles in shaping a child's or adolescent's political views. Choice (C) is the best answer because geography plays the least significant role in political socialization.

8. **A** According to the data in the table, 39 percent of likely voters in 2004 identified as Republicans; in 2008, only 29 percent of likely voters identified as Republicans. Similarly, 48 percent of likely voters identified as Republicans or leaned Republican in 2004, while only 42 percent did so in 2008. This information supports choice (A). On the other hand, black voters comprised 8 percent of the likely voter population in 2004 and 12 percent in 2008; therefore, choice (E) is incorrect. From 2004–2012, 15–20 percent of likely voters held a college degree only and 16–20 percent held a postgraduate degree; since the sum of these two numbers is less than 50 percent in any given election year, choice (B) is incorrect. In 2004, 13 percent of likely voters were aged 18–29 and 38 percent were aged 30–49; therefore, 51 percent (the sum of 13 and 38 percent) of likely voters in 2004 were under age 50, and choice (D) is incorrect. There is no data in the table to support choice (C): Midwestern voters comprised only 23, 22, and 23 percent of likely voters in 2004, 2008, and 2012. Although it appears that Midwestern voters were equally likely to vote in all three elections, there isn't actually enough data to reach this conclusion. The data in the table tells us only what percentage of the likely voter population was comprised of Midwestern voters, not what percent of Midwestern voters were likely to vote.

Free-Response Question 1

Students may earn a total of six points for this question: three points for part (a) and three points for part (b).

In part (a), you may earn one points for identifying a Democratic stronghold. Possible answers include

- West coast
- Midwest
- Northeast
- New England
- Mid-Atlantic or Chesapeake

It's a good idea to identify a couple of individual states to make it clear what region you're referring to. You may then earn one point for each reason for this voting pattern that you describe, up to a maximum of two points. Some of these reasons may include

- Strong presence of unions or organized labor
- Large populations of racial/ethnic minorities
- High urban concentrations
- Environmental concerns of voters
- Liberal political philosophy
- Long history of supporting Democrats (be careful on this one and make sure you know your history if you choose this reason)

In part (b), you may earn one points for identifying a Republican stronghold. Possible answers include

- South
- Southeast
- Gulf coast
- Plains states

You may then earn one point for each reason for this voting pattern that you describe, up to a maximum of two points. Many of these could simply be opposites of the reasons listed in the previous part of this question. These factors include

- "Right-to-work" states, or those with few unions
- Rural
- Conservative political philosophy
- Hunting tradition or strong support among voters for gun rights
- Solid Christian/Protestant/Fundamentalist identification
- Social/religious conservatives
- Long history of supporting Republicans (be careful on this one and make sure you know your history if you choose this reason)

Note: It is not enough on this question to say that John McCain is from Arizona or Barack Obama is from Illinois. You should evaluate the political identities of the regions based on the aforementioned factors.

Chapter 7
Political Parties, Interest Groups, and Mass Media

DRILL 1

1. Which of the following is usually true about the relationship between presidential and vice-presidential candidates?

   (A) They are from different parties.
   (B) They are from different states.
   (C) They are from the same state.
   (D) The vice-presidential candidate usually makes most of the campaign decisions.
   (E) The vice-presidential candidate served in the prior administration's cabinet.

2. Which of the following is NOT a tactic used by interest groups to persuade elected members of government?

   (A) Lobbying for issues
   (B) Endorsing candidates
   (C) Voting directly on bills
   (D) Filing lawsuits in the courts
   (E) Making political donations to candidates

3. Which of the following best describes an informal government action?

   (A) Elections for national offices
   (B) Judicial nominations
   (C) Impeachment proceedings
   (D) Congressional votes on legislation
   (E) Conversations with lobbyists

4. The increasing use of presidential primaries in the past four decades has had which of the following effects?

   (A) Decreased spending on political campaigns
   (B) Decreased spending by PACs
   (C) More control over the presidential nomination process by the elite political class
   (D) Elimination of national party conventions
   (E) Decreased importance of state conventions

5. Which of the following is a function of political parties?

   (A) Congressional lobbying
   (B) Giving citizens a link to the political process
   (C) Writing opinions for the Supreme Court
   (D) Ensuring that the elite class runs the government
   (E) Suppressing minority rights

6. Which of the following categories of campaigns do NOT have the option to be partially financed by public money?

   I. Congressional
   II. Gubernatorial
   III. Presidential

   (A) I only
   (B) II only
   (C) I and II only
   (D) II and III only
   (E) I, II, and III

7. An election that changes the balance of government power from one party to the other in America's two-party system is called

   (A) party dealignment
   (B) a critical election
   (C) a primary election
   (D) split ticket voting
   (E) a coalition

8. Politicians use all of the following tactics to generate positive media stories EXCEPT

   (A) holding meetings to address pressing issues
   (B) extra-marital affairs
   (C) television interviews
   (D) press releases
   (E) photo-ops

9. Which of the following factors contributes most directly to split-ticket voting in America?

(A) More third party candidates with little public support
(B) More voter decisions based on party identification
(C) Stronger national party organizations and weaker state party organizations
(D) Decreasing voter identification with the Democratic and Republican parties
(E) Higher reliance on parties support by candidates

10. Interest groups presently represent which of the following causes?

  I. Environmentalism
  II. The Right to Bear Arms
  III. The Right to Forbid the Quartering of Soldiers
  IV. The Right to Free Speech

(A) II only
(B) IV only
(C) I, II, and III only
(D) I, II, and IV only
(E) I, II, III, and IV

11. Which of the following was true before the 1960s' increase in popularity of states using primary election systems to select presidential candidates?

(A) Political parties didn't exist.
(B) The cost of running for office was higher.
(C) U.S. voters played a larger role in the nomination process.
(D) State party organizations played a smaller role in the nomination process.
(E) State party leaders had more control over the nomination process.

12. Which of the following is a function of the two major political parties in the United States?

(A) To act as a check on the other party
(B) To represent a single political issue
(C) To de-emphasize their national conventions
(D) To select juries in criminal trials
(E) To represent a narrow portion of the electorate

13. All of the following describe the organization of the major parties in the United States EXCEPT:

(A) Party decisions are top down from the national level to the local level.
(B) The majority of a party's leaders are local activists.
(C) All levels of a political party are represented at the party's convention.
(D) Local and state participants may exercise power in their national party system.
(E) National elected officials frequently campaign for local candidates in their parties.

14. Advising legislators on the technical components of particular issues is the primary job of

(A) the media
(B) lobbyists
(C) campaign coordinators
(D) the courts
(E) cabinet members

DRILL 2

Questions 1-2 refer to the following table.

Trends in National House Vote, 2004-2010

	2010 Dem	2010 Rep	2008 Dem	2008 Rep	2006 Dem	2006 Rep	2004 Dem	2004 Rep
Protestant/Other Christian	38%	59%	45%	53%	44%	54%	42%	57%
White Protestant/Other Christian	28	69	35	63	37	61	34	65
Catholic	44	54	55	42	55	44	49	50
White Catholic	39	59	46	52	50	49	45	54
Unaffiliated	68	30	72	25	74	22	65	31
White evang. or born-again Christians*	19	77	28	70	28	70	25	74

*Includes Catholics and members of other faiths in addition to Protestants
Figures for third party candidates not shown.
Source: 2010, 2008, 2006, and 2004 National Election Pool exit polls, Pew Research Center's Forum on Religion and Public Life. 2010 data from CNN.com.

1. Which statement about voting behavior is best supported by the table shown above?

   (A) Those who identify as Protestant are largely sympathetic to the Democratic Party platform.
   (B) Catholic voters are a reliable voting block for the Republican Party.
   (C) Those with little religious affiliation tend to vote Republican.
   (D) There is no discernible relationship between religious identity and voting behavior.
   (E) Voting behavior based on religious identification is at least somewhat divided along racial lines.

2. Which generalization about congressional elections in the first decade of the twenty-first century does the table support?

   (A) Support for Democratic candidates rose to a peak in the middle of the decade before dropping.
   (B) Catholic voters participated less in congressional elections in the early part of the decade than they did in the later part.
   (C) The 2008 presidential election created a lasting wave of support for Democratic candidates.
   (D) Republicans gained more congressional seats in the 2006 election than they did in any other year.
   (E) The presidential candidates at the top of the ticket in 2004 and 2008 hurt their respective parties on down ticket voting.

3. Duverger's law holds that

   (A) the candidate who spends the most money will win an election
   (B) a plurality system supports the success of third parties
   (C) the number of votes a party receives dictates the number of legislators who represent that party in the legislature
   (D) the popular vote winner and electoral vote winner are one in the same in a general election
   (E) a single-member plurality system necessarily leads to a two-party system

4. "Horse race journalism" is problematic due to the fact that it

   (A) shifts the media focus from the issues of a campaign to the results of public opinion polls
   (B) relies on speculative information rather than fact-based data
   (C) encourages news outlets to break stories before verifying the facts
   (D) highlights the negative aspects of a candidate rather than the candidate's virtues
   (E) focuses on narrow interests that are not relevant to the general public

5. Since the mid-1980s, which of the following interests has experienced the greatest increase in political action committee membership?

(A) Labor unions
(B) Trade groups
(C) Corporations
(D) Civil rights advocates
(E) Health care

6. Elections in which political alignments fundamentally change are referred to as

(A) critical elections
(B) blanket primaries
(C) dealignments
(D) closed primaries
(E) realignments

7. All of the following regarding *amicus curiae* briefs are true EXCEPT:

(A) Qualified individuals can file such briefs in lawsuits to which they are not party.
(B) *Amicus curiae* briefs are referred to as "friend of the court" briefs.
(C) Judges may consider such briefs if the information directly affects the case.
(D) Interest groups may both file lawsuits to advance their interests and submit amicus curiae briefs.
(E) *Amicus curiae* briefs are an ineffective means of influencing the outcome of a case.

8. Which of the following is true regarding the nation's electoral system?

(A) It allows third parties to make a significant impact on presidential elections.
(B) It has led to the successful rise of bolter parties.
(C) It is mandated by the Constitution.
(D) It has little impact on the political parties.
(E) It strengthens America's two-party system.

9. All of the following statements regarding gerrymandering are true EXCEPT:

(A) Gerrymandering refers to the partisan redrawing of congressional district borders.
(B) Due to gerrymandering, a number of House incumbents run for reelection unopposed.
(C) Gerrymandering affects members of the House more than members of the Senate.
(D) When legally allowable, the legislature will gerrymander the district boundaries to give the majority party an advantage in future elections.
(E) Gerrymandering is allowable in all 50 states.

10. Which of the following statements regarding political action committees (PACs) is FALSE?

(A) They were formed in order to give people a voice in government policy meetings.
(B) PACs must raise money from at least 50 contributors and must donate to at least five different candidates.
(C) Unions and corporations can grant limited amounts of money to candidates of their choice.
(D) PACs may not donate more than $5,000 to a single candidate per year.
(E) The Federal Election Campaign Act allows corporations, unions, and trade associations to form PACs in order to raise campaign funds.

11. All of the following are effects of media consolidation EXCEPT:

(A) Political news coverage is increasingly similar.
(B) The concentration of ownership allows the media to suppress stories that do not serve their interests.
(C) The majority of the media's political coverage has become increasingly liberal.
(D) Critics of consolidation question whether the media benefits the public interest.
(E) The public may not be adequately informed of crucial issues.

12. All of the following groups have influenced the platform of the Republican since 1950 EXCEPT

   (A) The Congressional Hispanic Conference
   (B) Physicians' Council for Responsible Reform
   (C) Hoover League
   (D) Capitol Hill Club
   (E) Evangelical Christians

13. While political parties run candidates for office who represent the political agenda of the party members, interest groups

   (A) try to influence policy via political action and donation to sympathetic candidates
   (B) work with congressional committees and executive agencies to enforce federal regulations
   (C) aim to raise the standard of living for America's poorest residents through Great Society Programs
   (D) meet for the purpose of choosing delegates to the national convention
   (E) solely focus on issues related to job security, taxes, wages, and employee benefits

14. Interest groups can influence the government in all of the following ways EXCEPT

   (A) direct lobbying through private meetings with government officials
   (B) socializing with government officials
   (C) submitting *amicus curiae* briefs to the court
   (D) sending out propaganda promoting their views
   (E) providing unlimited campaign contributions

DRILL 3

1. Which of the following is the LEAST accurate statement about political parties in the United States?

   (A) Americans have become increasingly uncertain that the two-party system can effectively handle major issues facing the country and represent the public interest.
   (B) The percentage of voters who identify as independent has decreased since the 1960s.
   (C) Ethnic and racial groups can become aligned with particular political parties.
   (D) Support for third parties has increased over the past decade.
   (E) Individuals with strong party affiliation tend to practice straight-ticket voting.

2. Which of the following was a direct result of the Federal Election Campaign Act?

   (A) Congress is allowed to pass laws necessary and proper to the performance of its duties.
   (B) Poll taxes were outlawed.
   (C) Corporations, unions, and trade associations were allowed to raise campaign funds via political action committees.
   (D) The federal government could register voters in states or counties that had been using literacy tests to prevent individuals from voting.
   (E) Soft money rules were changed for 527 groups.

3. A sound bite would most likely be used during a presidential election in order to

   (A) avoid "horse race" politics
   (B) provide the audience with a candidate's view in a limited amount of time
   (C) reduce the amount of negative advertising used
   (D) ensure a candidate is presented in the best light
   (E) emphasize who won and lost presidential debates

4. Critical elections often lead to

   (A) party dealignment
   (B) the formation of a coalition government
   (C) party neutrality
   (D) the establishment of linkage institutions
   (E) party realignment

5. Public funding is used for which of the following?

   I. Presidential candidates in the primary election
   II. Presidential candidates in the general election
   III. National nominating conventions

   (A) I only
   (B) II only
   (C) I and II only
   (D) II and III only
   (E) I, II, and III

6. All of the following statements are true regarding the role of the vice president EXCEPT:

(A) The vice president has the ability to influence legislation in the Senate.

(B) Former Democratic vice presidents are ex officio super-delegates to the Democratic National Convention.

(C) Over the past couple of decades, the vice presidency has been used to launch bids for the presidency.

(D) Since the early 1970s, most vice presidents have become politically inactive after leaving office.

(E) A vice president is often selected because he or she has qualities that help the presidential candidates appeal to a broader voting base.

7. What do political parties and interest groups have in common?

(A) They accurately represent diverse and specific interests.

(B) They are difficult to join without a lot of funding for media exposure.

(C) They give their members direct access to the executive branch.

(D) They work with the Supreme Court to combat bad policies.

(E) They widen accessibility to politicians and the political process.

8. The process of selecting presidential nominations is different now than it was 50 years ago primarily because

(A) corruption in campaign financing allows a few powerful individuals to select a party's nominee

(B) primaries, rather than state conventions, are a more influential part of the process

(C) ballot access has becoming greatly simplified

(D) opposition to the Electoral College has intensified

(E) party members are more likely to nominate people with little political experience than they were in the past

Free Response

Time—25 minutes

1. Many interest groups focus their political efforts on a single issue or an ideology that is specific to that group of people. Their focus on that issue or ideology can sometimes mean that they overlook the greater good of the public.

    (a)   Describe each of the following two tactics that interest groups use to affect the outcome of elections.

- PACs
- "Get out the vote" efforts

    (b)   Describe each of the following two tactics that interest groups use to persuade decision-makers to act in the best interest of the group.

- Litigation
- Economic leverage

    (c)   Describe each of the following informal methods of limiting the power that interest groups have over politics.

- Pluralism
- Media coverage

DRILL 4

1. Which of the following is true of lobbyists?

   (A) A significant source of funding is not an important factor to be successful.
   (B) Lobbyists are forbidden from testifying at congressional hearings.
   (C) Most lobbyists represent a wide range of interests.
   (D) Lobbyists cannot gain access to speak with the president directly.
   (E) Filing an *amicus curiae* brief is an effective lobbying technique.

2. If an issue has low intensity and low saliency for much of the public, then an interest group will

   (A) not be able to convince any member of Congress to care about it
   (B) not invest any time or money in promoting the issue
   (C) be more likely to influence members of Congress
   (D) use television media to raise as much awareness of the issue as possible
   (E) form a coalition with other interest groups whose issues have low intensity and low saliency

3. Which of the following accurately describes a consequence of the rise of the primary system used to select presidential candidates?

   I. State party leaders have lost authority in the nomination process.
   II Fewer people are willing to register with either the Democrat or the Republican parties.
   III. The cost of running a presidential campaign has declined.

   (A) I only
   (B) II only
   (C) III only
   (D) I and II only
   (E) II and III only

4. All of the following are roles of political parties in the United States EXCEPT

   (A) encouraging voter registration and turnout
   (B) educating voters about political issues
   (C) setting rules and procedures at polling places
   (D) establishing commonalities among diverse groups of people
   (E) determining which candidates will be successful in elections

5. A legal filing that presents an argument in favor of a particular issue is known as

   (A) a writ of *certiorari*
   (B) a concurring opinion
   (C) an *amicus curiae* brief
   (D) a bill of attainder
   (E) a motion of cloture

6. Which of the following presidential elections is NOT considered a critical election?

   (A) 1932, Roosevelt v. Hoover
   (B) 1968, Humphrey v. Nixon
   (C) 1980, Carter v. Reagan v. Anderson
   (D) 1992, Clinton v. Bush v. Perot
   (E) 2000, Bush v. Gore

7. Which of the following economic sectors has created the smallest number of political action committees?

   (A) Agribusiness
   (B) Commercial Banks
   (C) Public Sector Unions
   (D) Defense Aerospace
   (E) Masons

8. The practice of mixing subjective analysis with objective reporting of the facts is known as

   (A) yellow journalism
   (B) horse race journalism
   (C) interpretive reporting
   (D) watchdog journalism
   (E) partisan reporting

Free Response

Time—25 minutes

1. For every presidential election, the two major political parties host national conventions during which they select their nominees. The parties choose delegates, through various methods, to formally vote on the nominee during the convention.

    (a)   Explain the difference between a primary and a caucus as they are used by presidential candidates to win delegates.

    (b)   Explain what superdelegates are and how superdelegates give more authority to party leaders.

    (c)   What is one outcome, positive or negative, of a winner-take-all primary?

    (d)   Why do presidential candidates sometimes seem to have different opinions about political issues when they are seeking the party nomination than they do after they win it?

DRILL 5

Questions 1-2 refer to the table below.

Support For Democratic Party
Percent Change From 1988-2008

	Percent Change
Large Metro Area	+ 21
Core Urban	+ 29
Inner Suburbs	+ 25
Mature Suburbs	+ 27
Emerging Suburbs	+ 13
True Exurbs	+ 1
Medium Metro Area	+ 15
Small Metro Area	+ 7
Small Town Rural Area	+ 2
Deep Rural Area	- 6

1. The table best supports which of the following statements about support for the Democratic Party over the time period shown?

   (A) More people from Core Urban areas than from Inner Suburbs or Mature Suburbs support the Democratic Party.
   (B) The lowest level of support for the Democratic Party comes from True Exurbs.
   (C) No region outside of Large Metro areas has seen as great an increase in support as those within.
   (D) The Democratic party is unlikely to win federal elections in Small Town Rural areas.
   (E) The level of support for the Democratic party generally increased across the United States during the twenty year period shown.

2. The table best supports which of the following statements about party identification?

   (A) A decline in viable third-party candidates during the time period shown boosted support for the Democratic party.
   (B) In 2008, the Democrats received more votes than the Republicans did in Large Metro areas for all federal elections.
   (C) In 2008, a greater percentage of the population was willing to identify as Democrat than was in 1988.
   (D) In 1988, a very small portion of the population living in True Exurbs supported the Democratic party.
   (E) Most of the positive change in support for the Democratic party can be attributed to the election of President Barack Obama.

3. One benefit of multiple-member districts, such as exist in the state legislatures of Arizona and Maryland, is that they

   (A) encourage more diverse candidates who can better represent unique constituents
   (B) give an advantage to candidates from the two major political parties
   (C) lead to political parties that attempt to appeal to as wide a voter base as possible
   (D) provide incumbency advantages in a way that single-member districts cannot
   (E) ensure that only candidates who receive a majority of the votes can serve in office

4. All of the following are ways in which ordinary citizens attempt to pressure their legislators to take action EXCEPT

   (A) writing a petition and collecting signatures
   (B) contributing money to an interest group, which donates those funds to a candidate for office
   (C) travelling with a group of people to Washington, D.C. to meet with a legislator
   (D) starting letter writing campaigns
   (E) rallying voters to all vote the same way on a certain issue

5. Which of the following is NOT a formal organization within the two major political parties in
the United States?

   (A) National party
   (B) State party
   (C) County party
   (D) Electoral board
   (E) Congressional party committee

6. All of the following categories of interest groups
represent types noneconomic views EXCEPT

   (A) professional associations
   (B) public interest
   (C) single-issue
   (D) ideological
   (E) government

7. An average citizen wishing to effect change in
the way small businesses are regulated should
become more active in

   (A) an interest group because interest groups
       tend to focus on local politics
   (B) an interest group because interest groups
       have access to more financing than
       political parties do
   (C) an interest group because interest groups
       work hard to promote a narrow set of
       interests
   (D) a political party because political party
       affiliation will allow him or her to speak
       directly with his or her representatives
   (E) a political party because political parties
       don't represent a wide range of interests

8. Which of the following is NOT a widely accepted
Republican political belief or value?

   (A) Strong military and aggressive foreign
       policy
   (B) Little government intervention in domestic
       matters
   (C) More states' rights
   (D) Traditional notion of family values
   (E) A progressive tax structure

New England Voting Preferences in United States Presidential and Senate Elections

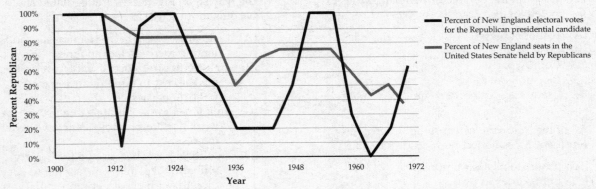

States counted in this graphic are Connecticut, Maine, Massachusetts, New Hampshire, Rhode Island, and Vermont.

Source: The United States Senate and the National Archives.

1. Since 1900, there have been changes in the demographics of the supporters of the two major political parties. Certain demographic groups that voted Republican for much of United States history now vote Democratic. Changes in party preferences among certain groups have occurred at different rates, depending on the type of election.

   (a)   Describe the similarities and differences shown in the trend lines in the figure above.

   (b)   Choose two of the following factors that influence the outcome of elections. Use them to provide possible explanations for the differences in the levels of support for Republicans between the state senatorial races and the presidential races for the time period shown.
   - Redistricting
   - Term limits
   - Differences between state and national politics

   (c)   Choose two of the following demographic groups and explain how their party affiliations have changed since 1900.
   - African Americans
   - Southerners
   - Women
   - Labor union members

   (c)   Use each of the following factors that influence the outcome of elections them to provide possible explanations for the differences in the levels of support for Republicans between the senatorial races and the presidential races for the time period shown.
   - Redistricting
   - Term limits
   - Differences between state and national politics

DRILL 6

1. Which of the following statements regarding the role of the media in reporting political news is inaccurate?

   (A) The media can help hold government officials accountable to the people.
   (B) The media have the ability to set the public agenda for debate.
   (C) The media facilitate two-way communication between government officials and citizens.
   (D) Consolidation of media providers means that coverage now has a clear liberal bias.
   (E) Attack journalism and yellow journalism undermine the role of the media.

2. Which of the following is a difference between regular political action committees (PACs) and Super PACs?

   (A) Super PACs are not regulated by the Federal Election Commission.
   (B) There is no legal limit on the size of a donation that can be made to a Super PAC.
   (C) Corporations only donate to regular PACs, not to Super PACs.
   (D) Only Super PACs can be affiliated with unions.
   (E) Super PACs can mask the identity of their donors, but regular PACs cannot.

3. One way that the Supreme Court has attempted to limit the practice of gerrymandering is by ruling that

   (A) congressional district lines will be redrawn every 20 years instead of every ten
   (B) permanent district lines must be drawn in districts where the population has remained stable for at least 50 years
   (C) gerrymandering based solely on racial data is illegal
   (D) gerrymandering cannot be practiced in districts where representatives have served more than 5 consecutive terms
   (E) an independent commission must redraw all district boundaries

4. Which of the following is a representational system in which there is no advantage to placing second in an election?

   (A) Single-member district
   (B) Multiple-member district
   (C) Popular sovereignty
   (D) Presidential democracy
   (E) Professional legislature

5. All of the following are common ways that interest groups lobby to influence decisions made by the federal government EXCEPT

   (A) meeting privately with representatives and government officials to propose legislation
   (B) offering political donations to candidates or parties that support their cause through political action committees
   (C) endorsing political candidates who support their cause
   (D) publishing press releases, which promote their views among the general public
   (E) meeting privately with members of a jury on a pending court case regarding their views

6. The last major party realignment occurred during which of the following presidential election years?

   (A) 1932
   (B) 1960
   (C) 1996
   (D) 2000
   (E) 2004

7. All of the following are traditional ideological views of the Republican Party EXCEPT

   (A) increased spending and allocations for the military
   (B) tax relief for everyone, especially wealthy individuals and corporations
   (C) limiting spending on social and welfare programs
   (D) increased regulation on the ownership of firearms.
   (E) limiting spending on government-run health programs

Free Response

Time—25 minutes

1. One of the rights that the Constitution protects is the right to assemble. People often join together in order to advance a particular cause or interest among their elected representatives.

   (a) What are two rights, in addition to right to assemble, enumerated in the Bill of Rights that protect people who join together to advance a cause?

   (b) Explain one way in which efforts to advance a particular interest are regulated by the federal government.

   (c) There are several common tactics used by special interest groups to sway politicians. Describe the purpose of each of the following tactics.
   - Lobbying
   - Grassroots campaigns
   - Media campaigns

Chapter 8
Political Parties, Interest Groups, and Mass Media: Answers and Explanations

ANSWER KEY

Multiple-Choice Questions

Drill 1
1. B
2. C
3. E
4. E
5. B
6. C
7. B
8. B
9. D
10. D
11. E
12. A
13. A
14. B

Drill 2
1. E
2. A
3. E
4. A
5. D
6. A
7. E
8. E
9. E
10. A
11. C
12. C
13. A
14. E

Drill 3
1. B
2. C
3. B
4. E
5. E
6. D
7. E
8. B

Drill 4
1. E
2. C
3. A
4. C
5. C
6. E
7. E
8. C

Drill 5
1. E
2. C
3. A
4. B
5. D
6. A
7. C
8. E

Drill 6
1. D
2. B
3. C
4. A
5. E
6. A
7. D

EXPLANATIONS

Drill 1

1. **B** Usually, when presidential candidates select someone to run for vice president, they seek to add a person that will "balance" the ticket. Part of this balance comes from choosing someone from a different region of the country. For example, the moderate Arizonan Republican John McCain chose the more ideologically conservative Alaskan Republican, Sarah Palin, as his running mate. McCain's choice was made, in part, in response to Republicans who didn't think he was conservative enough. You can pick (B) and eliminate choice (C). As for the other false answers, presidential and vice-presidential candidates are almost always of the same party, so eliminate (A). While a presidential candidate coordinates with a vice-presidential candidate, the presidential candidate usually gets to make final decisions on campaign issues, so eliminate choice (D). Finally, the vice president can come from many prior occupations including congressional (Joseph Biden and Paul Ryan) and gubernatorial (Sarah Palin) positions. Not all have served in the prior administration's cabinet.

2. **C** While interest groups hire lobbyists to support or fight issues, endorse candidates who support their interests, file lawsuits in the courts, and make donations to political candidates, they cannot vote directly for a bill because they are not elected members of Congress. Eliminate choices (A), (B), (D), and (E).

3. **E** Of all the choices, choice (E) is the only informal action taken by government. There is no official record kept of conversations between lobbyists and members of Congress. The topics of most of those conversations are usually not known by the general public. However, elections for national offices, judicial nominations, impeachment proceedings, and congressional votes on legislation are all governed by the Constitution and federal or state laws. The results and proceedings of those four functions are published in the media. Therefore, eliminate choices (A), (B), (C), and (D).

4. **E** During the first 150 years and more of America's history, states' parties held nominating conventions that were controlled by state party leaders. Participants in these conventions selected each state's presidential candidates, often through high-level political deal-making in literal "smoke filled rooms." Now citizens vote in state primaries and caucuses in order to send delegates to national nominating conventions. The primary system drove the cost of spending on campaigns way up because candidates have to spend to get their messages out to the states' electorates, often through advertising, so eliminate (A). Some of this increased spending is financed through increased spending by Political Action Committees (PACs), so (B) can be eliminated as well. The rise of primaries shifts some the balance of power of the process from state leaders to voting U.S.

citizens, so choice (C) is incorrect. National party conventions are held every four years, with the most recent in 2012, so eliminate choice (D).

5. B   Political parties provide ways for citizens to participate in government by acting as an intermediary between them. For example, a citizen can join a party as an activist member, which puts the citizen in touch with other like-minded people and gives the citizen a louder "voice" in the democracy. Eliminate (A) because interest groups lobby Congress, not political parties. Supreme Court justices write opinions, so choice (C) is also incorrect. The task of political parties is not to ensure that elites run the government, so eliminate choice (D). Finally, suppressing minority rights, or any rights, is also not a function of parties, so cross off choice (E) as well.

6. C   By law, only presidential campaigns have the option of being financed by public funds, even though both Mitt Romney and Barack Obama eschewed the public funds in 2012. Notice that this is a NOT question, so eliminate part III of the answer and choice (D) and (E) along with it. Neither congressional nor gubernatorial candidates have the option of being financed by public funds, so the correct choice is (C).

7. B   Party dealignment occurs when individual citizens stop voting based on party preferences and start voting based on the positions of individual candidates, so eliminate choice (A). Choice (B), a critical election, on the other hand, is an election that changes the balance of power from one major party to the other and is the correct answer to the question. A primary election is an intraparty election that selects candidates to run in a general election, so eliminate choice (C). Split ticket voting is an action taken by voters when they vote for some candidates from one party and other candidates from another party and choice (D) is not the correct choice. Choice (E) is also incorrect because a coalition describes a group of people from different parties or factions who come together to increase their numbers and power in governmental bodies.

8. B   Politicians use meetings, television interviews, press releases, and photo-ops to generate positive media stories to improve their public images, so eliminate choices (A), (C), (D), and (E). However, having extra-marital affairs usually generates negative media stories and has ruined the careers of many politicians, leaving choice (B) as the correct choice.

9. D   Split-ticket voting is when a citizen votes for candidates from different parties on the same ballot. Split-ticket voting is less likely to happen when voters identify strongly with parties and more likely to happen when voters identify weakly with parties, so eliminate choice (B) and keep choice (D) for now. While more third party candidates could arguably contribute to split ticket voting, the connection is not as strong as decreasing voter identification. Third party candidates tend to draw people who will vote for the party for all candidates on the ballot, so choice (A) is not as strong as choice (D) and you can eliminate it. Choice (C) is also not as good as choice (D) because it mentions stronger national party organizations, which reduces split-ticket voting. Finally, choice (E)

contributes to voters casting all of their votes for one party, known as straight-ticket voting, which is the opposite of split-ticket voting.

10. **D** While Environmentalism, Gun Rights, and Free Speech Rights are well represented by interest groups, the Right to Forbid the Quartering of Soldiers doesn't have enough relevance to have an interest group today, so choice (D) is the correct answer.

11. **E** Political parties have existed in America since the late eighteenth century, so eliminate choice (A). You can also cross off choice (B) because the cost of running a campaign has consistently risen over the past decades. Presidential nominations in early American history were controlled more by state party leaders than they are under today's primary system. Any registered party member can vote in closed primaries, and any voter can vote in open primaries, which gives more power (and a larger role) to U.S. citizens today. Therefore, eliminate choice (C). On a similar note, primaries decreased the role of state party organizations in presidential nominations as compared to pre-primary systems, so get rid of choice (D). This leaves us with the correct answer, choice (E), which is correct because the party leaders of each state used to choose candidates to support, distribute ballots for candidates, and, in many cases, even hire people to physically intimidate the supporters of opposing candidates. The system was run from the top-down. The bottom line is that the primary system for presidential nominations replaced a system heavily controlled by state party leaders.

12. **A** The framers of the U.S. Constitution designed the U.S. government with built in checks and balances in mind. While not explicitly created by the Constitution, the two-party system helps to fulfill the function of checks because one party can often stop the actions and intentions of the other party. For example, if the president and the Senate majority are in different parties, the president can veto congressional legislation or, conversely, senators can filibuster a bill the president supports. Choice (A) is correct. Choices (B) and (E) are both wrong because parties in a two-party system must represent many issues and a broad portion of the electorate—that is how they get elected. Parties try to promote their national conventions, so eliminate choice (C). Choice (D) is wrong because parties do not select juries in criminal trials.

13. **A** Political parties exist from the local to the national level, with decision-making distributed across all levels; therefore, choice (A) is a false statement and the credited response to this question. The national party represents only a small part of a political party's structure, so choice (B) is a true statement. Choices (C) and (D) are also true statements, as many local activists are invited to a party's national convention and are welcome to vote on matters such as the party platform. Choice (E) is also a true statement, as the president can help a governor in a tough race by attending a campaign event or a senator may give an endorsement to a member of his or her party running in a local mayoral race.

14. **B** Although we cynically view lobbyists as those who wine and dine politicians to achieve their interest groups' goals, the primary function of lobbyists is to give advice to legislators on the specifics

of the interests they represent. The media provides nontechnical information to the general public, so answer choice (A) is incorrect. Choice (C) is wrong because campaign coordinators work with the legislator during the campaign season, participate in fundraising, and should be able to advise the candidate on a wide array of issues. Choice (D) is incorrect because it is the job of the courts to rule on civil and criminal cases, as well as the constitutionality and applicability of laws. While cabinet members do advise a president on issues, they are appointed by a politician and work within the executive branch, so answer choice (E) is incorrect.

Drill 2

1. **E** The table shows that white Protestants and white Catholics vote more solidly Republican than Protestants in general and Catholics in general, respectively. Therefore, we can conclude that there are some racial factors at play in these voting behaviors. This makes choice (E) the best answer. We see data that shows a strong correlation between some religions and their voting patterns, so eliminate answer choice (D). According to the table, Protestants tend to vote for Republican candidates, so answer choice (A) is incorrect. Choice (B) is not true because Catholics tend to split their votes between Democrats and Republicans. The table also shows a very high proportion of those who identify as Unaffiliated voting for Democrats, which would contradict answer choice (C).

2. **A** We can observe a slight bell curve throughout the decade, as support for Democrats among all groups on the table rises after the 2004 election. That support then drops in the 2008 and 2010 elections. The table cannot support the generalization in choice (B) because it does not provide data about how many Catholics voted: the data indicates only which party Catholic voters supported. Choice (C) is incorrect because a lower percentage of each group in the table voted for Democrats in 2010 than in 2008. Choice (D) is incorrect because voters in all groups shifted their support toward the Democrats in 2006; this would suggest that Republicans lost seats in 2006. Choice (E) is incorrect because a higher percentage of most groups voted Republican in 2004 and 2008 than in 2006; this would suggest that the Republican presidential candidates may have garnered more support for Republican House candidates.

3. **E** Duverger's law explains the inevitability of a two-party system whenever an election is decided by a plurality. Choice (B) contradicts this principle. Choice (C) is not applicable to Duverger's law because it explains a proportional representation system, which we see in some European democracies. Choices (A) and (D) explain phenomena that are not necessarily true and are contradicted by several historic examples. Even if you'd never heard of Maurice Duverger or his law, choice (E) best describes the American political system, making it your best guess.

4. **A** Horse race journalism refers to in-depth coverage of the polling leading up to an election. It is criticized for its commitment to predicting winners and not analyzing the issues of the campaign.

While choices (B), (C), (D), and (E) may be problems in political journalism, they do not involve the focus on polling that horse race journalism does.

5. **D** Since the mid-1980s, political action committees focused on civil rights have experienced the greatest increase in membership. Accordingly, the correct answer is choice (D) and all other choices can be eliminated.

6. **A** A pair, or series, of elections during which political alignments substantially change is referred to as a critical election. A blanket primary is a primary election in which voters may select a candidate from any party for each office; eliminate choice (B). Eliminate choice (C) because dealignment refers to the recent trend in which voters act increasingly independent of party affiliation. Choice (D) can be eliminated because a closed primary is a primary election in which voting is restricted to registered members of a political party. Realignment, which has not occurred since the New Deal, occurs when a party undergoes a major shift in its electoral base and political agenda; eliminate choice (E).

7. **E** *Amicus curiae*, or "friend of the court," briefs that pertain to a particular case can be submitted by qualified individuals or organizations in an effort to persuade justices on a specific matter; such briefs can be quite influential in determining the outcome of the case. Accordingly, all of the answer choices are correct except for choice (E).

8. **E** The two-party system in America is strengthened by the nation's electoral system. Election rules, which have been agreed upon by members of both major parties, make it difficult for all but Republicans or Democrats to gain ballot access, let alone win an election. Accordingly, answer choices (A), (B), and (D) can be eliminated. The framers of the Constitution disliked political parties and hoped to prevent them; thus, choice (C) can be eliminated.

9. **E** While choices (A), (B), (C), and (D) are all true statements regarding gerrymandering, choice (E) is untrue. Iowa and California, for example, use independent commissions to form district boundaries.

10. **A** PACs were created to allow corporations, unions, and trade associations to raise campaign funds. All of the following statements are true except for choice (A). The purpose of creating PACs was not to have a voice in government policy meetings. Rather, the purpose was to raise campaign funds for the committees chosen candidates.

11. **C** All of the statements regarding the effects of media consolidation are true except for answer choice (C). Whether the coverage be liberal or conservative is irrelevant; the point is that the coverage is similar across all forms of media due to the increasingly monopolistic state of the media.

12. **C** All of the following groups listed, except for the Hoover League, have steadily increased their influence on the Republican party platform. While the Hoover League did have an influence on the Republican party platform, it was established in 1928 and failed to last past the late 1930s.

13. **A** An interest group is a political group structured around a certain political goal and/or philosophy. Interest groups try to influence public policy through activism and political donations to candidates who align with their goals. Eliminate choice (B) because it defines an iron triangle; a working relationship with interest groups, congressional committees, and executive agencies that enforce federal regulations. The Great Society was a social/economic program aimed at raising the standard of living for America's poorest residents; eliminate choice (C). Choice (D) refers to a caucus and, thus, can be eliminated. While interest groups may focus on issues related to job security, taxes, wages, and employee benefits, such issues are not the *sole* focus of interest groups; rather such issues are considered "bread-and-butter issues" that are the daily concerns of most Americans. Accordingly, eliminate choice (E).

14. **E** Any interest group can directly lobby, testify before Congress, socialize with government officials, endorse specific candidates, file class action suits and *amicus curiae* briefs, rally members, and disperse propaganda. While interest groups can provide political donations to parties that support certain platforms, there are limits to the amount of money that can be provided by corporations, trade groups, and unions; thus, choice (E) is incorrect.

Drill 3

1. **B** The percentage of voters who identify as independent has *increased*, not decreased, since the 1960s. All of the remaining statements are accurate as written and, therefore, can be eliminated.

2. **C** The Federal Election Campaign Act grants corporations, unions, and trade associations to form political action committees in order to raise campaign funds. Choice (A) can be eliminated because it is refers to the elastic clause. Eliminate choice (B) because poll taxes were outlawed with the passage of the Twenty-fourth Amendment. Choice (D) can be eliminated because the federal government was granted the right to register voters in states implementing literacy tests with the passage of the Voting Rights Act of 1965. Finally, eliminate choice (E) because soft money rules were changed for 527 groups with the passage of the Bipartisan Campaign Reform Act of 2002.

3. **B** A sound bite refers to a brief remark, extracted from a longer piece of audio, that summarizes a politician's comments, views, or beliefs. Accordingly, choice (B) is the correct answer. "Horse race" politics occurs when the press is more concerned about who is up or down in the polls than with reporting information on the candidates' positions and qualifications. Eliminate choice (A). Sound bites can be negative or positive, so neither choice (C) nor choice (D) is necessarily correct. Choice

(E) does not reflect a reason that sound bites are used; polling data shows who the public believes won or lost.

4. **E**   Critical elections, during which new issues become important and coalitions occur, often result in party realignment, or the displacement of the majority party by the minority party. Eliminate choice (A) because party dealignment refers to the gradual disengagement of people and politicians from a particular party. Choices (B) and (D) can be eliminated because critical elections do not lead to the establishment of either coalition governments or linkage institutions. Eliminate choice (C) because party neutrality refers to the idea that many Americans are indifferent to the two main political parties.

5. **E**   Qualified presidential candidates receive public funding in both the primary and general elections. Furthermore, national political parties receive public money for their national nominating conventions. Accordingly, all three statements are correct.

6. **D**   All of the statements are true regarding the office of the vice president except for choice (D). In fact, the opposite is true. Since the 1970s, many former vice presidents have had politically active careers after leaving office. For example, consider the political careers of former Vice Presidents Humphrey, Quayle, Gore, and Cheney; after leaving office, all of the aforementioned individuals pursued political careers.

7. **E**   Choice (E) is correct because people can get involved with both interest groups and political parties in a variety of ways, some very low cost. Eliminate choice (B). Seldom, though, does that include direct access to the executive branch or the Supreme Court, so eliminate choices (C) and (D). Political parties cannot accurately represent diverse interests because they need to appeal to as wide of a voter base as possible. Eliminate choice (A).

8. **B**   The rise of primaries took away power from state party leaders and their conventions. Choice (A) can be eliminated for the same reason since nominees are chosen by popular vote in primaries. Ballot access has not been simplified, opposition to the Electoral College does not influence the nomination process, and people with no political experience are almost never nominated to run for president. Accordingly, eliminate choices (C), (D), and (E).

Free-Response Question 1

Students may earn a total of six points on this question. Two points are available for part (a), two for part (b), and two for part (c).

Part (a) asks you to describe two tactics that interest groups use to affect the outcome of elections. You will receive 1 point for each description. Here are the points you need to make: PACS enable interest groups to donate money to candidates they support. In close races, that donation can make a big difference. PACs can also donate to a candidate's opponent if they want to punish that candidate for not supporting an interest group. "Get out the vote" efforts help ensure that voters who support the same candidates that an interest group supports get to the polls on election day.

Part (b) asks you to describe two tactics that interest groups use to persuade decision-makers to act in the best interest of the group. You will receive 1 point for each description. Here are the points you need to make: Interest groups may file *amicus curiae* briefs with a court to present an argument in favor of an issue. They may also file lawsuits related to their interests against the government or other parties. Interest groups can use their economic power to pay for advertisements during political campaigns, to donate to candidates through PACs, or to pay for research that supports their cause. Encouraging labor strikes and boycotts are other forms of economic leverage you could discuss.

Part (c) asks you to describe two informal methods of limiting the power that interest groups have over politics. You will receive 1 point for each description. Here are the points you need to make: Media coverage is costly and some interest groups don't have the funds to get their message on television or in print. Opponents of interest groups can use the media to respond to advertising or messaging run by that group. Pluralism refers to the vast number of unique interest groups. They are all competing for the attention of the public and of politics, but not all will be heard.

Drill 4

1. **E** Lobbyists generally represent a specific corporation or interest. For that reason, there are literally thousands of them. Eliminate choice (C). Funding is one of the most crucial factors for success lobbying, so eliminate choice (A). Some, though not many, do meet with the president and many testify at congressional hearings on matters that are important to their clients, so eliminate choices (B) and (D).

2. **C** Congressmen want to be reelected, so on issues that are very important (high intensity and saliency) to their constituents, they are unlikely to be swayed by interest groups. But on issues that matter to a small group of people and aren't relevant to the majority, they are more amenable to changing their minds to appease that small group and gain votes. Choice (A) is the opposite of the correct answer, choice (B) goes against the mission of interest groups, and choice (D) depends on the group's funding and many interest groups are quite small with limited funds. Finally, eliminate choice (E) because if the causes aren't related, they won't derive any real benefit from a coalition.

3. **A** Only Roman Numeral I is true since the power now lies more in the hands of the voters in primaries. Numeral II is increasingly true, but is not a consequence of the primary system, especially given that close primaries require registration with a party to participate. Numeral III is not true because the process is not lengthier and costlier because of the need to campaign just for the nomination. Numeral I alone is correct, so select choice (A).

4. **C** Polling rules and regulations are set by state election boards and must be in compliance with the Constitution and other federal laws. All of the remaining choices accurately describe a role of political parties and can be eliminated.

5.   **C**   An *amicus curiae* brief is often filed by an interest group in the hopes of affecting the outcome of a case. A writ of *certiorari* is an order to a lower court to send a case to the Supreme Court for review. A concurring opinion is an opinion written by a Supreme Court justice who votes with the winning side, but disagrees with the majority opinion about the case. A bill of attainder is a bill passed by a legislature declaring a person guilty of a crime. Finally, a motion of cloture is a motion to end debate in the Senate.

6.   **E**   A critical election is one in which dramatic change occurs to the balance of power between parties in the government or there is a drastic realignment of party loyalties. Although the 2000 election of Bush was controversial because of ballot issues and Bush's failure to win the popular vote, it was not a critical election under the correct definition. In 1932, Roosevelt's New Deal dramatically shifted support toward the Democrats. In 1968, Nixon finally succeeded in recapturing for the Republican Party much of the support that had been lost to the New Deal. In 1980, despite a strong third-party challenger, Reagan completed the realignment that Nixon had begun and received 90 percent of the electoral votes. Finally, the 1992 election of Clinton, again even in the presence of a strong third-party challenger, shifted 10 states in favor of the Democrat party and they have remained that way since.

7.   **E**   Every choice except choice (E) is very well represented by political action committees (PACs). In 2012, there were 15 PACs representing specialized trade contractors and only 1 of those represented masons. In contrast, there were 274 agribusiness PACs, 111 commercial bank PACs, 48 public sector union PACs, and 14 defense aerospace PACs.

8.   **C**   The question accurately defines interpretive reporting. Eliminate choice (A) because yellow journalism is the practice of reporting shocking stories to attract more readers. Eliminate choice (B) because horse race journalism is the practice of focusing its reports on how candidates fare relative to each other in public opinion polls rather than on substantive issues in the campaigns. Eliminate choice (D) because watchdog journalism occurs when a newspaper reports on the misdeeds of elected officials, thereby holding them accountable for their actions. Eliminate choice (E) because partisan reporting occurs when a newspaper essential serves as the voice of a political party.

Free-Response Question 1

Students may earn a total of five points on this question. Two points are available for part (a), one for part (b), one for part (c), and one for part (d).

Part (a) asks you to describe the difference between a primary and a caucus. You will receive 1 point for your explanation of each process. Here are the points you need to make: in a primary, votes are cast for a candidate and the ballots are then counted to decide the winner. Primaries may be open (voters from any party can participate) or closed (only members of that party can participate). A caucus is a meeting of party members in which participants meet to deliberate and decide on the nominee.

Part (b) asks what superdelegates are and how superdelegates give more authority to party leaders. You will receive 1 point for your answer. To earn credit, you must state that superdelegates are those who are not pledged to vote for a certain candidate. They are often the party leaders themselves and have an automatic vote in the national conventional, which means they can swing the convention in favor of whichever candidate they support.

Part (c) asks you to describe one outcome of a winner-take-all primary. You will receive 1 point for your answer. A positive point you can make to earn credit is that there is a faster conclusion to the nomination process so that the candidate can prepare for the national race. A negative point you can make to earn credit is the difficulty of success for less well-known candidates.

Part (d) asks you to explain why presidential candidates sometimes change their mind about issues when they are in different parts of the election cycle. You will receive 1 point for your answer. Some points you can discuss to earn credit include the differences in demographics between those voting in the primary and those voting in the general election, opponents in the two races, financing available to candidates in the two races, media coverage of the campaigns, and the politically relevant events that occur during the campaign.

Drill 5

1. **E** Choice (E) is correct because support for the Democratic Party increased in all areas but one: deep rural areas. Support for the Democratic Party increased in all metro areas and small town rural areas, which together comprise the vast majority of the population. The table shows levels of percent change over the twenty-year time span, not actual numbers of supporters, so eliminate choices (A) and (B). Choice (D) can be eliminated for a similar reason: support for the Democratic party grew by only 2 percent, but we can't determine what percent of voters in small town rural areas support the Democratic party. Finally, choice (C) can be eliminated because Medium Metro areas increased their support more than Emerging Suburbs or True Exurbs did. Small Metro areas and Small Town Rural areas also saw a greater increase than True Exurbs did.

2. **C** Choice (C) is correct because almost every area has seen a significant increase in the portion of its population that identifies with the Democratic Party. Eliminate choices (A) and (E) because the causes for the increases shown in the table are not mentioned. Eliminate choice (B) because the table doesn't provide any actual numbers or starting values. Choice (D) is incorrect because we only know the percent change, not the starting percentage.

3. **A** In multiple-member districts, minor parties which allow for more accurate representation of a diverse constituency, can be more successful because more than one seat is awarded per district. This is unlike a winner-take-all system, or single-member district, which choices (B) and (C) describe. Choice (D) is incorrect because if there are more seats to be won overall, while an incumbent may still have an advantage, the possibility of winning a seat is more equitable. Finally, choice (E) is incorrect because when multiple candidates can win a seat, the chances of getting a majority of votes is less likely. What is more likely is that those who win seats will win with a plurality of votes, not a majority.

4. **B** Interest groups are forbidden from donating directly to political campaigns, although they can contribute through PACs. All other answer choices describe activities that are a regular part of what ordinary citizens and interest groups do in order to influence politicians and create change, so they can all be eliminated.

5. **D** State electoral boards are bipartisan organizations that administer and enforce election laws. They operate independently of the political parties. All of the remaining answer choices describe organizations that are part of the formal structure of the Democratic and Republican parties. The national party is the nominal head, although it doesn't have any formal authority over the other organizations.

6. **A** Professional associations are considered economic interest groups because they work to ensure good material benefits for their members only. An example of this would be the National Education Association which helps ensure good salaries and benefits for school teachers. The other categories are all noneconomic interest groups because they fight for public, or collective, goods, such as solidarity among those interested in the cause or distribution of information. An example of each is Greenpeace (public interest), the National Rifle Association (single issue), the Christian Coalition (ideological), and a state government lobby (government).

7. **C** Interest groups exist to help people with specific issues promote those issues among legislators and work for positive change. Eliminate choices (A), (B), and (E) because they do not accurately describe interest groups and political parties. Interest groups don't limit themselves necessarily to local politics and generally have less money than parties do. Political parties have to represent a wide range of interests to earn voter support. Eliminate choice (D) because party affiliation is not directly linked to having access to one's representatives. It may help in some circumstances, but there is a wide range of avenues through which someone can attempt to contact a congressperson.

8. **E** A progressive tax structure, under which those who earn more money pay a higher percentage of that money in taxes, is typically favored by the Democrats. Republicans favor a flat tax structure under which everyone pays the same percentage, regardless of income. All of the other answers accurately describe the typical Republican platform and thus can be eliminated.

Free-Response Question 1

Students may earn a total of six points on this question. One point is available for part (a), two for part (b), and three for part (c).

Part (a) asks you to describe the relationship between the trend lines in the graph. You will receive 1 point for your explanation. To earn credit, you need to state that while in both kinds of races the percentage of support that has gone to Republicans has been declining, in state senatorial races, that decline has been much steadier.

Part (b) asks you to describe two changes in the demographics composition of the major political parties. You will receive 1 point for each group you describe. You need to make the following points:

- African Americans—They have voted overwhelmingly for the Democrats since 1964 (you don't have to give the exact dates to earn credit). They initially overwhelmingly voted for Republicans at a time when most white landowners in the south voted Democrat.
- Southerners—They have switched from voting for Democrats to overwhelmingly voting for Republicans.
- Women—They don't always vote for Republicans as consistently as they used to. There are also more of them who vote now, so they constitute a larger portion of all Democrats.
- Labor Union Members—They don't always vote for Democrats as consistently as they used to. There are also fewer of them now, so they constitute a smaller portion of all Democrats.

Part (c) asks you to describe each of the factors that could account for the differences in the trend lines in the graph. You will receive 1 point for each part of the answer. The following points are the ones you will need to make:

- Redistricting—Redistricting is used to create voting lines that will favor the candidate from one party over another. Consistent grouping of voters in favor of Republican candidates for state offices would lead to more stability in the senatorial trend line. They could also be used to create safe seats for senators, which would also lead to more stability in the senatorial trend line.
- Term limits—The president only serves two terms, so the incumbency advantage helps the president only once. Senators can serve indefinitely, so they have a continuous incumbency advantage, which is why the graph shows fewer wild swings in percent of support for Republicans in the Senate races. Senators also serve two years longer than the president does, so there is less opportunity for change in the graph on the senatorial trend line.
- Differences between state and national politics—Candidates running for local office can be more responsive to the needs of their constituents. Candidates and voters of different parties may disagree on national issues yet share views on local issues. Republican candidates for state office can use their closeness with the constituents to win more votes and stay in office. Candidates running for national office have to appeal to a wider range of people and are more likely to conform to the party line.

Drill 6

1. **D** While television stations and radio channels clearly promoting either the liberal or the conservative viewpoint exist, most news is reported objectively. Choice (A) describes watchdog journalism. Choice (B) is a natural consequence of the space limits of print and time limits of television and radio slots. The media have to choose which stories to report and which to omit, thereby influencing what the public discusses and what they are relatively unaware of. Choice (C) is accurate because the public learns about government actions through the media and the government learns about public opinion. Finally, choice (E) is accurate because attack journalism and yellow journalism often show a heavy bias and create distrust among the public in the stories then offered by that media outlet.

2. **B**   The Super PAC, which came to public consciousness in 2010, is a PAC that can raise funds from individuals, corporations, unions, and other groups, without any legal limit on donation size. Like regular PACs, they are still regulated by the FEC, so eliminate choice (A). Because of the Taft-Hartley Act of 1947, corporations cannot spend money to influence federal elections, but they can help pay for administrative costs of both regular PACs and Super PACs. Eliminate choice (C). Choice (D) is incorrect, although there are more limitations on PACs that are union-affiliated. Finally, choice (E) is incorrect because all PACs are federally required to reveal the identities of their donors, although donors themselves may make donations in such a way that their identities remain hidden.

3. **C**   In both *Shaw v. Reno* (1993) and *Miller v. Johnson* (1995), the Supreme Court ruled that because of the equal protection clause in the Fourteenth Amendment, drawing district lines based solely on racial data would be unconstitutional. District lines are redrawn every 10 years when the census is conducted to ensure equal representation in places that experienced population changes, so eliminate choices (A) and (B). There are no rules about gerrymandering that relate to length of term in office, so eliminate choice (D). Finally, eliminate choice (E) because in most states, the state legislature is responsible for drawing district lines.

4. **A**   The question accurately describes a single-member district, so answer (A) is correct. In a single-member district, one candidate wins the seat, unlike a multiple-member district in which several of the top vote-earners will have a seat in the legislature. Eliminate choice (B). Popular sovereignty refers to any system in which the government must respond to the fill of the people. Eliminate choice (C). A presidential democracy is one in which the executive and legislative branches are separate. Eliminate choice (D). Finally, a professional legislature is one in which members are paid a salary and have staff members. Eliminate choice (E).

5. **E**   Interest groups are not permitted by law to meet with a jury as a means to persuade them regarding the outcome of a court case. All of the other choices describe common ways that interest groups lobby the government.

6. **A**   Party realignment is a dramatic change in the composition of the two major political parties. It is signaled by a critical election, in which large parts of the majority party's coalition switch to the minority party. Party realignments are rare, triggered by traumatic events (such as a war or severe economic recession), and have long-lasting effects on the two-party system. The Great Depression triggered the most recent party realignment in 1932. Women, liberals, African Americans left the Republican Party to join the New Deal coalition of Franklin Roosevelt and the Democratic Party. The Democratic Party continued to be the dominant party for the next three decades. No party realignment has occurred since 1932, so choice (A) is the best answer.

7. D The Republican Party and its supporters are strong advocates of the Second Amendment, which gives citizens the right to bear arms. Democrats tend to be against private ownership of assault-type weapons and promote increased regulation of ownership of firearms. All other choices describe core ideological stances of the Republican Party.

Free-Response Question 1

Students may earn a total of six points on this question. Two points are available for part (a), one for part (b), and three for part (c).

Part (a) asks you to describe two ways that the Constitution protects special interest groups. You will receive 1 point for each method you explain. Some of the possible rights you can discuss are the freedom of speech, freedom of the press, the right to petition the government, protection from unreasonable search and seizure, or the right to due process of the law.

Part (b) asks you to describe one way the government regulates interest groups. You will receive 1 point for this answer. Some of the possible methods you can discuss are requirements for candidate disclosure of funding and activities, registration requirements for lobbyists and PACs, limits on dollar amounts of donations and other campaign finance laws, or the prohibition of bribery.

Part (c) asks you to describe three tactics used by special interest groups. You will receive 1 point for each description you provide. Here are the points you need to cover to earn credit.

- Lobbying—meeting directly with lawmakers to talk about a group's interest.
- Grassroots campaigns—organizing citizens to stage protests, sign petitions, write letters, and engage in other activities to influence lawmakers.
- Media campaigns—placing ads on television, radio, and in print to either support a particular candidate or give negative publicity to the opponents' campaigns.

Chapter 9
Institutions of Government

DRILL 1

Voter Turnout in the 1998 Texas Primary Elections
(R = Republican   D = Democrat)

Education	Gender				Age							
	Male		Female		18-25		26-45		46-60		61+	
	R	D	R	D	R	D	R	D	R	D	R	D
Some high school	5%	16%	8%	21%	2%	12%	8%	12%	9%	16%	12%	15%
High school	10	25	12	32	4	14	10	14	15	24	20	22
Some college	18	34	19	40	8	22	8	10	24	38	32	31
College	25	42	26	50	11	26	15	30	36	45	46	42
Master's	30	48	34	56	15	32	18	32	38	48	52	53
Doctorate	45	52	40	60	19	38	22	44	46	52	58	60

1. Which of the following statements is best supported by the table above?

   (A) Men who held a college degree were just as likely to vote in the Republican primary as were females who held a college degree.
   (B) Males with some high school education were half as likely to vote in the Republican primary as females with some high school education were to vote Democrat.
   (C) Regardless of educational attainment, individuals over the age of 61 were more likely to turn out for the Democrat primary.
   (D) The greater the educational attainment of females, the more likely they were to vote in the 1998 primary elections.
   (E) Individuals under the age of 25 who held a doctorate were more likely to vote in the Democrat primary than were individuals between the ages of 26-45.

2. What is the role of a bill's sponsor in Congress?

   (A) Hold a committee vote on the bill
   (B) Find compromise to pass the bill
   (C) Defend the bill of from compromise
   (D) Determine how long Congress will debate the bill
   (E) Introduce the bill to Congress

3. The committee system is less important in the Senate than the House because the

   (A) Senate approves nominees to the Federal Courts
   (B) Constitution gives more power to House committees
   (C) Senate has fewer members
   (D) Senate has no committees
   (E) Senate has a seniority system, but the House does not

4. When the Supreme Court decides to take a case on appeal it

   (A) issues a writ of *habeas corpus*
   (B) issues a writ of *certiorari*
   (C) issues *amicus curiae* briefs
   (D) engages in judicial review
   (E) engages in judicial activism

5. What power do presidents have regarding the federal judiciary?

   (A) Three extra votes during Senate confirmation
   (B) The power to overrule court opinions that directly involve the president
   (C) Impeachment power
   (D) Appointment power
   (E) The ability to alter written judicial opinions

6. Permanent, subject-matter-specific committees are referred to as

   (A) standing committees
   (B) select committees
   (C) joint committees
   (D) political action committees
   (E) conference committees

7. Which of the following resulted from the Budget and Impoundment Control Act?

   (A) Clear guidelines for the settlement of new territories were established.
   (B) Congress was granted the power to prevent the president from refusing to fund congressional initiatives.
   (C) Government employees were allowed to vote in government elections.
   (D) Declassified government documents were made available for public use.
   (E) Congress was provided with the authority to regulate and break up monopolies.

8. All of the following actions could occur when proposing and ratifying Constitutional amendments EXCEPT:

   (A) The proposed amendment must be approved by two-thirds of the House.
   (B) Three-fourths of the state legislatures must approve the amendment.
   (C) Elected delegates can vote on a proposed amendment if Congress mandates that each state use a ratifying convention.
   (D) The proposed amendment must be approved by two-thirds of the Senate.
   (E) Three-fourths of the state legislatures can petition Congress to call a constitutional convention.

9. All of the following statements about Congress are true EXCEPT:

   (A) Only Congress can pass laws.
   (B) A proposed amendment must be approved by two-thirds of the delegates in both houses of Congress.
   (C) Congress can override a presidential veto if two-thirds of the House and Senate agree to do so.
   (D) Congressional power over the bureaucracy is less than that of the president.
   (E) Congress cannot establish an official church of the United States.

10. Which of the following statements about War Powers Act of 1973 is false?

    (A) Congress must declare war if the president wants to send more than 10,000 troops to hostile areas.
    (B) Congress has invoked the War Powers Act twice since its ratification to force the president to withdraw troops.
    (C) The president must receive congressional approval before making war.
    (D) Unless Congress grants an extension, troops must return home from hostile areas within 90 days.
    (E) The Supreme Court has never ruled on the War Powers Act.

11. Which of the following groups experienced the greatest increase in congressional membership in the 1992 election?

    (A) Women and minorities
    (B) Conservative democrats
    (C) Green party
    (D) Libertarians
    (E) Liberal Republicans

12. The principle that mandated that the states cannot tax the national bank and, therefore, the federal government, was established in

    (A) *McCulloch v. Maryland*
    (B) *Fletcher v. Peck*
    (C) *Roe v. Wade*
    (D) *Schneck v. United States*
    (E) *Griswold v. Connecticut*

13. Which of the following statements regarding incumbency in a congressional election are true?

 I. The majority of Americans believe incumbents to be more politically active than the challengers are.
 II. Challengers receive fewer monetary campaign contributions than incumbents do.
 III. Incumbents are always endorsed by the president when running for reelection.
 IV. Incumbent representatives who run for reelection win approximately 90% of the time.
 V. House incumbents have a greater advantage than do incumbent senators

(A) I and III only
(B) II and IV only
(C) II, IV, and V only
(D) II, III, IV, and V only
(E) All of the above

14. All of the following statements regarding Congress are true EXCEPT:

(A) Elections for the 435 seats in the House of Representatives occur every four years.
(B) A senator's term lasts for six years.
(C) The rules of the Senate are more informal that those of the House.
(D) Congress is responsible for writing the laws of the nation.
(E) Senate elections are generally more competitive than House elections.

15. The House of Representatives has initiated impeachment proceedings for which of the following federal offices?

 I. President
 II. Member of the House of Representatives
 III. Senator
 IV. Federal Judge

(A) I only
(B) I and IV only
(C) II and III only
(D) I, II, and III only
(E) I, II, III, and IV

16. How often does congressional redistricting usually occur?

(A) Every 2 years
(B) Every 4 years
(C) Every 6 years
(D) Every 8 years
(E) Every 10 years

DRILL 2

1. Which of the following would most directly lead to an increase in presidential power?

   (A) Economic weakness, such as unemployment
   (B) Domestic problems, such as civil unrest
   (C) Congressional gridlock
   (D) A larger role for the United States in international affairs
   (E) The Supreme Court invoking judicial review

2. Which of the following departments uses the largest percentage of the federal budget?

   (A) Department of Defense
   (B) Department of Justice
   (C) Department of Agriculture
   (D) Department of Education
   (E) Department of Labor

3. How are the electoral votes of most states apportioned in a general presidential election?

   (A) The winner of the state receives electoral votes in proportion with his or her percentage of the state's popular vote.
   (B) The winner of the state receives a few votes for winning the state, plus an extra vote for each congressional district won.
   (C) The winner of the state receives all of the state's electoral votes.
   (D) The winner of the state receives 75% of the state's electoral votes.
   (E) Electoral votes aren't apportioned; the winner of the nation's popular vote becomes president.

4. What is a joint committee?

   (A) A committee of presidential advisors
   (B) A committee with members from both the president's cabinet and the Senate
   (C) A committee with members from both the president's cabinet and the House
   (D) A committee with members from all three branches of government
   (E) A committee with members from both the Senate and the House

5. What is a plurality election?

   (A) An election in which a candidate must win with more than half of the vote
   (B) An election in which the candidate who gets the most votes wins, even if the winning candidate doesn't get more than half of the vote
   (C) An election in which electors are assigned to vote for candidates
   (D) A primary election
   (E) A run-off election

6. Cabinet departments are created by

   (A) the Declaration of Independence
   (B) the Articles of Confederation
   (C) the Constitution
   (D) the legislative branch
   (E) the judicial branch

7. Incumbents who run for reelection in the House of Representatives win about

   (A) one-quarter of the time
   (B) one-third of the time
   (C) half of the time
   (D) two-thirds of the time
   (E) nine-tenths of the time

8. Who would be most likely to agree with the theory of supply-side economics?

   (A) A Democratic politician from an urban area
   (B) A Republican politician interested primarily in law-and-order policies
   (C) A Democratic politician interested in Keynesian economics
   (D) A moderate Independent politician interested in a balanced approach to economics
   (E) A Republican politician interested in laissez-faire economics

9. What is a pocket veto as used by the president?

   (A) A veto that allows the president to strike individual parts of a bill
   (B) When a president threatens to veto a bill, hoping to sway public opinion
   (C) A regular veto signed by the president
   (D) When a congressional session ends 10 or fewer days after passing legislation and the president doesn't sign the legislation
   (E) When the president directs the Supreme Court to strike down congressional legislation

10. What is the income tax?

   (A) A tax on money earned by people and businesses
   (B) A tax on goods bought by people and businesses
   (C) A tax on money made in the stock market or other securities investments
   (D) A tax on property
   (E) A tax on the transferred estate of a deceased person

11. Which of the following best describes the House Rules Committee?

   (A) It is a permanent committee in the House in which members hold expertise in a particular area of policy, such as tax policy.
   (B) It is a temporary committee with members of both the House and the Senate.
   (C) It is a permanent committee that determines the length and terms under which debate will proceed in the House.
   (D) It is a temporary committee in the House organized for a special purpose that arises due to an emergency.
   (E) It is a temporary committee formed to reconcile House and Senate versions of a bill.

12. How can Congress override a presidential veto?

   (A) Two-thirds vote in both houses
   (B) Majority vote in the Senate
   (C) Two-thirds vote in the House of Representatives
   (D) Majority vote in both houses
   (E) Two-thirds vote in the Senate

13. One of the consequences of the electoral college system is that

   (A) presidential candidates don't spend a lot of time campaigning in states with small populations
   (B) politics in some states are dominated by one party
   (C) presidential candidates rely more heavily on media campaigns than they used to
   (D) third-party candidates have difficulty gaining ballot access in some states
   (E) the result of the popular vote rarely aligns with the election result

14. The committee in the House of Representatives that is responsible for establishing the terms of debate on any matter up for consideration is the

   (A) Rules Committee
   (B) Ways and Means Committee
   (C) Oversight and Government Reforms Committee
   (D) Appropriations Committee
   (E) House Administration Committee

15. Which group is the president's chief staff members usually a part of?

   (A) House Administrations Committee
   (B) Delegates from the president's political party
   (C) Appointees of the Senate and House majority leaders
   (D) Senate Appropriations Committee
   (E) White House Staff

THE LAW-MILLS AGAIN AT WORK.

16. Which of the following statements best represents the point of the cartoon above?

(A) The legislative branch has more power than do the other two branches of American government.

(B) Federal judges often hand down rulings that contradict recently passed legislation.

(C) Members of Congress lack respect for the judicial branch.

(D) Federal judges have a difficult time staying knowledgeable on all of the legislation passed.

(E) Members of Congress work harder than do employees in the judicial branch.

DRILL 3

Presidential Federal Judicial Nominations
(As Of June 2013)

	Clinton		W. Bush		Obama	
	Number	Percent of Total	Number	Percent of Total	Number	Percent of Total
Asian	5	1.3%	4	1.2%	17	7.2%
Black	62	16.4%	24	7.3%	43	18.1%
Hispanic	25	6.6%	30	9.1%	43	18.1%
Women	111	29.4%	71	21.8%	102	43.1%

1. The information in the table above supports which of the following statements?

   (A) President Bush made more federal judicial appointments than did President Clinton.
   (B) Democrats are more likely to appoint Hispanics to the judiciary than are Republicans.
   (C) President Obama appointed the highest percentage of minorities in every category to the judiciary.
   (D) President Clinton appointed the lowest number of minorities to the judiciary.
   (E) Republicans appoint fewer women to the judiciary than they do people from any other group.

2. Congress is likely to overturn a presidential veto when

   (A) the president is in his or her first term
   (B) the number of Democrats and number of Republicans in Congress is nearly equal
   (C) citizens in multiple states have started petitions in favor of the legislation
   (D) the president appointed at least two members of the Supreme Court
   (E) more than two-thirds of the members of each house voted in favor of the legislation

3. Which of the following groups is usually responsible for redrawing the boundaries of congressional districts?

   (A) Individual state election boards
   (B) Office of Planning, Evaluation, and Policy
   (C) Individual state legislatures
   (D) The Federal Election Commission
   (E) The U.S. Election Assistance Commission

4. According to the Constitution, the president alone has the power to

   (A) declare war
   (B) lead the political party of which he or she is a member
   (C) grant reprieves and pardons
   (D) propose new taxes
   (E) withhold information that relates to national security

5. After Abraham Lincoln was elected president in 1860 with only 39.8 percent of the popular vote, which of the following had to take place before he was formally declared the winner?

   (A) Districts were redrawn to change the number of electoral votes in states where more people had voted.
   (B) Members of Congress decided which candidate would be declared the winner.
   (C) A runoff was held between the two candidates who had received the most votes in the first election.
   (D) No further action was necessary because Lincoln received a majority of the electoral votes.
   (E) The candidate from the Constitutional Union party was allowed to transfer his votes to Lincoln.

6. Which of the following best describes franking?

(A) The privilege of members of Congress to mail information to their constituents at government expense
(B) The selection of congressional staff members and interns
(C) The right of the spouse of a deceased member of Congress to occupy the seat until the next election
(D) The forcible removal of a Congress member from office
(E) The process through which members of the House of Representatives are assigned to special committees

7. Which of the following is NOT a possible consequence of gerrymandering?

(A) an increase in the wasted vote effect
(B) creation of an advantage for third parties in winner-take-all elections
(C) increased likelihood of reelection for incumbents
(D) confinement of minority interests to a few districts
(E) districts that give a distinct advantage to one party

8. One of the ways in which the legislative branch provides checks and balances on the executive branch is that

(A) the House must approve presidential treaties
(B) Congress can vote to remove presidential appointees at any time
(C) the Senate can limit the number of staffers the president is allowed to have
(D) the House can conduct an impeachment trial of the president
(E) the Senate must approve presidential nominations

9. Which of the following statements about the party affiliations of nominees to the Supreme Court is true?

(A) Nominees generally have party affiliations that are similar to those of the president who nominates them.
(B) Nominees with strong party affiliations to one of the two major parties are ineligible to serve on the Supreme Court.
(C) Nominees who are confirmed often switch their party affiliations while serving on the Supreme Court.
(D) Nominees are prohibited from discussing their party affiliations during the nomination and confirmation process.
(E) Nominees who have served in a leadership role in their party are more likely to be confirmed than those who have not.

10. Which of the following presidential powers is shared with the Senate?

(A) Deploying troops
(B) Drafting appropriations bills
(C) Negotiating treaties
(D) Forcing Congress into session
(E) Nominating vice presidents

11. A significant way in which the House of Representatives differs from the Senate is that

(A) debate can continue indefinitely in the Senate
(B) the number of members a state has in the Senate is based on a state's population
(C) the Senate can impeach a president and the House conducts the impeachment trial
(D) the House is responsible for confirming presidential appointees
(E) revenue bills can only be introduced in the Senate

12. Which of the following is NOT true about the line-item veto?

   (A) It allows an executive to approve only select parts of a bill.
   (B) It violates the Presentment Clause.
   (C) Congress passed laws granting it to the president.
   (D) Like the president, state executives are barred from holding this power.
   (E) The Supreme Court ruled it an unconstitutional power for the president to have.

13. Which of the following presidential appointees must be confirmed by the Senate before they can assume the office?

   I. White House Chief of Staff
   II. Inspector General of the Environmental Protection Agency
   III. Secretary of the Department of the Interior
   IV. Governor of the Federal Reserve System

   (A) I only
   (B) I, III, and IV only
   (C) III and IV only
   (D) II, III, and IV only
   (E) All appointments must be confirmed

14. Which of the following is NOT a way that the power of federal courts can be limited?

   (A) An amendment or law that renders a court decision illegal
   (B) The failure of local or state executives to enforce a ruling of the court
   (C) The appointment of new judges with certain political affiliations
   (D) Impeachment proceedings
   (E) A special election to oust a federal judge

15. Individual entitlements are

   (A) federal benefits that must be paid by Congress to all eligible citizens
   (B) federal income tax dollars that are redistributed through charity networks
   (C) discretionary spending programs that vary by state
   (D) expenditures in the federal budget that must be approved by Congress every year
   (E) federal appropriations administered by states

16. Appeals to the Supreme Court usually result in

   (A) a challenge to the constitutionality of related laws
   (B) a review of the case without hearing arguments
   (C) a rejection of the appeal
   (D) the decision of the lower court being overturned
   (E) the resignation of the judge who made the initial decision

DRILL 4

1. The prominent form of federalism since the passage of the Fourteenth Amendment is

    (A) cooperative federalism
    (B) layer-cake federalism
    (C) dual federalism
    (D) creative federalism
    (E) competitive federalism

2. All of the following are true of the Electoral College system EXCEPT:

    (A) It is often referred to as the "winner-take-all" system.
    (B) The Electoral College system places equal emphasis on election results in all states.
    (C) The framers created it in order to shield the government from the less-educated public.
    (D) Critics of the Electoral College feel the system is antiquated.
    (E) The number of electors provided to each state is equal to the sum of its federal legislators.

3. Which of the following statements is false regarding the principle of *stare decisis*?

    (A) *Stare decisis* is the policy of a court to rule by precedent.
    (B) The principle of *stare decisis* is most flexible in constitutional cases.
    (C) Generally, the courts will overturn the previous ruling rather than cite to *stare decisis*.
    (D) The principle requires that judges apply identical reasoning to lawsuits as has been used in prior, similar cases.
    (E) The principle was not uniformly adhered to in the case of *Planned Parenthood of Southeastern Pennsylvania v. Casey*.

4. In the United States, divided government refers to

    (A) the two legislative houses
    (B) the belief that the Constitution should be interpreted loosely when concerning the restrictions it places on federal power
    (C) the separation of powers amongst the executive, judicial, and legislative branches of government
    (D) a scenario in which one political party controls the executive branch, while another party controls the House, Senate, or both
    (E) the point at which a party experiences a significant shift in its political agenda and electoral base

5. Which of the following is required to disclose campaign finance information, enforce the provisions of the law such as the limits and prohibitions on contributions, and oversee the public funding of presidential elections?

    (A) McGovern-Fraser Commission
    (B) Bipartisan Campaign Reform Commission
    (C) Congressional Budget Office
    (D) Federal Reserve Board
    (E) Federal Election Commission

6. Non-legislative tasks of Congress include the following:

    I. Oversight
    II. Public education
    III. Sponsoring a bill
    IV. Representing constituents within the government

    (A) II only
    (B) I and IV only
    (C) II and III only
    (D) I, II and IV only
    (E) I, II, III, and IV

7. All of the following statements about the Senate are true EXCEPT:

   (A) The vice president is the president of the Senate.
   (B) International treaties must receive a three-fourths approval from the Senate.
   (C) The president of the Senate only votes on Senate issues as a tiebreaker.
   (D) Each state has two representatives in the Senate.
   (E) The Senate has the sole power to approve cabinet and judicial appointments.

8. All of the following are true regarding the attorney general EXCEPT:

   (A) The Constitution does not explicitly impose any duties or powers to the attorney general.
   (B) A general election for the position of attorney general occurs every four years.
   (C) The attorney general is nominated by the president and confirmed in the Senate.
   (D) The attorney general is the sole member of the president's cabinet who is not given the title secretary.
   (E) The office of Attorney General was established by Congress by the Judiciary Act of 1789.

9. Which of the following is not a criticism of the Electoral College?

   (A) The Electoral College makes the national popular vote irrelevant.
   (B) The winner-takes-all system favors less populous states.
   (C) The Electoral College encourages campaigns to focus on swing states.
   (D) The way in which the Electoral College functions dissuades voter turnout and participation.
   (E) The Electoral College system promotes stability via the two-party system.

10. Of the following, the most important informal power of the president is

    (A) to set economic policy and influence policy agenda.
    (B) his or her role as commander-in-chief of the military
    (C) to appoint cabinet members, judges, and ambassadors
    (D) to commission military officers
    (E) to veto legislation

11. Which of the following is FALSE about congressional oversight?

    (A) The General Accounting, Congressional Budget Office, and Congressional Debt Consolidation Office are the administrative offices within Congress used in the congressional oversight process.
    (B) The process of congressional oversight was developed in order to gain some control over agencies in the executive branch.
    (C) The short-lived Congressional Oversight Panel was created to review the current state of financial markets and the regulatory system.
    (D) One purpose of congressional oversight is to oversee the budget and appropriations process.
    (E) Congress has an oversight role over federal agencies.

12. All of the following events gave rise to concept of cooperative federalism EXCEPT

    (A) the enactment of Roosevelt's New Nationalism initiative
    (B) the passage of Ronald Regan's New Federalism: Phase II initiative
    (C) the establishment of Roosevelt's New Deal program
    (D) Woodrow Wilson's creation of the New Freedom Program
    (E) the passage of the Fourteenth Amendment

13. A motion of cloture can be used to

   (A) call roll and establish whether a quorum is present
   (B) permanently kill a pending matter and halt any future debate on the matter.
   (C) overcome a filibuster
   (D) bring up a bill or other legislation for consideration
   (E) instruct conference committee members to take a certain position in the conference

14. Which of the following scenarios does not violate the principle of separation of powers?

   (A) Roosevelt's attempt to increase the number of justices on the Supreme Court in order to pass New Deal legislation
   (B) Truman's effort to seize and operate the nation's steel mills without statutory authority
   (C) Jackson's action to destroy the National Bank of the United States
   (D) Congress's passage of the War Powers Act of 1973
   (E) Obama mandating recess appointments when the Senate was in session

15. Which of the following is not true of an appellate court?

   (A) Juries are not used to determine the outcome.
   (B) A panel of three judges hears the case.
   (C) Such courts review only the record and no new evidence is considered.
   (D) The most common appellate court judgments are to affirm, vacate, reverse, or remand rulings.
   (E) The judges must reach, and issue, a unanimous decision.

DRILL 5

1. Of the following criteria, which is not true regarding pork barrel spending?

   (A) It is competitively awarded.
   (B) It is not the subject of congressional hearings.
   (C) It significantly increases the cost of legislation beyond the president's annual budget request.
   (D) It aids only a local area or a certain interest group.
   (E) It is requested by only one chamber of Congress.

2. Which of the following powers is implied, rather than enumerated, in the Constitution?

   (A) Regulate the value of money
   (B) Oversee Congress
   (C) Maintain a Navy
   (D) Collect taxes
   (E) Declare war

3. In order to be appointed to the Supreme Court, justices must be nominated by the

   (A) president without a confirmation process
   (B) Senate without a confirmation process
   (C) president and confirmed by the Senate
   (D) president and confirmed by the House of Representatives
   (E) Senate and confirmed by the House of Representatives

4. The committees that are concerned with revenue bills are the

   (A) House Appropriations and Senate Budget Committees
   (B) House Ways and Means and Senate Budget Committees
   (C) House Budget and Senate Finance Committees
   (D) House Ways and Means and Senate Finance Committees
   (E) House Financial Services and Senate Finance Committees

5. Which of the following is NOT true about the National Security Advisor?

   (A) The role of National Security Advisor is a staff position within the Executive Office of the president.
   (B) The National Security Advisor serves as chief advisor to the president on national security issues.
   (C) During times of crisis, the National Security Advisor operates in the White House Situation Room.
   (D) The National Security Advisor holds a significant role in the National Security Council.
   (E) The National Security Advisor is appointed by the president and confirmed by the Senate.

6. Which of the following federal officials are subject to term limits?

   (A) Supreme Court justice
   (B) President
   (C) Senator
   (D) Member of the House of Representatives
   (E) Federal court judge

7. A rider to a congressional appropriations bill that brings federal money to a home state is called

   (A) a pocket veto
   (B) a filibuster
   (C) a killer amendment
   (D) cloture
   (E) pork barrel spending

8. Which of the following defines coalition building?

   (A) Different interest groups working together toward a shared goal
   (B) One party calling for a vote recount
   (C) Lobbying a member of Congress to improve the small business climate
   (D) Denying a confirmation vote to a presidential appointee
   (E) Removing a federal official from office

9. Which of the following is true about the Senate majority leader?

(A) The Senate majority leader is the president of the Senate.
(B) The Senate majority leader controls the Senate's legislative agenda.
(C) The Senate majority leader is not more powerful than the other senators.
(D) The Senate majority leader never acts as a power broker.
(E) The Senate majority leader has great power in the U.S. House of Representatives.

10. Which of the following Supreme Court cases established the principle of judicial review?

(A) *Fletcher v. Peck*
(B) *McCulloch v. Maryland*
(C) *Marbury v. Madison*
(D) *Mapp v. Ohio*
(E) *Gibbons v. Ogden*

11. A committee with members from both the House and Senate that comes together to reconcile differences in bills is known as a

(A) standing committee
(B) conference committee
(C) select committee
(D) joint committee
(E) political action committee

12. The judicial branch is most strongly influenced by the executive branch through the power of the president to

(A) appoint judges to the federal judiciary
(B) nullify Supreme Court rulings
(C) bring impeachment proceedings against a judge
(D) set term limits for federal judges
(E) use the media to guide public opinion on important decisions

13. The Supreme Court most often decides to accept cases for review

(A) at the request of the attorney general
(B) at the request of the president
(C) any time an *amicus curiae* brief is filed
(D) when a case involves a constitutional matter
(E) when a federal appellate court is not able to hear a case in a prompt manner

14. The Budget and Impoundment Control Act of 1974 was passed to

(A) decrease the amount of money that lobbyists are allowed to spend each year
(B) help put an end to the Vietnam War by cutting off military funding
(C) prevent the president from refusing to fund congressional initiatives
(D) establish the House Committee on Ways and Means
(E) establish a debt ceiling

15. What is the primary reason that the committees in the House of Representatives are more influential than they are in the Senate?

(A) The difference in size between the two chambers means that more work in done on the floor in the Senate and more work is done in committees in the House.
(B) The Senate as a whole has confirmation powers that the House does not have.
(C) Members are appointed to the committee in the House but are elected to committees in the Senate.
(D) A member of any party can serve a committee in the House, but only major party members can serve on committees in the Senate.
(E) Committee membership enables members of Congress to work for the special interests of their constituents.

DRILL 6

Presidential Election Results (1896-1996)

Year	Winner	Total Electoral Votes	Incumbent?	Main Opponent	Total Electoral Votes
1896	W. McKinley	271	No	W. Bryan	176
1900	W. McKinley	292	Yes	W. Bryan	155
1904	T. Roosevelt	336	No	A. Parker	140
1908	W. Taft	321	No	W. Bryan	162
1912	W. Wilson	435	No	T. Roosevelt	88
1916	W. Wilson	277	Yes	C. Hughes	254
1920	W. Harding	404	No	J. Cox	127
1924	C. Coolidge	382	No	J. Davis	136
1928	H. Hoover	444	No	A. Smith	87
1932	F. Roosevelt	472	No	H. Hoover	59
1936	F. Roosevelt	523	Yes	A. Landon	8
1940	F. Roosevelt	449	Yes	W. Wilkie	82
1944	F. Roosevelt	432	Yes	T. Dewey	99
1948	H. Truman	303	Yes*	T. Dewey	189
1952	D. Eisenhower	442	No	A. Stevenson	89
1956	D.Eisenhower	457	Yes	A. Stevenson	73
1960	J. Kennedy	303	No	R. Nixon	219
1964	L. Johnson	486	Yes*	B. Goldwater	52
1968	R. Nixon	301	No	H. Humphrey	191
1972	R. Nixon	520	Yes	G. McGovern	17
1976	J. Carter	297	No	G. Ford	240
1980	R. Reagan	489	No	J. Carter	49
1984	R. Reagan	525	Yes	W. Mondale	13
1988	G. Bush	426	No	M. Dukakis	111
1992	W. Clinton	370	No	G. Bush	168
1996	W. Clinton	379	Yes	B. Dole	159

*F. Roosevelt died in office and Vice President H. Truman filled the office until the next election.
*J. Kennedy died in office and Vice President L. Johnson filled the office until the next election.

1. Which of the following conclusions about presidential election results from 1896 to 1996 is best supported by the information provided in the table above?

   (A) Incumbent presidents always received at least twice as many electoral votes as their challengers do.
   (B) Challengers who run for election at least twice eventually win the presidency.
   (C) Incumbency provides no advantage in presidential elections.
   (D) The incumbent won in the three presidential races with the highest number of electoral votes awarded to the winner.
   (E) Challengers may win the presidency narrowly but never by a landslide.

2. The War Powers Act of 1973 restricted the ability of the president to do which of the following?

(A) Lower the minimum age required to serve in the military to sixteen
(B) Send more than 5,000 troops into combat without congressional approval
(C) Keep troops in combat for more than 90 days without congressional approval
(D) Appeal to the American public through the media to support a war
(E) Use members of the armed forces to combat private state militias

3. The decision of which of the following Supreme Court cases was based on the supremacy clause of the Constitution?

(A) *McCulloch v. Maryland*
(B) *Gideon v. Wainwright*
(C) *District of Columbia v. Heller*
(D) *Schenck v. United States*
(E) *Texas v. Johnson*

4. All members of Congress have the power to

(A) propose as many amendments to a bill as they want
(B) cast a vote of cloture to stop a filibuster
(C) to vote on a discharge petition to override a committee's decision to kill a bill
(D) veto a presidential nominee to the Supreme Court
(E) establish rules for debate of bills

5. In 1992, members from what group of people were elected to Congress in such a large number as to noticeably modify the makeup of Congress?

(A) People under 30 years old
(B) Libertarians
(C) Southerners
(D) Foreign-born nationals
(E) Minorities

6. Which of the following statements about the advantages of incumbency is FALSE?

(A) Incumbents do not need to work as hard to solicit campaign donations are challengers do.
(B) Incumbents can use their staff members to manage their campaigns.
(C) Incumbents have proven their willingness and ability to help constituents.
(D) Incumbents are not as reliant on media for name recognition as their challengers are.
(E) Incumbents are always experienced in running a successful election campaign.

7. After a federal law has been declared unconstitutional in a Supreme Court case

(A) the president can choose to nullify the decision of the Court
(B) members of Congress who passed the law are subject to a recall election
(C) a constitutional amendment is generally proposed to help ensure that such a law won't be passed again
(D) Congress must formally repeal the law before it is cleared from the record
(E) a two-thirds vote in both houses of Congress can reinstate the law

8. All of the following accurately describe differences between the House and the Senate EXCEPT:

(A) The Senate has confirms presidential appointments while the House does not.
(B) Tax bills originate in the House, not in the Senate.
(C) Senators serve longer terms than do Representatives.
(D) Rules of debate in the Senate are less formal than those in the House.
(E) The House has a minority leader but the Senate does not.

1. The Supreme Court is expected to be immune to political pressure; however, this is not always the case.

    (a)   Describe one way in which the Supreme Court is insulated from politics and one way in which the Supreme Court is affected by politics.

    (b)   Explain one way in which the confirmation process affects which justices serve on the Supreme Court.

    (c)   Identify one way the president can limit the power of the Supreme Court.

    (d)   Identify one way the Congress can limit the power of the Supreme Court.

DRILL 7

1. Which of the following statements about congressional committees are true?

    I. Select committees are the most common type of congressional committee.
    II. Committees cannot be composed of members from both chambers.
    III. Party leaders determine who serves on a committee.
    IV. Serving on certain committees can benefit of member of Congress during elections.

    (A) I and II only
    (B) II and III only
    (C) I and IV only
    (D) III and IV only
    (E) II, III, and IV only

2. Authorization of spending and appropriations bills are used by Congress to

    (A) override presidential vetoes
    (B) engage in oversight of the bureaucracy
    (C) set the federal budget
    (D) justify pork barrel projects
    (E) decrease inflation

3. Gerrymandering occurs

    (A) every 2 years when congressional elections are held
    (B) every 10 years when congressional redistricting occurs
    (C) after requesting approval from the Federal Election Commission (FEC)
    (D) after requesting approval from the Committee on House Administration
    (E) never since it was declared unconstitutional in the Voting Rights Act of 1965

4. Due to greater involvement of the United States in international affairs since World War II

    (A) domestic problems and civil unrest have intensified
    (B) the president has seen an increase in his or her power
    (C) the Supreme Court has relied more on judicial activism than judicial review
    (D) Congress has been more likely to enforce checks and balances on the executive branch
    (E) government has been divided in almost every administration

5. The Senate will conduct an impeachment trial of the president when

    (A) a majority of representatives pass articles of impeachment
    (B) a majority of senators pass an article of impeachment
    (C) two-thirds of the representatives vote in favor of holding the trial
    (D) a majority of senators and representatives vote in favor of holding the trial
    (E) two-thirds of the senators vote in favor of holding the trial

6. During presidential elections, Maine and Nebraska are different from most states in that

    (A) they conduct caucuses, not primaries, to select the nominees
    (B) they allow vote-by-mail
    (C) they have ballot access laws that limit the number of third parties that appear on the ballot
    (D) their polls are open for more than just one day
    (E) they do not apportion votes on a winner-take-all basis

7. Which of the following statements about cabinet departments is FALSE?

(A) They are established by the legislative branch.

(B) Their members often don't have much influence over presidential decisions.

(C) They cannot all be run by leaders who belong to the same political party the president does.

(D) Not every federal agency is a cabinet department.

(E) Their heads are appointed, and fired, by the president.

8. Members of a standing committee in Congress

(A) handle most of the legislative issues in that committee's jurisdiction

(B) serve only for a short time before the committee is disbanded

(C) reconcile different the different versions of a bill that come from the two chambers

(D) represent the Democrats and Republicans equally

(E) must consult the party majority leader before making a decision

Free Response

Time—25 minutes

1. In addition to creating legislation, members of Congress are charged with overseeing the federal bureaucracy, educating the public, and representing their constituents.

   (a) Explain the role of each of the following committees in the legislative process.

   - House Ways and Means Committee
   - Conference committee

   (b) Identify one way in which members of Congress oversee the federal bureaucracy.

   (c) Describe how members of Congress use their position to educate the public. Explain what role the House Rules Committee plays in this task.

   (d) Explain how members of Congress may represent their constituents beyond voting decisions.

DRILL 8

1. In both 1992 and 1996, Bill Clinton won the presidential election by

   (A) avoiding an indirect election
   (B) a proportional distribution of electoral votes
   (C) a plurality of votes
   (D) a run-off in the House of Representatives
   (E) losing the popular vote but winning the electoral vote

2. Members of the House Rules Committee have significant influence in Congress because they are able to

   (A) closely interact with constituents to ensure to combat waste in government
   (B) oversee federal elections
   (C) write new tax bills and gain prestige from serving on the oldest House committee
   (D) determine for how long a bill can be debated and how many amendments to the bill can be proposed
   (E) collaborate with the president to set the federal budget

3. Which of the following accurately states one reason that incumbent members of Congress are more likely to win an election than their challengers are?

   (A) Incumbents are allotted a certain amount of free airtime for television and radio advertising.
   (B) Incumbents are more likely to get campaign contributions from a variety of sources than their challengers are.
   (C) Most voters are apathetic towards non-presidential elections and are unwilling to go to the polls to vote for a challenger.
   (D) Many voters have a personal relationship with their senators and representatives and would feel uncomfortable voting them out of office.
   (E) The most successful campaign managers prefer to work with incumbents than with challengers.

4. How does a bill proceed following a presidential veto?

   (A) It returns to a congressional committee.
   (B) It is typically overturned by Congress.
   (C) The Supreme Court decides on its constitutionality.
   (D) The veto is generally sustained.
   (E) It moves to the cabinet for approval.

5. Research shows that the most influential factor in a Congressperson's voting behavior is

   (A) the will of his or her constituents
   (B) the lobbyists who consult him or her
   (C) party identification
   (D) media coverage
   (E) his or her religious affiliation

6. What must happen in order for the president to use a veto message?

   (A) A bill must fail to pass the House of Representatives.
   (B) The president must write to Congress to articulate his or her objections to a bill.
   (C) After a bill is passed, a president must first sign it into law.
   (D) The president must ignore a bill for over ten congressional working days.
   (E) The president must offer his or her own bill to Congress after an original fails to pass the Senate.

7. Which of the following is a regressive tax?

   (A) Estate tax
   (B) Federal income tax
   (C) Corporate tax
   (D) State income tax
   (E) Sales tax

8. Which of the following types of federalism gained traction in the 1970s?

   (A) Dual federalism
   (B) Cooperative federalism
   (C) Marble-cake federalism
   (D) Regulated federalism
   (E) New federalism

Free Response

Time—25 minutes

1. The Constitution separates power between the president and Congress, which means that both branches of government must work together in order to govern. This can be difficult during times of divided government.

    (a)   Define divided government.

    (b)   Explain how divided government may occur.

    (c)   Explain the effect of divided government on each of the following:
- Recess appointments
- Executive orders
- Signing statements
- Budgeting process

DRILL 9

Number Of Nominations To The Supreme Court, By Party Of The President

	1900-1949		1950-Present	
	Republicans	Democrats	Republicans	Democrats
Chief justice	3	2	4	1
Associate justice	16	14	20	9

1. Which of the following conclusions can be drawn from the data above?

    (A) There are currently more justices on the Supreme Court appointed by Democrats than by Republicans.
    (B) Over the last 100 years, the Supreme Court has been dominated by conservative thinkers.
    (C) Republican presidents have had more opportunities to nominate justices to the Supreme Court than Democratic presidents have.
    (D) More Republican nominees failed confirmation by the Senate than Democratic nominees did.
    (E) Fewer justices resign when there is a Democratic president than when there is a Republican one.

2. The "rule of four" refers to the

    (A) minimum number of cabinet members who must be present for the president to hold an official cabinet meeting
    (B) minimum number of interest groups that must join forces in order to create an officially recognized political action committee
    (C) number of committee members on a Senate committee who must agree to send a bill to the Senate floor for debate
    (D) usual number of Supreme Court justices that have to be interested in a case for it to be accepted for review
    (E) most common number of candidates who attempt to win a party's nomination for president

3. Which of the following fiscal issues does NOT need to be voted on by Congress before funds can be paid out?

    (A) The annual federal budget
    (B) Individual entitlements
    (C) Appropriations bills
    (D) Continuing resolutions
    (E) Discretionary spending

4. Which of the following is NOT part of the system of checks and balances outlined in the Constitution?

    (A) The Senate must approve judges nominated by the president.
    (B) The president can pardon those whom the courts have convicted.
    (C) Congress can impeach and remove a federal judge.
    (D) The Supreme Court can declare a presidential act unconstitutional.
    (E) The president can remove a justice from the Supreme Court.

5. All of the heads of the following organizations are appointed by the president and confirmed by the Senate EXCEPT the

    (A) Department of State
    (B) National Aeronautics and Space Administration
    (C) Bureau of the Census
    (D) Center for Disease Control and Prevention
    (E) Nuclear Regulatory Commission

6. Which of the following accurately outlines the roles of the House and Senate in regards to tax laws and spending bills?

(A) Tax and spending bills must originate in the Senate and the House may only amend revenue bills.

(B) Tax and spending bills must originate in the House and the Senate may only amend revenue bills.

(C) Tax bills must originate in the House and spending bills must originate in the Senate, however each body of legislature has the power to amend them.

(D) Tax bills must originate in the Senate and spending bills must originate in the House, however each body of legislature has the power to amend them.

(E) Tax bills and must originate in the House, but spending bills can originate in either chamber of Congress.

7. All of the following are key differences between the line-item veto and the pocket veto EXCEPT:

(A) Specific provisions of a bill could become law with a line-item veto, whereas no provisions of a bill may become law with a pocket veto.

(B) The president currently retains the power to use the pocket veto, but can no longer use a line-item veto.

(C) A line-item veto requires executive action, whereas a pocket veto does not.

(D) The pocket veto is a power provided to the president by the Constitution, whereas a line-item veto is not.

(E) A pocket veto may be overridden, whereas a line-item veto may not.

8. As commander-in-chief, the president may do which of the following without the approval of Congress?

(A) Declare war
(B) Deploy troops
(C) Ratify peace treaties
(D) Acquire money to wage war
(E) Suspend *habeas corpus* during peacetime

1. As representatives of the people, members of Congress are attuned to public opinion. However, members of Congress do not always vote in accordance with the wishes of their constituents.

    (a)   Define each of the following aspects of public opinion:
- Saliency
- Intensity
- Stability

    (b)   Describe two ways in which public opinion affects the voting decisions of members of Congress.

    (c)   Explain why a member of Congress may vote contrary to the opinion of the majority of his or her constituents.

    (d)   Although representatives are generally thought to be more responsive to their constituents than senators are, sometimes this is not that case. Describe one reason that public opinion might have a greater effect on the way senators choose to vote.

DRILL 10

1. Why does the Supreme Court grant *certiorari* to only a small fraction of the appeals submitted?

   (A) The majority of appeals don't require a jury trial.
   (B) The Court usually agrees with the decision of the lower courts.
   (C) The cases fail to provide convincing oral arguments to warrant such a decision.
   (D) The Court receives far too many appeals and fails to evaluate all of them.
   (E) The majority of the petitioners do not file *amicus curiae* briefs.

2. All of the following are accurate examples of the system of checks and balances incorporated into the Constitution EXCEPT:

   (A) Congress may override a presidential veto with approval of a two-thirds majority.
   (B) The Supreme Court may rule a law signed by the president unconstitutional.
   (C) The president is commander-in-chief of the armed forces; however, only Congress may declare war.
   (D) Proposed amendments to the Constitution require approval of a three-fourths majority of both Congress and the state legislatures.
   (E) Presidential nominees to the Supreme Court must be confirmed by Senate in order to serve.

3. Which of the following is a role of the president as outlined by the U.S. Constitution?

   (A) Draft legislation
   (B) Declare war
   (C) Regulate commerce
   (D) Negotiate treaties with foreign nations
   (E) Establish post offices

4. Of the following, which best explains the process of congressional redistricting?

   (A) New districts are formed by the House Ways and Means Committee after the census every 5 years.
   (B) New districts are formed by the House Ways and Means Committee after the census every 10 years.
   (C) New districts are formed according to individual state constitutions after the census every 5 years.
   (D) New districts are formed according to individual state constitutions after the census every 10 years.
   (E) New districts are formed by the Senate Judiciary Committee after the census every 10 years.

5. The presidential elections of 1824, 1876, 1888 and 2000 were unusual because

   (A) they were decided by a candidate receiving a majority of the electoral college votes
   (B) a third party candidate received electoral college votes
   (C) they were delayed by a mandatory recount due to a small margin of victory in a single state
   (D) they resulted in the a change in political party that controlled the presidency
   (E) the eventual winner of the presidential election failed to win plurality of the popular vote

6. Which of the following best explains the purpose for congressional franking?

   (A) To simplify the process of communicating with constituents
   (B) To decide the salaries of the subsequent Congress
   (C) To mark designate money for use in a specific state
   (D) To establish a system of seniority with regards to voting and committee selection
   (E) To permit the incorporation of earmarks in funding allocation bills

7. All of the following are reasons for the decennial U.S. census EXCEPT

(A) Redistribution of Electoral College votes to reflect changes in state populations
(B) Redistricting of congressional districts
(C) Accurate determination of the U.S. population
(D) Determination of federal funding allocations for social and educational programs
(E) Redefining the dates for elections of U.S. senators

8. Presidential vetoes

(A) can affect only part of a bill if the president agrees with other parts
(B) are explained to Congress through a veto message
(C) cannot occur when Congress is not in session
(D) have never been the subject of a Supreme Court case
(E) are the final authority on a bill

Time—25 minutes

1. The United States Supreme Court hears appeals through the process of judicial review.

    (a) Define judicial review, and describe what role it plays in the system of checks and balances.

    (b) Explain how the Court decide which cases to hear.

    (c) Describe the principles of *stare decisis* and judicial activism. Explain how they shape how justices make decisions.

DRILL 11

1. Which of the following best articulates the message of the 1880 cartoon shown above?

   (A) The economy is on the verge of collapse.
   (B) Franchise must be extended.
   (C) Health care reform is needed more than ever.
   (D) The two-party system is flawed.
   (E) Conservation should be a primary goal of government.

2. Which of the following statements about the White House Office staff members is true?

   (A) They must be confirmed by the Senate before taking office.
   (B) They are independent of the other Executive Offices of the Presidency.
   (C) The roles of the staff members are consistent from one administration to the next.
   (D) They do not interact with Congress or the cabinet departments.
   (E) They are frequently some of the president's friends and most trusted acquaintances.

3. Which Senate committee has the biggest role to play in considering presidential nominations?

   (A) Committee on Homeland Security and Governmental Affairs
   (B) Committee on the Judiciary
   (C) Senate Budget Committee
   (D) Committee on Appropriations
   (E) Committee on Rules and Administration

4. In which of the following election years did a third party presidential candidate succeed in winning at least one electoral vote?

   I. 1968
   II. 1980
   III. 1992
   IV. 2000

   (A) I only
   (B) III only
   (C) III and IV only
   (D) I, III, and IV only
   (E) I, II, III, and IV

5. The federal courts do NOT have original jurisdiction over cases involving

   (A) a foreign national and a U.S. state
   (B) maritime law
   (C) legality of state laws
   (D) international trade
   (E) military appeals

6. One of the most influential coalitions in the
American political history was the

   (A) Shays's coalition
   (B) Minority coalition
   (C) Populist coalition
   (D) New Deal coalition
   (E) Virginia coalition

7. Which of the following members of Congress is
in the presidential line of succession?

   (A) Speaker of the House
   (B) Senate majority leader
   (C) House majority leader
   (D) Democratic conference committee chair
   (E) Republican conference committee chair

8. In *Clinton v. City of New York* (1998), what was
the main reason that the Supreme Court struck
down the line-item veto as unconstitutional?

   (A) The decision was an example of judicial
review, though it was not affirmed by all
justices on the Court.
   (B) The Line Item Veto Act of 1996 was
intended to help enforce fiscal
conservatism by allowing the president to
nullify certain appropriations.
   (C) Republicans had taken control of both
houses of Congress in the midterm
elections of 1994.
   (D) The Supreme Court at the time was
dominated by conservative justices.
   (E) The line-item veto gave the president
unilateral power that violated the powers
given to Congress in the Constitution.

Free Response

Time—25 minutes

1. The executive branch of the federal government contains administrative agencies that oversee bureaucracies. These bureaucracies are characterized by a merit-based system.

    (a)   Describe a merit-based system.

    (b)   Describe one way in which the structure of federal bureaucracy promotes its bureaucratic independence.

    (c)   Explain how discretionary authority promotes bureaucratic independence.

    (d)   Describe how each of the following can balance the power of the bureaucracy.
- Congress
- The judiciary
- Private citizens

DRILL 12

1. Which of the following is LEAST important to the president when nominating federal judges?

   (A) Experience
   (B) Birthplace
   (C) Political affiliations
   (D) Public opinion
   (E) Senatorial courtesy

2. If the president's press secretary resigned, what would need to happen before a new person could fill that role?

   (A) The Senate would have to confirm any presidential appointee.
   (B) The president would have to hire a person he or she felt was right for the job.
   (C) The White House Human Resources office would have to accept applications from the public.
   (D) A special election in the District of Columbia would need to be held.
   (E) The House of Representatives would have to vote on an appointee.

3. Which of the following Supreme Court nominees was NOT confirmed by the Senate?

   (A) Earl Warren
   (B) William Rehnquist
   (C) Robert Bork
   (D) Sandra Day O'Connor
   (E) Clarence Thomas

4. Which of the following is NOT one of the roles of the Senate Committee on Appropriations?

   (A) Allocating funds to government agencies
   (B) Reviewing the president's budget request
   (C) Writing spending plans for the coming fiscal year
   (D) Creating emergency spending legislation
   (E) Drafting bills to raise revenue

5. Which of the following might interfere with the system of checks and balances established by the Constitution?

   (A) Executive privilege
   (B) The exclusionary rule
   (C) Congressional oversight
   (D) Expressed powers
   (E) A filibuster

6. Which of the following is a term for discretionary federal money that serves only a small portion of the population and is a tool for members of Congress to enhance their reputations?

   (A) Reapportionment
   (B) Pork barrel spending
   (C) Private goods
   (D) A progressive tax
   (E) Public assistance

7. The U.S. Courts of Appeals are also known as

   (A) federal claims courts
   (B) judicial districts
   (C) trial courts
   (D) circuit courts
   (E) judicial agencies

8. A motion for cloture must be approved by

   (A) a majority of representatives
   (B) a majority of senators
   (C) at least 60 representatives
   (D) at least 60 senators
   (E) the president

1. Every ten years, following the U.S. Census, congressional districts are reapportioned and redistricted.

    (a)   Define reapportionment.

    (b)   Define redistricting.

    (c)   Define gerrymandering, and explain two reasons why politicians might engage in gerrymandering.

    (d)   Explain two ways that the Supreme Court has responded to gerrymandering.

DRILL 13

1. Which of the following clauses in the Constitution is related to the separation of powers?

   (A) The elastic clause
   (B) The due process clause
   (C) The presentment clause
   (D) The equal protection clause
   (E) The full faith and credit clause

2. Which of the following is another term for cooperative federalism?

   (A) Dual federalism
   (B) Layer-cake federalism
   (C) Marble-cake federalism
   (D) New federalism
   (E) Fiscal federalism

3. Which of the following is NOT a type of presidential power?

   (A) Expressed power
   (B) Delegated power
   (C) Emergency power
   (D) Inherent power
   (E) Formula power

4. Under which circumstances is the president NOT chosen through a general election?

   (A) Whenever there is a third party candidate
   (B) In elections with at least one controversial candidate
   (C) Whenever all of the swing state electoral votes go to the same candidate
   (D) In elections involving an incumbent president
   (E) Whenever no candidate receives a majority of electoral votes

5. All of the following organizations play a role in congressional oversight of the federal bureaucracy EXCEPT the

   (A) Government Accountability Office
   (B) Congressional Research Service
   (C) Congressional Budget Office
   (D) Senate Committee on Finance
   (E) Senate Committee on Appropriations

6. Which of the following is NOT one of the federal courts?

   (A) Juvenile Court
   (B) District Court
   (C) Tax Court
   (D) Court of International Trade
   (E) Court of Appeals

7. Congress does NOT exercise legislative oversight over which of the following organizations?

   (A) Department of Homeland Security
   (B) American Civil Liberties Union
   (C) Office of Fair Housing and Equal Opportunity
   (D) Veterans Health Administration
   (E) National Renewable Energy Laboratory

8. Which of the following statements about the House of Representatives is FALSE?

   (A) Members must live in the states they represent.
   (B) There can never be more than 435 members in the House.
   (C) Amendments that allow for pork barrel spending can be attached to any House bill.
   (D) The House of Representatives is more responsive to the public than is the Senate.
   (E) Adherence to the views of one's political party is strongly encouraged among House members.

Free Response

Time—25 minutes

1. The United States Constitution outlines a federal system.

    (a)   Define federalism.

    (b)   Choose two of the following and explain how each has been used to expand federal power.
- The interstate commerce clause
- Categorical grants
- The Fourteenth Amendment

    (c)   Explain how one of the following has been used to limit the power of the state governments.
- Voting Rights Act
- The incorporation doctrine
- Clean Air Act

DRILL 14

1. All of the following regulate contributions to political campaigns EXCEPT

   (A) the Federal Election Campaign Act of 1971
   (B) the Federal Election Campaign Act amendment of 1975
   (C) the Federal Election Commission
   (D) the Bipartisan Campaign Reform Act of 1994
   (E) the Bipartisan Campaign Reform Act of 2002

2. Which of the following is NOT an action that a federal court might make after hearing a case?

   (A) Issue a concurring opinion
   (B) Affirm a ruling
   (C) Cite *stare decisis*
   (D) Act as a common-carrier
   (E) Encourage Congress to repeal a law

3. The process of approving presidential appointees generally slows down when there is

   (A) dual federalism
   (B) hyperpluralism
   (C) divided government
   (D) due process
   (E) horizontal federalism

4. Which of the following statements about the federal judiciary is addressed in the Constitution?

   (A) The Supreme Court has original jurisdiction over cases involving ambassadors.
   (B) There must be nine justices on the Supreme Court.
   (C) There must be 13 judicial circuits, each with a court of appeals.
   (D) Crimes committed by United States citizens in another country will be tried in the Supreme Court.
   (E) The Supreme Court can use the power of judicial review to invalidate laws passed by Congress.

5. The purpose of a discharge petition is to

   (A) remove a member from a conference committee
   (B) prevent a bill from being voted on
   (C) take control of a bill away from its committee
   (D) send a bill to a joint committee
   (E) get rid of an outdated standing committee

6. Which of the following pieces of legislation most limited the office of the president, while empowering Congress?

   (A) The Budget and Impoundment Control Act of 1974
   (B) Hatch Act
   (C) Freedom of Information Act
   (D) Federal Election Campaigns Acts
   (E) Gramm-Rudman-Hollings Bill

7. In *McCulloch v. Maryland*, the Supreme Court made a ruling based on the

   (A) Supremacy Clause
   (B) Equal Protection Clause
   (C) Free Exercise Clause
   (D) Commerce Clause
   (E) Establishment Clause

8. Once a bill is engrossed, the next step in the legislative process is

   (A) the conference committee's approval
   (B) for the president to sign or veto it
   (C) the addition of riders
   (D) to reconcile the differences between the House bill and the Senate bill
   (E) to return the bill to a standing committee

1. Historically, presidents have been given wide latitude in how they exercised their war making powers. Congress passed the War Powers Resolution in 1973 in order to limit these powers.

   (a) Describe the two ways in which the War Powers Resolution limits the president's war making powers.

   (b) Describe the primary way the Constitution balances the war making powers of Congress and the president.

   (c) Besides the constitutional power mentioned in part (b), identify and explain two other formal powers granted to Congress in regards to the decision to go to war.

DRILL 15

Congressional Approval Ratings and President's Party Seat Changes, Recent Midterm Elections

Year	President's Party	Majority party in House	% Approve of Congress	Seat gain/loss in U.S. House for president's party
2006	Republican	Republican	26	-30
2002	Republican	Republican	50	+6
1998	Democrat	Republican	44	+5
1994	Democrat	Democrat	23	-53
1990	Republican	Democrat	26	-8
1986	Republican	Democrat	42	-5
1982	Republican	Democrat	29	-28
1978	Democrat	Democrat	29	-11
1974	Republican*	Democrat	35	-43

*The president (Ford) took office less than 3 months before the midterm elections

Source: The Gallup Organization

1. Which of the following statements is best supported by the data in the table above?

   (A) When the president's party has the majority in the House, that party gained seats in the midterm elections between 1974 and 2006.
   (B) When Democrats held the presidency and the House, they never gained seats during midterm elections between 1974 and 2006.
   (C) Republican presidents have never overseen Republican gains in the House during midterm elections between 1974 and 2006.
   (D) When Congress had its lowest approval between 1974 and 2006, the majority party gained seats.
   (E) The highest congressional approval rating between 1974 and 2006 occurred while Democrats held the majority.

2. Which of the following factors is LEAST likely to help a congressional candidate in an election?

   (A) Being an incumbent
   (B) The coattail effect during a general election year
   (C) Large contributions from PACs
   (D) Membership in the president's party during a midterm election
   (E) Running in a district that was gerrymandered by a state legislature of the candidate's own party

3. In the past four decades, the membership of Congress has seen an increase in the number of all of the following EXCEPT

   (A) women
   (B) African Americans
   (C) active duty military veterans
   (D) Hispanics
   (E) Asian Americans

4. Every amendment to the Constitution

   (A) was first passed by a national convention called by the states
   (B) was first passed by a two-thirds majority in each chamber of Congress
   (C) was ratified by the legislatures of three-fourths of the states
   (D) was initially proposed by the president
   (E) increased the rights of citizens

5. A power created for the president by a congressional action is known as

   (A) a statutory power
   (B) a constitutional power
   (C) an inherent power
   (D) an expressed power
   (E) an emergency power

6. One of the privileges experienced by members of Congress is franking, which is the ability to

   (A) fund their campaigns through the donations of political action committees
   (B) fly to their home districts for free
   (C) receive insider trading information without penalty
   (D) use their congressional aides to work on their campaigns
   (E) send material through the mail to their constituents by using their signatures instead of postage

7. When each house of Congress passes a different version of the same bill, the bills must be reconciled in a

   (A) select committee
   (B) conference committee
   (C) joint committee
   (D) standing committee
   (E) rules committee

8. When the Supreme Court remands a case, it

   (A) declares that the lower court's ruling is valid
   (B) sends the case back to the lower court
   (C) refuses to issue a writ of *certiorari*
   (D) reverses the ruling of the lower court
   (E) agrees to hear the oral arguments

Free Response

Time—25 minutes

1. Since the ratification of the Constitution, the principle of federalism has been used to either expand or limit the power of the federal government relative to that of the states.

    (a)   Describe two of the following and explain how each has limited the power of the federal government.

          • The Tenth Amendment
          • The Eleventh Amendment
          • Welfare Reform Act of 1996

    (b)   Explain how one of the following has encouraged states to implement federal policies.

          • Children's Health Insurance Program
          • National Minimum Drinking Age Act of 1984
          • The No Child Left Behind Act of 2001

Chapter 10
Institutions of Government:
Answers and Explanations

ANSWER KEY

Multiple-Choice Questions

Drill 1
1. D
2. E
3. C
4. B
5. D
6. A
7. B
8. E
9. D
10. B
11. A
12. A
13. C
14. A
15. B
16. E

Drill 2
1. D
2. A
3. C
4. E
5. B
6. D
7. E
8. E
9. D
10. A
11. C
12. A
13. A
14. A
15. E
16. D

Drill 3
1. C
2. E
3. C
4. C
5. D
6. A
7. B
8. E
9. A
10. C
11. A
12. D
13. D
14. E
15. A
16. C

Drill 4
1. A
2. B
3. C
4. D
5. E
6. D
7. B
8. B
9. E
10. A
11. A
12. B
13. C
14. D
15. E

Drill 5
1. A
2. B
3. C
4. D
5. E
6. B
7. E
8. A
9. B
10. C
11. B
12. A
13. D
14. C
15. A

Drill 6
1. D
2. C
3. A
4. C
5. E
6. B
7. D
8. E

Drill 7
1. D
2. B
3. B
4. B
5. A
6. E
7. C
8. A

Drill 8

1. C
2. D
3. B
4. D
5. C
6. B
7. E
8. E

Drill 9

1. C
2. D
3. B
4. E
5. D
6. E
7. E
8. B

Drill 10

1. B
2. D
3. D
4. D
5. E
6. A
7. E
8. B

Drill 11

1. D
2. E
3. B
4. E
5. C
6. D
7. A
8. E

Drill 12

1. B
2. B
3. C
4. E
5. A
6. B
7. D
8. D

Drill 13

1. C
2. C
3. E
4. E
5. D
6. A
7. B
8. C

Drill 14

1. D
2. D
3. C
4. A
5. C
6. A
7. A
8. B

Drill 15

1. B
2. D
3. C
4. B
5. A
6. E
7. B
8. B

EXPLANATIONS

Drill 1

1. **D** According to the chart, as educational attainment increases, so too does the female voter turnout for both the Republican and Democratic primary elections. Choice (A) can be eliminated because men who held a college degree were less likely to turnout for the Republican primary than were females who held a college degree. Eliminate choice (B) because males with some high school education were only a quarter as likely to turnout for the Republican primary as females with some high school education were for the Democrat primary. Choice (C) can be eliminated because individuals over the age of 61 with a college degree were less likely to vote in the Democrat primary; the turnout for Democrats was 42 percent versus 46 percent for the Republican. Eliminate choice (E) because individuals under the age of 25 who held a doctorate were less likely to vote in the Democrat primary than were individuals between the ages of 26–45 with a doctorate (44 percent).

2. **E** A sponsor of a bill may or may not write the bill (an interest group, for example, may be the author of the bill), but a sponsor does introduce a bill to Congress, by definition. Choice (E) is the correct answer. Committee chairs hold committee votes on bills—while the sponsor of a bill may be a committee, the bill's sponsor isn't always the committee head, so you can eliminate choice (A). Choices (B) and (C) represent subjective situations that depend on the bill at issue. Some bills pass or fail after the original version is heavily compromised, while other bills pass or fail with the original language intact. Since the amount of compromise depends on many factors, neither option is the correct answer. Choice (D) is also wrong because the sponsor usually doesn't determine how long a bill will be debated.

3. **C** The Senate has 100 members while the House has 435 members. Considering these numbers, it is more difficult to make laws and allow everyone to have a say with 435 voices. To make legislative processes easier in the House, much of the law-making work is delegated to committees, where a smaller number of specialists attempt to hash out details. Since the Senate has fewer members, the general assembly can accommodate all members and committee work is less important, so select choice (C). While choice (A) is true, the fact that the Senate approves nominees to Federal Courts doesn't affect its committee system. Choice (B) is a false statement because the Constitution doesn't mention House committees. Choice (D) is also a false statement because the Senate does have committees. Choice (E) is only half-right, which makes it all wrong: both the Senate and the House employ seniority systems.

4. **B** The U.S. Supreme Court only reviews cases on appeal if four of the nine justices agree to review it. If so, the court issues a writ of *certiorari*, which functions as a request for lower court transcripts of a case. Choice (A), habeas corpus, is incorrect because it is a legal term used to describe the

principle that an accused person must be brought before a judge in criminal court. Amicus curiae briefs are legal documents filed by third parties in the hope of swaying the court toward one decision or the other, so eliminate choice (C). Judicial review is a power that permits the U.S. Supreme Court to repeal congressional legislation that it finds unconstitutional while judicial activism describes judges who often use judicial review to repeal congressional legislation, so choices (D) and (E) can be eliminated as well.

5. **D** Presidents have the constitutional power to appoint judges to the federal judiciary, though the president's appointments must be confirmed by the Senate. Presidents don't get three extra votes during confirmation proceedings, so eliminate choice (A). Choices (B) and (E) are incorrect because the separation of powers keeps judicial opinions free from presidential interference. Congress has impeachment power, but the president doesn't, so you can also eliminate choice (C).

6. **A** A standing committee is a permanent congressional committee focused on specific subject matter. Choice (B) can be eliminated because a select committee is a temporary committee, created by Congress to investigate specific issues. Eliminate choice (C) because a joint committee is comprised of members from both houses of Congress to investigate and research specific subjects. Eliminate choice (D) because corporations, unions, and trade associations form political action committees to raise campaign funds. Eliminate choice (E) because a conference committee is a temporary panel composed of both House and Senate members, formed for the purpose of reconciling differences in legislation that has passed both chambers of Congress.

7. **B** The Budget and Impoundment Control Act (1974) established congressional budget committees, created the Congressional Budget Office, and gave Congress the power to prevent the president from refusing to fund congressional initiatives. Eliminate choice (A) because the Northwest Ordinance legislation provided guidelines for the settlement of new territories. Eliminate choice (C) because the Hatch Act allowed government employees to vote in government elections, but prohibited them from partaking in partisan politics. Choice (D) can be eliminated because the Freedom of Information Act declassified government documents for public use. Eliminate choice (E) because the Sherman Anti-Trust Act gave Congress the power to regulate and break up monopolies.

8. **E** All of the choices can be part of the amendment process except for choice (E). While the state legislatures can petition Congress to call a constitutional convention, only two-thirds, not three-fourths, of the states are needed for such a convention to occur.

9. **D** All of the statements about congressional powers are true except for choice (D). When it comes to control of the bureaucracy, Congress has more power than the president. For example, Congress has the power to affirm or reject presidential appointments, abolish agencies, determine the funding an agency receives, and change agency jurisdiction if unsatisfied with policy implementation.

10. B Passed by Congress in 1973, the War Powers Act was established in an effort to force the president to seek congressional approval prior to making war. All of the statements about the War Powers Act are true except for choice (B). Since its establishment, the War Powers Act has never been invoked to force the president to withdraw troops.

11. A In the 1992 election, there was significant change to the makeup of Congress. One of the most significant changes in congressional membership was the increase in minority and women members. The results of the election led to the addition of ten African American and five Hispanic lawmakers. The 1992 election was also deemed the "Year of the Woman" because 28 new women were elected.

12. A In *McCulloch v. Maryland* (1819), the court ruled that the states did not have the power to tax the national bank and the federal government. The outcome of *McCulloch v. Maryland* reinforced the supremacy clause of the Constitution. Eliminate choice (B) because *Fletcher v. Peck* established the Supreme Court's right to apply judicial review to state laws. Choice (C) can be eliminated because *Roe v. Wade* decriminalized abortion. Eliminate choice (D) because *Schenck v. United States* established the "clear and present danger" principle with regards to the type of speech that is restricted. Finally, eliminate choice (E) because the Supreme Court ruled that the constitution implicitly guarantees a citizen's right to privacy in *Griswold v. Connecticut*.

13. C There are a number of advantages of incumbency in congressional elections. Incumbents receive more campaign contributions than do challengers, incumbents in the House who run for reelection win approximately 90 percent of the time, and, while incumbent Senators do have an advantage against challengers, House incumbents face less serious challengers due to gerrymandering. Choices I and III are respectively incorrect because there is no evidence that most Americans believe incumbents to be more politically active than challengers and the president does not always endorse incumbents.

14. A All of the statements regarding Congress are true except for choice (A). Elections for the 435 seats in the House of Representatives occur every two years, not every four years.

15. B The Constitution provides that the House of Representatives can initiate impeachment proceedings for "[t]he president, vice president, and all civil Officers of the United States…for…Treason, Bribery, or other High Crimes and Misdemeanors." At the federal level, impeachment proceedings have been brought against Presidents Johnson and Clinton as well as more than 15 federal judges, most recently Judge Thomas Porteous, who was successfully removed from the bench in 2010. While representatives and senators can suffer removal from office, the process is called "expulsion" and handled differently than impeachment. Choice (B) is correct.

16. E Every ten years, the Constitution requires the federal government to take a census. Congressional redistricting occurs in the House of Representatives every ten years and is based upon the results of

the census, so the correct choice is (E). States that lose population might lose representatives while states that gain population might gain representatives. The Senate is immune from redistricting since each state gets two senators regardless of population.

Drill 2

1. **D** While in office, the president has more control over handling international affairs than he or she has over most issues that occur within the United States, such as economic or domestic problems, so eliminate choices (A) and (B) on that basis. While congressional gridlock may lead to presidential action taken through executive orders, it may also mean that no federal action is taken, depending on the situation. Since choice (C) is so heavily dependent on the situation, it is not as strong as choice (D). You can also cross off choice (E) because judicial review is the principle by which the Supreme Court can strike down congressional law. This decreases the power of Congress, but only affects presidential power indirectly. Since the president is responsible for handling foreign policy, acting as Head of State, and commander-in-chief duties, a larger role in international affairs most directly increases presidential power.

2. **A** The Department of Defense (DOD) and the Department of Health and Human Services (DHHS), together with the Social Security Administration (SSA) agency, account for about two-thirds of total federal spending within the United States's budget. The DOD handles all expenses dealing with national security and the U.S. Armed Forces, the DHHS handles all expenses involving Medicare and Medicaid, and SSA handles America's Social Security program. Each of these individually is more than four times as large as the fourth largest U.S. budget expense in the 2012 budget, the Department of Agriculture. These same three are predicted to remain the most expensive into the foreseeable future. Since the Department of Defense is the only one of the three that appears as an answer choice, select choice (A).

3. **C** With only two exceptions, Maine and Nebraska, almost all of the states use a winner-take-all system when apportioning electoral votes. That means that the winner of New Jersey gets all of its electoral votes whether the vote percentages are 99–1 percent or 50.1–49.9 percent in that state. If you know that most states use a winner-take-all system, you can eliminate choices (A), (B), (D), and (E).

4. **E** A joint committee is a type of congressional committee with members from both the Senate and the House. Joint committees are usually used either to communicate with the public or for investigations. They do not usually write bills to be voted upon in congressional chambers. Choice (E) is the correct answer. Joint committees do not involve members from the executive branch, so all of the remaining choices can be eliminated.

5. **B** A candidate wins an election with a plurality of the vote when that candidate gets more votes than any other candidate. This happens most often when three or more candidates with popular support run for the same office. An election which requires a candidate to get more than half the vote is a majority election, so eliminate choice (A). Choice (C) describes the general presidential election, which is a majority election because a candidate must win a majority of electors to become president. If no one receives a majority of electoral votes, the House of Representatives selects the winner from the top three vote-earners. Primary elections select candidates to run in general elections, so choice (D) can be eliminated. Run-off elections are usually held when there are so many candidates with popular support that none of the candidates gets a high enough percentage of the vote to be considered a winner. Run-off elections are usually elections that are re-run, but with fewer candidates, so a minimum percentage of the vote can be achieved by the winner.

6. **D** While cabinet level departments mainly serve the executive branch, all departments are created by the legislative branch, making choice (D) correct. For example, the Department of Homeland Security was created by a piece of legislation called The Homeland Security Act in 2002. Neither the Declaration of Independence, nor the Articles of Confederation, nor the U.S. Constitution mentions cabinet departments, so choices (A), (B), and (C) are incorrect. The judicial branch doesn't have a hand in creating cabinet departments, so choice (E) can also be eliminated.

7. **E** Incumbent members of the House who run for reelection almost always win. On average they win slightly more than 90 percent of the time. The other choices are too low to model the overwhelming proportion of successful House incumbents in their bids for reelection.

8. **E** Supply-side economics is a theory that espouses creating economic policies that benefit producers of goods. Broadly speaking, the theory aims to keep inflation down and the price of goods cheaper. It usually requires tax cuts and fewer regulations which are also the hallmarks of laissez-faire economics. Supply-side economics is usually favored by Republicans and its recent lineage runs from Republican President Ronald Regan to 2012's Republican vice-presidential candidate Paul Ryan. Choice (E) is the correct answer. Of the two dominant economic theories, Democratic politicians tend to reject supply-side economics and accept Keynesian economics, so you can eliminate choices (A) and (C). A moderate Independent would most likely favor policies that balance the two approaches, so eliminate choice (D). Finally, a Republican interested in law-and-order policies probably won't care about supply-side economics as much. In fact, the law-and-order Republican may favor policies that spend on police, fire departments, and prisons, making them less likely to support supply-side policies, so eliminate choice (B).

9. **D** The U.S. Constitution directs that a president must sign or veto legislation within 10 days of passage, "Sundays excepted." If the president fails to act within those 10 days, the legislation becomes law by default. However, the rules change if a congressional session ends during those 10 days. If a congressional session ends within 10 days of passage and the president doesn't sign the bill, then

the legislation doesn't become law and Congress must re-legislate the entire bill. This situation is known as a pocket veto. The pocket veto is a rare maneuver, but James Madison was the first to use it in 1812. Choice (D) is the correct answer. Choice (A) is the definition of a line-item veto and choice (C) is the definition of a regular veto (usually just called a "veto"), so you can eliminate both choices. A threat of a veto is not the same as a pocket veto, so you can eliminate (B) as well. Choice (E) is wrong because it violates the Constitution's principle of separation of powers—the president doesn't have the ability to direct the Supreme Court to strike down congressional legislation because the Supreme Court is an independent branch of government.

10.   **A**   The income tax is a tax on money earned by people and businesses, so choice (A) is the correct answer. Choice (B) describes a sales tax, choice (C) describes a capital gains tax, choice (D) describes a property tax, and choice (E) describes an estate tax.

11.   **C**   Choice (A) describes a congressional standing committee, choice (B) describes a congressional joint committee, choice (D) describes a congressional select committee, and choice (E) describes a congressional conference committee, so all of those choices can be eliminated. Choice (C) is an accurate description of the House Rules Committee—it determines the length of debate in the House and the terms of the debate, including whether to allow an open or closed rule for amending the bill.

12.   **A**   In order for Congress to override a presidential veto, both Houses must pass the legislation after the veto by a two-thirds vote. Since a two-thirds vote by just one congressional house isn't enough, you can eliminate choices (C) and (E). A majority vote in both congressional houses doesn't suffice to override a presidential veto, so choices (B) and (D) are also wrong. Choice (A) is the correct answer.

13.   **A**   Because the electoral college system is winner-take-all, presidents focus their campaigns on the states with the biggest populations, which means the most electoral votes. Choice (A) is correct. The electoral college system does not influence people's individual politics, so choice (B) is incorrect. The electoral college system also does not influence the ways in which candidates reach out to people, so choice (C) is incorrect. Choice (D) is incorrect because while it is true, ballot access rules are established by states and not related to the electoral college. The electoral college prevents third party candidates from winning electoral votes. Finally, choice (E) is untrue because the popular vote usually does align with the electoral college results.

14.   **A**   Choice (A) is correct. The Ways and Means Committee is a tax-writing committee, the Oversight and Government Reforms Committee watches how tax payer money is spent and how efficient the government is, the Appropriations Committee oversees all appropriations bills, and the House Administration Committee oversees federal elections and day-to-day operations of the House.

15.   **E**   The chief staff members are individuals from key departments that represent a wide array of policy issues. They are not primarily limited to one department, as in choices (A) and (D). They generally

are members of the same political party as the president, since they are appointees, but they are not delegates, as choice (B) says. They are also not appointed by Congress, so choice (C) is incorrect.

16. **D** The cartoon depicts justice as being buried in legislation. There are simply too many laws for justice to stay on top of, which is what choice (D) says. Choice (B) is very close to the correct answer, but it is a little too detailed to be supported. The cartoon doesn't precisely depict rulings and recent legislation. Choice (A) is incorrect because the executive branch is not depicted in the cartoon. Choice (C) is incorrect because nothing in the cartoon indicates that members of Congress aren't merely doing their jobs. Finally, choice (E) is incorrect because the quantity of final products produced doesn't always equate to effort.

Drill 3

1. **C** Choice (A) requires some calculations before you can eliminate it, but if you work with the other statements first, you won't have to calculate anything. Choice (C) is clearly true based on the percentages given. Bush appointed more Hispanics than Clinton did, but fewer minorities total, so eliminate choices (B) and (D). Choice (E) is incorrect because women represent the highest category of appointees for President Bush.

2. **E** Congress requires a two-thirds majority in both houses to overturn a presidential veto. Therefore, if more than two-thirds of the members were in favor of the legislation when it was passed, obtaining that majority vote to overturn a veto is highly likely. The part of a term a president is in, with the exception of the lame duck period, has no effect on overturning a veto. The number of Supreme Court appointees is also irrelevant. Eliminate choices (A) and (D). Partisanship is often related to voting in favor of or against certain pieces of legislation, but not necessarily. Choice (B) is not as relevant or specific as choice (E). The same is true of choice (C). Citizens can influence the way the way legislators vote, but the two-thirds majority is what is most relevant to this question.

3. **C** District boundaries are set by individual states. The election boards of individual states enforce the boundaries and other election laws, but they don't create the laws or draw boundaries. The Office of Planning, Evaluation, and Policy is an education department, the Federal Election Commission governs campaigning financing, and the U.S. Election Assistance Commission helps ensure that people can register to vote.

4. **C** Article II, Section 2 of the Constitution gives the president the power to grant reprieves and pardons. Congress has the power to declare war, although in some circumstances the president has unconstitutionally done so. Choice (A) is incorrect. The president does serve as the leader of his or her political party, but this is not a role granted to him or her by the Constitution, so choice (B) is

not correct. The House of Representatives is granted the power to propose new taxes, so choice (D) is not correct. Choice (E) may be common practice, but is not a constitutionally granted power.

5. **D** If a candidate receives a majority of electoral college votes, no further action is required. That candidate becomes the next president. According to the Twelfth Amendment, the House of Representative will elect the president from the top three candidates if there is a tie in the electoral college, but there is never a run-off, a transfer of votes, nor any other action taken.

6. **A** Choice (A) accurately describes what franking is, as drafted into law by Congress in 1789. Staff members and interns are hired and Congress members can be impeached. If a senator dies in office, the governor of his or her state, in most cases, can appoint someone to take his or her seat, but there is no official term for that process. There is also no special term for the process by which Congress members are selected for committees.

7. **B** Gerrymandering is the process of drawing voting districts in a way that favors one candidate over another by either isolating those who won't vote for the candidate or spreading them out in such a way that they will always be in the minority. This process decreases the chances of a third-party candidate getting enough votes to the winner, since third party candidates have fewer supporters than do the Democrats and Republicans. Choice (B) is correct.

8. **E** The Senate is responsible for approving treaties, so choice (A) is incorrect. Only the president can remove his or her own appointees, so choice (B) is incorrect. Congress controls the budget, which can indirectly limit the number of people on the president's staff, but the Senate cannot directly set a limit on the staff. Choice (C) is incorrect. The House impeaches the president, but the trial is held in the Senate, so choice (D) is incorrect. Choice (E) is the only accurate statement.

9. **A** Appointing judges with similar political affiliations is one way that the president can influence the power of the Supreme Court. Therefore, choice (A) is correct and choice (C) is definitely incorrect. The political activities and affiliations of a judge may make some Senate members more or less likely to confirm that person, but they don't represent any formal limitations to the ability to serve. Choices (B) and (D) are incorrect. Choice (E) completely depends on which party controls the Senate and which party the nominee is affiliated with, so that choice is not necessarily correct.

10. **C** Article II, section 2 of the Constitution says that two-thirds of the Senate must concur with a treaty, so choice (C) is correct. The president alone is responsible for deploying troops and forcing Congress into session. Congress is responsible for appropriations bills. Vice presidents are chosen by delegates at the parties' national conventions.

11. **A** A filibuster, in which senators can debate a measure indefinitely, exists only in the Senate, not in the House. Choice (A) is correct. Choices (B) and (E) describe the House, not the Senate and choice (D) describes the Senate, not the House. Choice (C) is the opposite.

12. **D** In 1998, the Supreme Court ruled the line-item veto unconstitutional because it violated the Presentment Clause in Article I, Section 7 of the Constitution, essentially circumventing the process by which a bill becomes a law. So choices (B) and (E) are true. Congress had attempted to legally grant that power to the president in the Line-Item Veto Act of 1996, making choice (C) correct. Choice (A) is an accurate description of what a line-item veto is. Choice (D) is the only choice that is not true because 43 states grant this power to their governors.

13. **D** Members of the White House staff do not need to be confirmed by the Senate, so only choice (I) should be eliminated. The remaining three positions are all in federal agencies that are either part of the president's cabinet or hold Cabinet rank. All such positions require Senate confirmation.

14. **E** Constitutional amendments do not have to be approved by the courts, so choice (A) is correct. Choice (B) is true as well, although individuals may choose to sue the state for not enforcing federal rulings. Choice (C) is a power given to the president and the Senate by the Constitution. Congress has the power to impeach any civil officer, including federal judges, so choice (D) is correct. However, impeachment is the only way that judges can be removed. A special election cannot be called, so choice (E) does not describe an accurate limitation.

15. **A** Individual entitlements, such as Social Security and Medicaid, must be paid to all eligible citizens. This is the only accurate definition among the answer choices. Choices (B) and (E) are incorrect because the funds are paid out through the federal government. They do not vary by state, as choice (C) states, and they are mandatory expenditures, which means they do not need to be approved in the budget each year, as choice (D) states.

16. **C** The Supreme Court hears less than 5 percent of the cases it receives requests for each year, so choice (C) is correct. Choice (A) and (B) describe cases that the Supreme Court agrees to hear, but is not accurate in relation to the number of appeals it receives every year. Choice (D) is also only a possible outcome after the court agrees to hear the case. Choice (E) is not a reasonable expectation. Judges do not need to resign if their decisions are overruled.

Drill 4

1. **A** Since the passage of the Fourteenth Amendment, cooperative federalism, a system in which national and state governments share many powers, has been the prominent form of U.S. federalism. The Fourteenth Amendment instigated the downfall of dual federalism by providing the national government the means to enforce the rights of citizens against state infringement; thus, eliminate choice (C). Choice (B) can be eliminated because layer-cake federalism refers to a system in which the national government takes the lead in regulating business and allows the states much of the power granted under the Tenth Amendment. Creative federalism refers to a system in which the national government imposes requirements for states to receive federal money, thus blurring

the line between national and state powers; eliminate choice (D). Choice (E) can be eliminated because competitive federalism refers to decentralizing the Great Society programs, thus forcing states to invent novel ways to implement social policy.

2. **B** The Electoral College system does not place equal emphasis on election results in all states. Rather, the system places greater emphasis on election results in states with larger populations. For example, California, which has a large population and 54 federal legislators, has a greater impact on an election than does Maine, whose population only received 5 electoral votes. All of the remaining answer choices are correct and, therefore, should be eliminated.

3. **C** *Stare decisis*, Latin for "let the decision stand," is a principle that requires the court to apply the same reasoning to lawsuits that has been used in prior, similar cases. Thus, choices (A) and (D) can be eliminated. Eliminate choice (B) because the principle of *stare decisis* is the most flexible in constitutional cases because correction through legislative action is exceedingly difficult in cases involving the Constitution. In the case of *Planned Parenthood of Southeastern Pennsylvania v. Casey*, the Court invalidated one of the regulations regarding the constitutional right to have an abortion but upheld the other four; thus, eliminate choice (E). Accordingly, choice (C) is false; generally the courts will cite to *stare decisis* rather than overturn a prior ruling.

4. **D** Divided government occurs when one party controls the executive branch, while another party controls either or both houses of Congress. Eliminate choice (A) because it refers to bicameral legislature. Broad constructionism is the belief that the Constitution should be interpreted loosely when concerning the restrictions it places on federal power; thus, eliminate choice (B). Choice (C) can be eliminated because it refers to the system of checks-and-balances. Eliminate choice (E) because the point at which a party experiences a significant shift in its political agenda and electoral base is referred to as realignment.

5. **E** The Federal Election Commission is required to disclose campaign finance information, enforce the provisions of the law such as the limits and prohibitions on contributions, and oversee the public funding of presidential elections. The McGovern-Fraser Commission was created by the Republican party in 1968 in order to promote diversity within the delegate pool; eliminate choice (A). Eliminate choice (B) because no such commission exists. Choice (C) can be eliminated because the Congressional Budget Office assesses the feasibility of the president's plan and helps create Congress's version of the federal budget. The Federal Reserve Board is an executive agency that is mainly responsible for the formulation and implementation of monetary policy; thus, eliminate choice (D).

6. **D** Three non-legislative tasks of Congress are oversight, public education, and representing constituents within the government. Sponsoring a bill, however, is part of the legislative process and, therefore, option III must be eliminated. Accordingly, choices (A), (B), (C), and (E) can be eliminated.

7. **B** International treaties must receive two-thirds approval from the Senate in order to be enacted. All of the other statements are correct as written and, therefore, can be eliminated.

8. **B** The attorney general is nominated by the president and confirmed by the Senate; thus, only choice (B) is not true. All of the other statements regarding the attorney general are correct as written and, therefore, can be eliminated.

9. **E** While there are numerous criticisms of the Electoral College, supporters feel that the way in which the system operates encourages stability through the two-party system. Critics of the Electoral College feel that the way in which the system functions is a disadvantage for third parties due to the winner-takes-all nature. Conversely, proponents of the system believe a two-party system provides stability and protects the country against radical minorities from implementing their views in legislation. Choices (A), (B), (C), and (D) can be eliminated because they are all critiques of the Electoral College.

10. **A** The most important informal, or inherent, power of the president is to influence policy agenda and set economic policy. Choices (B), (C), (D), and (E) are all formal powers of the president and, therefore, can be eliminated.

11. **A** The General Accounting, Congressional Budget Office, and Congressional Research Service Offices are the administrative offices within Congress used in the congressional oversight process; thus, choice (A) is incorrect. Eliminate all the other choices because they are correct as written.

12. **B** Cooperative federalism refers to a form of federalism in which the layers of government share responsibilities and policies. All of the events above gave rise to the concept of cooperative, or marble-cake, federalism except for the passage of Ronald Regan's New Federalism: Phase II initiative. Regan's New Federalism: Phase II initiative, which occurred during the 1980s, is an example of contemporary federalism. Contemporary federalism, which led from 1970 to 1997, is typified by changes in the intergovernmental grant system, the increase of unfunded federal mandates, concerns about federal regulations, and continuing disputes over the nature of the federal system.

13. **C** A motion of cloture is the sole process by which the Senate can stop a filibuster and bring a bill to a vote. Eliminate choice (A) because a quorum call is a call of the roll to establish whether or not a quorum is present. Choice (B) can be eliminated because a motion to table is used to permanently kill a pending matter and halt future debate on the matter. Eliminate choice (D) because the choice refers to the motion to consider. Choice (E) describes the motion to instruct and, therefore, can be eliminated.

14. **D** In the latter half of the twentieth century, Congress was concerned with the growing power and involvement of the executive branch and its tendency to involve the military in foreign affairs.

Accordingly, Congress passed the War Powers Act of 1973 in order to limit the president's ability to wage future wars and protect against overly zealous presidential decisions. All of the remaining answer choices violate the principle of separation of powers by demonstrating instances in which one branch of government has attempted to use power not ascribed to it or overstepping its bounds and, therefore, choices (A), (B), (C), and (E) can be eliminated.

15.   **E**   The final step in the appellate court procedure occurs when the three judges issue a decision on the case. However, judges in an appellate court do not need to reach a unanimous decision; i.e., there is possibility of both dissent, concurrence, or a mixture of the two. Choices (A), (B), (C), and (D) can be eliminated because they are true statements regarding appellate courts.

Drill 5

1.   **A**   Pork barrel expenses are budget items proposed by legislators to benefit individuals in their home state or district. While some expenses are unwarranted, they are passed anyway for political gain, such as campaign contributions. It does not go through a process of debate and consideration that competitively awarded funding would. Spending can be classified as pork barrel if it is requested by only one chamber of Congress, is not the subject of congressional hearings, greatly exceeds the president's budget request, and aids only a local area or special interest. Thus, choices (B), (C), (D), and (E) can be eliminated.

2.   **B**   Congressional oversight, the ability to review the work of federal agencies, investigate charges of corruption, hold hearings in which citizens discuss the government's problems and suggest solutions, among other actions, is an implied power in the Constitution. The primary purpose of congressional oversight is to check the actions of the executive branch. Among the many enumerated powers of the Constitution are the powers to regulate the value of money, provide and maintain a navy, collect taxes, and declare war. Accordingly, choices (A), (C), (D), and (E) can be eliminated.

3.   **C**   Justices to the Supreme Court are nominated by the president and confirmed by a majority vote in the Senate. Accordingly, choices (A), (B), (D), and (E) can be eliminated.

4.   **D**   Revenue bills, the way in which the federal government raises revenue in order to function, are handled by the House Ways and Means Committee and the Senate Finance Committee. Revenue bills must originate in the House Ways and Means Committee and both committees research and debate the bills.

5.   **E**   The National Security Advisor, who serves as the primary advisor to the president on national security issues and plays a major role in the National Security Council, is a staff position within the Executive Office of the President. During times of crisis, the National Security Advisor operates

from the White House Situation Room and updates the president on the most recent events related to the situation. While the president appoints the National Security Advisor, the position does not require Senate confirmation. Accordingly, the correct answer is choice (E).

6. **B** Term limits restrict the president to two terms in office. The Twenty-second Amendment created presidential term limits in 1951 in response to Franklin D. Roosevelt's four terms in the 1930s and 1940s. The president is the only one of the above answer choices with this restriction. Supreme Court justices and federal court judges get lifetime appointments, pending good behavior, so eliminate choices (A) and (E). The electorate elects senators and representatives of the U.S. House of Representatives to six- and two-year terms, respectively, and those officials can be elected as many times as they can win. Therefore, cross out choices (C) and (D).

7. **E** A pocket veto is used by the president to block a bill by not signing it after it passes at the end of a congressional session. A filibuster is a tactic designed to block the passage of legislation through the Senate. A killer amendment is an amendment tacked on to a bill to make it less likely to pass through a chamber of Congress. Cloture is a vote on whether to end a filibuster. That eliminates choices (A), (B), (C), and (D) and leaves us with the correct answer, choice (E). Pork barrel spending occurs when a member of Congress funds a project in his or her home district by adding a rider, also called an amendment, to a bill.

8. **A** Coalition building occurs when different groups work together toward the same goal. For example, socially liberal interest groups may work with Libertarian groups because both groups would like to strengthen civil liberties. Choice (A) is the correct answer. None of the other choices necessarily involve groups with different goals working together, so you can eliminate them.

9. **B** While it might be tempting to think the Senate majority leader is the president of the Senate, the vice president is actually the president of the Senate, so eliminate choice (A). However, the Senate majority leader does control the Senate's legislative agenda by choosing which pieces of legislation to vote upon and debate, which makes choice (B) the correct answer. The Senate majority leader has more power than other senators and often acts as a power broker, so you can eliminate choices (C) and (D). The Senate majority leader has no direct power in the House of Representatives, so eliminate choice (E) as well.

10. **C** The Constitution did not explicitly grant the Supreme Court the power of judicial review. Judicial review was established by Supreme Court Justice John Marshal in the *Marbury v. Madison* case in 1803, making choice (C) the best answer. *McCulloch v. Maryland* was the first case in which the Supreme Court used judicial review, but it did not establish the principle as *Marbury v. Madison* did. *Fletcher v. Peck* was the first case in which the Supreme Court ruled a state law unconstitutional, *Mapp v. Ohio* established that evidence collected illegally could not be used in trial, and *Gibbons v. Ogden* clarified the commerce clause as it related to interstate commerce.

11. **B** The question accurately describes a conference committee. A standing committee deals with permanent legislation, a select committee deals with a specific issue that exists only for a brief period, and a joint committee is similar to a select committee but has members from both chambers. A political action committee is a coalition of organizations that attempt to influence members of Congress. Therefore, all choices except choice (B) can be eliminated.

12. **A** Presidents use their appointment power to select judges whose views on key issues are similar to those of the president so that rulings will tend to coincide with the president's beliefs. Choices (B), (C), and (D) all describe powers that the president does not have. The president may appeal to the American people through the media, but judges, as appointees, are generally not influences by public opinion. Choice (E) is not the answer that provides the strongest influence the president can have.

13. **D** The Supreme Court receives thousands of cases a year and can only accept a small fraction of them. It generally accepts those cases that pertain to Constitutional issues or that involve an overturning of precedent. Many people may attempt to persuade the Supreme Court to hear a case, including lobbyists who file *amicus curiae* briefs but those are no guarantee. Accordingly, eliminate choices (A), (B), and (C). The Supreme Court is not a back-up court for other appellate courts, so eliminate choice (E).

14. **C** The Budget and Impoundment Control Act of 1974 was passed in response to President Nixon's refusal to disburse congressionally appropriated funds. Members felt that the president had too much power over budget matters. Nixon attempted to veto the Act, but Congress overrode the veto. Congressionally-appropriated funds are not relevant to spending by lobbyists, whose money comes from private organization, so eliminate choice (A). American military involvement in Vietnam ended in 1973, so eliminate choice (B). The House Committee on Ways and Means is the oldest committee in Congress, established in 1789, so eliminate choice (D). The idea of a debt ceiling was first established in 1917 with the First Liberty Loan Act, although not formalized until 1939. Eliminate choice (E).

15. **A** The large size of the House of Representatives means that more work can be done in committees than when all representatives are assembled on the floor. Confirmation powers are not relevant to committees, so eliminate choice (B). In both the Senate and the House, members to committees are assigned by the majority party, so eliminate choice (C). Committees in both the Senate and the House consist of members from both parties, although the majority party generally has more members. Eliminate choice (D). Finally, although choice (E) is true, it does not account for differences between the two chambers of Congress.

Drill 6

1. **D** The 1936 Roosevelt election, the 1972 Nixon election, and the 1984 Reagan election were those with the highest number of electoral votes awarded to the winner and all three were incumbents. Choice (A) can be disproven with the defeats of incumbents J. Carter in 1980 and G. Bush in 1992. Choice (B) can be disproven by looking at W. Bryan, T. Dewey, or A. Stevenson, all of whom ran at least twice and never won. Incumbents ran in 15 of the presidential elections shown and won in 11. Since incumbents won in more than two-thirds of their races, choice (C) is incorrect. Finally, choice (E) can be disproven by the election of W. Wilson in 1912, F. Roosevelt in 1932, or R. Reagan in 1980. In all cases, the winner was a challenger (not an incumbent) who won by a large margin.

2. **C** The War Powers Act was a response to prolonged U.S. involvement in the Korean and Vietnam Wars without a formal declaration of war by Congress. It states that after a president deploys troops, if Congress does not approve of involvement in the foreign conflict, the president will have 60 to 90 days to bring troops home. None of the remaining choices accurately describe the Act and should all be eliminated.

3. **A** In *McCulloch v. Maryland*, the Supreme Court ruled that states could not national banks or the federal government. It further stated that states must abide by any demonstration of power granted to the federal government by the Constitution. *Gideon v. Wainwright* was a case concerning the right to an attorney, *District of Columbia v. Heller* was a Second Amendment case, and *Schenck v. United States* and *Texas v. Johnson* were free speech cases. Accordingly, choices (B), (C), (D), and (E) can all be eliminated.

4. **C** The members of the House Committee on Rules can set a limit on how many amendments can be added to a bill, so eliminate choices (A) and (E). Filibusters only occur in the Senate, so eliminate choice (B). Only the Senate confirms presidential nominees, so eliminate choice (D). This leaves choice (C); discharge petitions can be voted on in both the Senate and House, and any member can vote on them.

5. **E** In 1992, ten African American and five Hispanic lawmakers were elected to Congress. This was a significant increase, so choice (E) is correct. None of the remaining groups contain members who increased their congressional presence in a very significant way.

6. **B** Incumbents cannot utilize their congressional staff for campaign work. They must hire campaign staffers separately. Incumbents have name recognition because they presently serve in Congress and work for their constituents, so it is easier for them to raise money and they do not rely on the media for name recognition as heavily as an unknown challenger would. Eliminate choices (A), (C), and (D). Incumbents clearly all have experience running successful campaigns simply due to the fact that they are in office. Eliminate choice (E).

7. **D**   When the Supreme Court declares a law unconstitutional, it is nullified and should no longer be enforced by any court or officer of the law. However, until it is formally repealed by the legislative body responsible for creating it, it remains on the books as a law. The president can never nullify a Supreme Court decision, so eliminate choice (A). Members of Congress can be recalled, but a recall is not linked to Supreme Court decisions. A recall requires petitions by citizens and can be initiated for many reasons. Eliminate choice (B). The Constitution is very difficult to amend; it has only been amended 27 times, but far more laws than 27 have been repealed. Eliminate choice (D). Finally, the law will not be reinstated once it has been declared unconstitutional, so eliminate choice (E).

8. **E**   Both chamber of Congress have a minority leader. Article II, Section 2 of the Constitution says that the Senate will confirm presidential appointments, so eliminate choice (A). Article I, Section 7 of the Constitution says that tax bills must originate in the House, so eliminate choice (B). Senators serve for six years and representatives for two, so eliminate choice (C). The House Committee on Rules sets rules for debate in the House, but such strict rules of debate don't exist in the Senate, so eliminate choice (D).

Free-Response Question 1

Students may earn a total of five points on this question. Two points are available for part (a), one for part (b), one for part (c), and one for part (d).

In part (a), you may earn one point for correctly describing one way in which the Supreme Court is insulated from politics and one point for correctly describing one way in which the Supreme Court is affected by politics. Possible descriptions of how the Court is insulated from politics include the following:

- Justices are appointed, not elected.
- Justices are appointed for life.
- Court decisions are not subject to veto by the other branches.

Possible descriptions of how the Court is affected by politics include the following:

- Justices base their decisions on the political "climate," not the "weather."
- Presidents appoint members of their own party to the Court.
- Nominees must be confirmed by the Senate.
- Presidents with longer tenures generally can appoint more justices.
- Extended periods in which the same party occupies the presidency result in more justices whose views are aligned with those of that party on the Court.

Part (b) asks you to explain one way in which the confirmation process affects the Supreme Court. Possible answers include

- Presidents nominate justices who are likely to be confirmed with little difficulty.
- Presidents avoid nominees with controversial opinions.
- Presidents nominate those with moderate views when their party lacks control of the Senate.
- Presidents tend to nominate people already serving as federal judges rather than attorneys or scholars.
- The vetting process eliminates from consideration those with scandals in their pasts.

Part (c) asks you to identify one way in which the president can limit the power of the Supreme Court. Possible answers include

- Nominate justices to the Court
- Appoint justices likely to issue opinions in the president's favor
- Refuse to enforce Court decisions

Part (d) asks you to identify one way in which Congress can limit the power of the Supreme Court. Possible answers include

- Pass new legislation to change the law that decisions will be based on
- Create Constitutional amendments, which are not subject to judicial review
- The Senate controls appointments through the confirmation process

Drill 7

1. **D** Select committees exist for a brief time to complete a specific task, so choices (A) and (C) can be eliminated since I is wrong. Standing committees are the most common type. Conference committees and joint committees include members from both chambers, so eliminate choices (B) and (E). Choice (D) is correct because party leaders choose committee members and serving on committees can enable members of Congress to work on issues that are important to their constituents, thus enhancing their reputation and helping to assure reelection.

2. **B** Congress can specify what funds must be used for and can withholding funding when necessary. These are both ways it engages in oversight of the bureaucracy. Authorization of spending and appropriations bills cannot override vetoes; Congress must vote to override vetoes. Eliminate choice (A). Spending is authorized after the annual budget has already been approved, so eliminate choice (C). Pork barrel spending is generally difficult to justify because, by nature, it is a pet project that serves only a small interest, and appropriations bills are not related to inflation; eliminate choices (D) and (E) respectively.

3. **B** Gerrymandering is the process of redrawing district lines to give certain candidates or parties an advantage. This can only occur every 10 years when district lines are redrawn following the census to ensure proportional representation. Eliminate choice (A). Gerrymandering is a controversial

practice and would not require formal approval from any organization, so eliminate choices (C) and (D). However, it is still legal, so eliminate choice (E).

4. **B** The Constitution gives the president the power to make treaties and to deploy troops, and the president is responsible for appointing ambassadors and other key international officials. Therefore, more involvement in foreign affairs leads to more power for the president. While all of the remaining choices may be true during certain points in U.S. history, they are not a result, as the question indicates, of heavier foreign involvement. Therefore, choices (A), (C), (D), and (E) are all incorrect in the context of this question.

5. **A** Although two-thirds of the Senate must vote to remove the president from office during an impeachment trial, the articles of impeachment that originate in the House and prompt a trial in the Senate only need to be passed by a simple majority. All choices except choice (A) refer to either the incorrect number of Congressmen or the wrong chamber.

6. **E** Maine and Nebraska do not use a winner-take-all system. Electoral votes in those states are awarded proportionately. This is in contrast to the rest of the states. Only five states caucus (Iowa, Texas, Nevada, Idaho, and Washington), so eliminate choice (A). Voting by mail and ballot access restricting are common practices, so eliminate choices (B) and (C). Polls are only open on the Tuesday after the first Monday in November, everywhere in the United States, so eliminate choice (D).

7. **C** The president appoints cabinet leaders and can appoint whomever he or she chooses; eliminate choice (E) and select choice (C) because he or she does not have to select people who belong to different political parties. Despite this connection, cabinet departments often have goals that differ from those of the president, so eliminate choice (B). Although the leaders are appointed, the departments are established by Congress, so eliminate choice (A). Finally, choice (D) is incorrect. There are 15 cabinet departments and numerous other sub-agencies or independent agencies with cabinet-rank status.

8. **A** A standing committee is one that deals with permanent legislative issues. Since they are permanent, eliminate choice (B). Choice (C) describes conference committees. Choice (D) is untrue; the majority party generally has more members on each committee. Choice (E) might happen, given that each committee is dominated by members of the majority party, but isn't required to happen, so eliminate this answer.

Free-Response Question 1

This question is scored on a scale of six points. Students can earn two points for part (a), one for part (b), two for part (c), and one for part (d).

In part (a), you may earn one point for explaining the role of each committee on the legislative process.

- The House Ways and Means Committee oversees taxing and spending legislation. All revenue bills must originate in the House (the Senate has the power only to amend revenue bills), and they begin in the Ways and Means Committee.
- A conference committee reconciles the different versions of a bill passed by the House and Senate. Before a bill can be sent to the president, it must be passed by both chambers of Congress in exactly the same form. Once the House and Senate have passed their own versions of a bill, the authors of each bill negotiate a compromise. The compromise bill is returned to both the House and Senate; each chamber must pass the bill in that form before the bill can be sent to the president for signing.

In part (b), you may earn one point for identifying a way in which members of Congress oversee the federal bureaucracy. Possible answers include

- The Senate confirms or rejects those nominated by the president to be directors of federal agencies.
- Congress establishes the budget for federal agencies.
- Congress may increase or decrease funding for federal agencies.
- Congress may hold committee hearings or launch investigations into the actions of a federal agency or its agents.
- Congress may change laws through new legislation.
- Congress may amend the jurisdiction of a federal agency through new legislation.

In part (c), you may earn one point for describing how members of Congress use their position to educate the public. You may earn one point for explaining what role the House Rules Committee plays in the public's education. Possible answers for describing how members of Congress use their position to educate the public include

- Committees and subcommittees can hold hearings on issues that members of Congress think the public should know about.
- Congress can hold floor debates to increase the public's awareness of a bill or issue.
- Committees and subcommittees can hold investigations into issues of public interest.
- The filibuster allows senators unlimited debate, in which issues important to one or more senators can be raised to the public.

Also in part (c), you may earn a point for explaining that the House Rules Committee determines how long a bill will be debated, if at all. The Rules Committee also decides whether amendments to a bill will be allowed. An open rule issued by the Rules Committee allows amendments to a bill, while a close rule prohibits amendments. By deciding whether and how long a bill will be debated and whether to allow amendments to a bill, the Rules Committee exercises great influence over how much the public will learn about a bill through floor debate.

In part (d), you may earn one point for explaining how members of Congress may represent their constituents beyond voting decisions. Possible answers include

- Members of Congress may author or sponsor bills of importance to their constituents.
- "Pork barrel" projects: Members of Congress may include funding in bills for local projects that benefit their constituents.
- Members of Congress may receive and act upon their constituents' complaints about federal services.
- Members of Congress may sponsor constituents who seek scholarships.
- Members of Congress may advocate on behalf of businesses that seek federal contracts.
- Members of Congress may sit on committees that oversee issues relevant to their constituents.
- Members of Congress may solicit the opinions of their constituents and take action based on those opinions.

Drill 8

1. **C** Due to Ross Perot, a strong third party candidate, Bill Clinton failed to receive over 50 percent of the popular vote both times he was elected. He still had the majority of the popular vote, so eliminate (E). A run-off occurs when no candidates receives a majority of the electoral votes, which Clinton did in both elections, even though he did not receive a majority of the popular vote. Eliminate choice (D). Only two states distribute electoral votes proportionately, so that was not a factor in either of Clinton's elections. Eliminate choice (B). Finally, the Electoral College system is an example of indirect voting, so eliminate choice (A).

2. **D** Choice (D) accurately describes one of the main functions of the House Rules Committee. Choice (A) describes the Committee on Oversight and Government Reform. Choice (B) describes the Committee on House Administration. Choice (C) describes the Committee on Ways and Means. Choice (E) describes the Committee on Appropriations.

3. **B** Incumbents historically have an easier time raising funds than their challengers do, partly because of name recognition and partly because they have had the opportunity to create real benefits for their constituents. Incumbents do not receive free airtime for advertising, so eliminate choice (A). Choice (C) can be eliminated because if everyone is apathetic toward voting, incumbents also are not receiving votes. Most voters have very limited access to members of Congress, so eliminate choice (D). Finally, eliminate (E) because there is no evidence that this is true.

4. **D** Most vetoed bills do not meet the two-thirds majority threshold in each house that is required for overturning a veto, making choice (B) untrue. Therefore, vetoes are typically sustained. When the president vetoes a bill, it goes back to both houses for a vote and no committee work is necessary at that time, so choice (A) is incorrect. Choice (C) is wrong, as the Supreme Court does not decide on the constitutionality of a law until it is passed, signed, and challenged in the lower courts. The cabinet is irrelevant to the veto process, so choice (E) is incorrect.

5. C   Research consistently suggests that a Congressperson's party is the primary factor in his or her voting decisions. In recent years, House and Senate votes have become more polarized, making this phenomenon more apparent. Even though constituents vote for their Congress members, politicians will often put the priorities of their party in front of those of the voters. After all, many voters are loyal to one of the two parties already and politicians assume that the few swing voters remaining can be persuaded with ads funded by party money. It is therefore in the interest of a congressperson to be in good standing in the party, despite what their constituents seem to want. Therefore choice (A) is not true. Lobbyists can exert a strong influence, but typically cannot override the pressure a candidate receives from party leaders, so choice (B) is incorrect. A member of Congress may monitor media coverage for information on a variety of issues but will still prioritize the will of his or her party. Eliminate choice (D). While religious identification can influence a member of Congress on many pressing issues, party affiliation is far more commonly a factor for a member of Congress. Eliminate choice (E).

6. B   A veto message is a presidential request for Congress to change certain aspects of a bill before he or she will sign it. He or she writes to Congress suggesting these changes and indicates that he or she will not veto the bill if his or her requested changes are made. If a bill fails to pass in either house, it will not even reach the president for a veto, so eliminate choices (A) and (E). Choice (C) is incorrect because after a bill is signed into law, a veto is not possible. If the president ignores the bill for over ten congressional working days, it will automatically become law, so eliminate choice (D).

7. E   A regressive tax places more of a burden on the less wealthy. A ten percent sales tax on a $1,000 television would disproportionately affect a person who makes minimum wage than it would a millionaire. An estate tax is a progressive tax because it only affects estates that are assessed at high value, so choice (A) is incorrect. Both federal and state income taxes are progressive taxes because the tax rate increases as one's income goes higher. Eliminate choices (B) and (D). Corporate tax is assessed relative to the revenue a corporation generates. Since it is also a progressive tax, choice (C) is incorrect.

8. E   Nixon promoted New Federalism during his tenure and the idea has caught on with many political leaders since. New Federalism is the idea of returning power to the states and decentralizing programs. Dual federalism, in which the federal government and the state governments each had clear and distinct roles, existed in the early history of the United States. Eliminate choice (A). Cooperative federalism, in which the roles of the federal and state governments are blurred and tend to overlap, existed in the middle of the twentieth century. Eliminate choice (B). Marble-cake federalism is just another term for cooperative federalism, so choice (C) can also be eliminated. Regulated federalism refers to the practice of the national government imposing standards and regulations on state governments, so eliminate choice (E).

Free-Response Question 1

This question is scored on a scale of six points. Students can earn one point for part (a), one for part (b), and four for part (c).

In part (a), you may earn one point for correctly defining divided government, which occurs when the president's party does not hold a majority in either one or both chambers of Congress.

In part (b), you may earn one point for explaining how divided government may occur. Possible answers include

- Midterm elections: The president's party loses support after the president's election or reelection, and the opposition party wins a majority in one or both chambers of Congress.
- Ticket-splitting: Voters elect a president and member of Congress of different parties.

In part (c), you may earn one point for explaining how divided government affects each of the actions mentioned.

- *Recess appointments*: The president is likely to make more recess appointments during times of divided government. Normally, the Senate must confirm the president's nominees before they can become ambassadors, judges, or heads of federal agencies; however, the president has the power to make appointments while Congress is in recess (not in session). If the Senate majority and the president are of different parties, then the president's nominees will face greater difficulty in getting confirmed. The process may take longer and/or the nominees may fail to be confirmed. Therefore, the president may choose to make an appointment during the congressional recess as a means of avoiding the Senate confirmation process (until the next session of Congress).
- *Executive orders*: The president may issue orders to the executive branch. These executive orders have the same effect as laws passed by Congress but do not require congressional approval. During times of divided government, the president is likely to issue more executive orders as a means of exercising influence over public policy without relying on Congress to pass a law—a law that Congress may fail to pass or may pass in a form different from the president's vision.
- *Signing statements*: Sometimes the president issues a statement upon signing a bill. While not actually part of the law, a signing statement clarifies the president's interpretation of a law and plans for its implementation. These signing statements can reflect interpretations or intentions significantly different from those of members of Congress. During times of divided government, the president is likely to issue more signing statements because the president and the congressional majority are more likely to disagree on key points of legislation.
- *Budgeting process*: The budgeting process is likely to be slower and more difficult during times of divided government. In the budgeting process, the president submits a budget to Congress, and Congress sends the budget to various committees to revise and approve it. In times of divided government, the congressional majority is likely to disagree with the president on revenue and appropriations issues; therefore, Congress is likely to make more revisions to the president's budget, increasing the likelihood that the president will veto the budget. This contention lengthens the budgeting process; for example, Democratic President Clinton and congressional Republicans failed to reach a consensus on the budget in 1995, resulting in a temporary shutdown of the federal government.

Drill 9

1. **C** Based just on the nomination numbers provided in the table, choice (C) is true in every category. Choice (A) is untrue (five were appointed by Republican presidents and four by Democrat presidents) and could not be inferred from the information provided in the table. Choice (B) can be eliminated because the table does not provide information about the length of justices' tenure or about justices' influence. Choice (D) discusses confirmation, which is beyond the scope of the table. Finally, eliminate choice (E) because the table doesn't offer enough information about why certain presidents were able to nominate justices. Justices may leave the Supreme Court due to resignation as well as retirement, impeachment, and death.

2. **D** While there is no hard and fast rule about which cases the Supreme Court must accept, in general, if four justices are interested in reviewing a case, the case will be accepted. There are no such rules about number of members for a cabinet meeting or number of interest groups needed to create a PAC, so eliminate choices (A) and (B). A majority of all members on a Senate committee must agree to send a bill for debate. Since some Senate committees have nine members, four would not be sufficient. Eliminate choice (C). Finally, presidential races generally start out with more than four members per party vying for the nomination, so eliminate choice (E).

3. **B** Individual entitlements, such as Social Security and Medicare, are a type of mandatory spending that Congress does not need to vote on. Any qualified individual can receive a payment. The annual budget must be approved by Congress every year, as must all discretionary spending, which is written into the budget, and the appropriations bill that actually allow the spending of budgeted funds to occur. Accordingly, eliminate choices (A), (C), and (E). If appropriations bills do not pass, Congress can pass a continuing resolution which allows operations of the affected organization to continue while Congress attempts to reach an agreement on the budget. Choice (D) can be eliminated.

4. **E** Supreme Court justices are appointed for lifetime tenures. A justice may be removed only if the House impeaches and the Senate convicts a justice; the president cannot unilaterally remove a justice from the bench. All other choices accurately describe checks and balances that were written into the Constitution.

5. **D** All answer choices except choice (D) are agencies or organizations whose leaders are selected through presidential appointment with Senate confirmation. Although the Center for Disease Control and Prevention (CDC) operates under the Department of Health and Human Services, whose leader is appointed by the president, the head of the CDC is a position for which one must apply and be hired.

6. **E**   Generally, the House and Senate share legislative powers as outlined in the Constitution. However, Article I, Section 7 of the Constitution specifically states that all bills for raising revenue originate in the House of Representatives and that the Senate may only amend them. However, both the House and the Senate have appropriations committees that draft spending bills.

7. **E**   The line-item veto permits the executive to veto specific provisions of a bill and sign the rest of the bill into law, rather than passing or vetoing the bill in its entirety; therefore, choice (A) is true. The governors of many states may make use of a line-item veto; however, the president may not. The Constitution grants the president the power to use a pocket veto but not a line-item veto; this makes choice (D) a true statement. As laid out in Article I, Section 7 of the Constitution, a pocket veto occurs when the president neither signs nor vetoes a bill and Congress is out of session. Thus, choice (C) is true because a pocket veto requires no executive action. Congress passed legislation in 1996 to grant the president the power of the line-item veto; however, the Supreme Court ruled the line-item veto unconstitutional in *Clinton v. City of New York* (1998). This makes choice (B) a true statement. A pocket veto may not be overridden because it occurs when Congress (the only body that may overturn a presidential veto) is out of session; thus, choice (E) is false and the correct response.

8. **B**   The president of the United States as Commander-in-Chief may deploy troops and oversee their operations without the permission of Congress, as is stated in Article II, Section 2 of the Constitution. However, the Constitution also specifies that only Congress may declare war, so eliminate choice (A). Since Congress also controls funding and appropriations, the president would have to request military funding; eliminate choice (D). The president has the right to negotiate treaties with other nations; however, the ability to ratify a treaty remains with the Senate, making choice (C) incorrect. Choice (E) is incorrect because Article I, Section 9 states that *habeas corpus* may be suspended only in cases of rebellion or invasion, not during peacetime.

Free-Response Question 1

This question is scored on a scale of seven points. Students may earn three points for part (a), two for part (b), one for part (c), and one for part (d).

In part (a), you can earn one point for each public opinion term you correctly define.

- *Saliency* refers to how important an issue is to the public. The public may have an opinion on a variety of issues, but only a few are truly important and which issues are important varies for individuals and groups. For example, Social Security and Medicare are salient issues for senior citizens, but not for young voters.
- *Intensity* refers to how strongly people feel about an issue. Groups who feel intensely about an issue are more likely to vote based on a candidate's position on that group and can have an oversized influence in elections and policymaking. For example, many Americans favor gun control, but the issue has a low level of intensity for them. On the other hand, the issue has a high degree of intensity for members of the National Rifle Association (NRA). This means that NRA members are more likely to vote for a candidate based on his or her position on gun control. Likewise, the NRA has proven to be a powerful lobby because its members, though few, have intense opinions regarding gun control.
- *Stability* refers to how steady people's feelings about a subject are. If public opinion can be easily changed, then the opinion has low stability. If the public's opinion remains unchanged for a relatively long time, then the opinion has high stability. For example, President George H.W. Bush had a public approval rating of 89 percent in early 1991 as a result of operations in the Gulf War; during his unsuccessful 1992 reelection campaign, his approval rating fell below 40 percent.

In part (b), you can earn one point for each description of a way in which public opinion affects the voting decision of members of Congress, for a maximum of two points. Possible answers include

- Members of Congress may vote in accordance with the opinion of the majority of their constituents.
- Members of Congress may vote in accordance with the opinion of a vocal minority of their constituents (those whose opinion holds a high degree of intensity).
- Members of Congress may vote in accordance with the opinion of swing voters in their districts.
- Members of Congress may vote in accordance with the opinion of voters who are in their districts and of the same party as the members of Congress.

In part (c), you may earn one point for explaining why a member of Congress may vote contrary to the opinion of the majority of his or her constituents. Possible answers include

- A member of Congress may vote in accordance with his or her party leadership, to the contrary of public opinion. This may be done to gain (or avoid losing) support from the party leadership.
- A member of Congress may vote in accordance with his or her past voting record, to the contrary of public opinion, in order to avoid appearing inconsistent.
- A member of Congress may view himself or herself as a trustee of the people. Some believe that members of Congress should act as delegates: that is, they should vote according to the wishes of their constituents. Others believe that members of Congress should act as trustees—that is, they are expected to use their own judgment in deciding how to vote.
- A member of Congress may vote to the contrary of public opinion if the opinion is believed to be unstable.

- A member of Congress may vote to the contrary of opinion of the majority if pressured by a minority that holds a contrary opinion with great intensity.
- A member of Congress may vote to the contrary of public opinion if the issue is believed to have low saliency among voters.

In part (d), you may earn one point for describing one reason that the public opinion might have an effect on the way that senators vote. Possible answers include

- Congressional districts are gerrymandered into "safe" districts (those that favor incumbents), while senators run for reelection in an entire state.
- Senatorial races are more competitive than House races.
- Members of the House benefit from an average reelection rate of over 90 percent.
- Congressional districts frequently feature a strong majority for one party, while states are usually more evenly divided.
- Senatorial races are more expensive than House races.

Drill 10

1. **B** The vast majority of appeals are not heard by the Supreme Court because the Court agrees with the decision of the lower courts. The Supreme Court does not hold trials and does not have a jury, so eliminate choice (A). The Court considers all appeals that have been sent, making choice (D) incorrect. Oral arguments are permitted only for those few cases that the Court hears, so eliminate choice (C). *Amicus curiae* briefs are helpful and common tactic used by interested parties to convince the Supreme Court to hear a case, but they are not mandatory. Eliminate choice (E).

2. **D** Choices (A), (B), (C), and (E) are examples of separations of power (checks and balances). Choice (A) is described in Article I, Section 7 of the Constitution. Choice (B) is an example of judicial review, established by *Marbury v. Madison*. The two parts of choice (C) are articulated in the Constitution in Article II, Section 2 and Article I, Section 1, respectively. Choice (E) describes the Senate's "advice and consent" role of Article II, Section 2. Choice (D) is incorrect because there are two methods of proposing constitutional amendments: by a two-thirds majority in Congress or by a convention called by two-thirds of the states. So far, only the first method of proposal has been used. Ratification of a proposed amendment may occur by the approval of three-fourths of state legislatures or three-fourths of state conventions (as prescribed by the proposed amendment); so far, 26 of the 27 amendments have been ratified by the state legislatures. Congress plays no role in ratifying amendments.

3. **D** Article II, Section 2 empowers the president to negotiate treaties, subject to ratification by the Senate. Choice (A) is incorrect because the Article I, Section 1 grants all legislative power to Congress. Choices (B), (C), and (E) are incorrect because they are all powers granted to Congress by Article I, Section 8.

4. **D** Congressional redistricting occurs every 10 years following the release of the decennial census as mandated by Article I, Section 2 of the Constitution, eliminating choices (A) and (C). Districting is decided by the individual states, eliminating choices (B) and (D). Most state constitutions permit the legislature to decide on new district borders. However, to reduce gerrymandering, many states now use independent commissions to designate fair district boundaries. The House Ways and Means Committee is responsible for writing tax code, defining tariffs, and overseeing funding of a large number of programs. The Senate Judiciary Committee is responsible for confirmation of federal judge appointments.

5. **E** In all four of these elections, the winner of the popular vote did not become president. All presidential elections (except the election of 1824) were won by the candidate having a majority of the electoral college votes, eliminating choice (A). Only in a very few elections have third-party candidates won electoral votes, and the 2000 election was not a year in which one did. Eliminate choice (B). The mandatory state recount delay in 2000 (in Florida) was not necessary in the other three elections, eliminating choice (C). Many presidential elections have resulted in a change in which political party controlled the executive office, although 1824 and 1876 did not, and therefore this event was not unique to these elections, eliminating choice (D).

6. **A** The congressional franking privilege permits the sending of mail without postage. Congressional appropriations reimburse the U.S. Postal service for mail sent in this manner. The establishment of franking dates to 1775 as a means of permitting legislators to keep in touch with their constituents from afar.

7. **E** The primary purpose of the U.S. census is to determine the population and distribution of individuals in the U.S. as a means of reallocating congressional seats, making choices (A), (B), and (C) correct. The statistics acquired during the U.S. census are used to understand the composition of the constituents of each state in order to more accurate allocate resources as needed, making choice (D) correct. Senate elections occur every two years with a term of six years as mandated by Article I, Section III of the Constitution. Dates for elections are not defined by the U.S. census.

8. **B** The president attaches a veto message to every veto explaining why he or she chose to veto a bill. If Congress doesn't have enough votes to override the veto, this information can help them draft a new bill that won't be vetoed. Because Congress can override a veto with a two-thirds majority vote in both houses, eliminate choice (E). Choice (A) refers to a line item veto, which the Supreme Court ruled unconstitutional in *Clinton v. City of New York* (1998). Eliminate choices (A) and (D). A pocket veto occurs when Congress is not in session and the president takes no action on a bill. Eliminate choice (C).

Free-Response Question 1

This question is scored on a scale of seven points. Students can earn two points for part (a), one point for part (b), and two points for part (c).

In part (a), students can earn one point for defining judicial review and another point for describing the role in plays in the system of checks and balances. In the United States, judicial review is the power of the Court to decide whether a law or act adheres to the Constitution. Judicial review allows the Court to overturn or limit acts of Congress or the Executive.

In part (b), students may earn one point for explaining how the Court decides which cases to hear. The Supreme Court hears cases by granting a writ of *certiorari*. A party can appeal a lower court ruling to the Supreme Court. If four justices agree to hear the case, the court will grant a writ of *certiorari* which orders the lower court to send the case to the Supreme Court for review.

In part (c), students may earn up to four points: one point for describing each principle (*stare decisis* and judicial activism) and one point for explaining how each shapes the way in which justices make decisions.

- *Stare decisis* means that the Court should defer to previous Court decisions by applying precedent.
- Judicial activism means that justices do not follow precedent and instead strike down an act of Congress or the Executive as unconstitutional based upon societal changes or policy considerations.
- *Stare decisis* encourages justices to be conservative in their rulings. This principle discourages justices from changing the law by deferring to previous decisions. Advocates of stare decisis cite the positive effects of stability of law and predictability of court decisions.
- Judicial activism presents justices with the opportunity to create new laws or alter/eliminate existing laws. This principle encourages justices to fix flawed legislation or correct executive-branch actions that create injustice. Opponents of judicial activism say that it is Congress's, not the Court's, role to create laws.

Drill 11

1. **D** The images of a dead elephant and a donkey attempting to jump off a cliff are allusions to the state of the Republican and Democratic parties of the late nineteenth century. The elephant, a longtime symbol of the GOP, represents a party that the cartoonist, Thomas Nast, feels has fallen into irrelevance. The donkey, by extension, represents a party that does not have any candidates who want to run in the 1880 election. There is no reference to the economy in the cartoon, so eliminate choice (A). Franchise refers to the right to vote, which is not at all indicated by the cartoon. Therefore, choice (B) is incorrect. Government involvement in either health care or conservation was not an issue in 1880 and is not referenced in the cartoon, so choices (D) and (E) are incorrect.

2. **E** The White House Office staff members are not subject to Senate approval but rather are hand-picked by the president, so eliminate choice (A) and select choice (E). The White House Office is part of the Executive Office of the President; it is not an independent office, so eliminate choice (B). The president is not required to fill all White House Office staff positions and he or she has

flexibility in what positions he or she offers, so eliminate choice (C). The president relies heavily on his or her staff to set his or her schedule and act as advisers, so the staff has a lot of interaction with Congress and cabinet members. Eliminate choice (D).

3. **B** The Committee on the Judiciary has the biggest role to play in considering presidential nominations to the federal courts, including the Supreme Court. The Committee on Homeland Security and Governmental Affairs is concerned with government contracts, municipal affairs of the District of Columbia, the census, the Postal Service, and many other issues completely unrelated to the judiciary. The Senate Budget Committee and the Committee on Appropriations deal with federal funding. The Committee on Rules and Administration is concerned with elections, Senate rules and regulations, the Senate library and many other issues completely unrelated to the judiciary. Choices (A), (C), (D), and (E) can all be eliminated.

4. **E** In 1968, George Wallace ran on the American Independent ticket: he won 13.5 percent of the popular vote and carried five Southern states, winning 46 electoral votes. Therefore, Numeral I is correct, and you may eliminate choices (B) and (C) because they do not include Numeral I. Although Ross Perot won 18.9 percent of the popular vote in 1992 and 8.4 percent in 1996, he did not receive a single electoral vote in either election. Therefore, Numeral III is incorrect, and you may eliminate choices (D) and (E). In 1980, John B. Anderson won 6.6 percent of the popular vote but did not receive a single electoral vote; therefore, Numeral II is incorrect. In 2000, Ralph Nader (Green) won 2.7 percent of the popular vote but did not win any electoral votes; therefore, Numeral IV is incorrect.

5. **C** Article III, Section 2 of the Constitution enumerates all of the cases in choices (A), (B), (D), and (E) specifically as being under federal jurisdiction. However, in claims concerning the legality of a law in one state, federal courts must defer to state courts for original jurisdiction, so choice (C) is correct.

6. **D** The New Deal coalition was a coming together of labor unions, Catholics, Southern whites, and African Americans that helped the Democrats dominate politics from the 1930s until the 1960s. Shays's rebellion was an uprising of farmers but was not a coalition since everyone involved was a farmer. Eliminate choice (A). While many minority interest groups may form coalitions to have more influence over lawmakers, there is no one well-known "Minority coalition." Eliminate choice (B). Choice (E) is also not a real coalition, so eliminate that answer. Finally, the Populists were a group that fought on behalf of the poor workers and farmers, and they fused with the Democratic Party in 1896 but they were not themselves a coalition group.

7. **A** The Presidential Succession Act of 1947 establishes the Speaker of the House as the second in line to the presidency, after the vice president. The president *pro tempore* of the Senate is the only other

member of Congress in the line of succession, which consists mostly of heads of the executive departments.

8.   E   Choice (E) is correct because the presentment clause in the Constitution gives Congress the power to make laws. If the president does not like a bill, he or she should send it back to Congress for further consideration. All of the other choices are true, but none provide a reason that the line item veto was deemed unconstitutional.

Free-Response Question 1

This question is scored on a scale of six points. Students can earn one point for part (a), one point for part (b), one point for part (c), and three points for part (d).

Part (a) asks the student to describe the merit-based system. Under a merit-based system, hiring and promotion decisions are based upon merit, experience, qualifications, and/or testing, rather than party affiliation.

Part (b) offers the student one point for describing one way in which the structure of the federal bureaucracy promotes independence. Acceptable answers include references to the bureaucracy's large size, specialization of certain divisions, tenure protections for employees, merit-based hiring and promotion, and the presence of regulatory commissions.

Part (c) asks the student how discretionary authority promotes independence. Since legislation often lacks details, the bureaucrats are often free to interpret it as they see fit and create policies related to the application of legislation.

In part (d), the student may earn three points: one point for describing how each group (Congress, the judiciary, and private citizens) can balance the power of the bureaucracy.

- Congress can limit the bureaucracy through providing or denying appropriations, passing additional legislation, the approval process for presidential appointments, and impeachment of officials in the bureaucracy.
- The judiciary can limit the bureaucracy through rulings that influence the power of the bureaucracy, judicial review, and injunctions.
- Private citizens can limit the bureaucracy through lobbying efforts, free speech, and public protests.

Drill 12

1.   B   A potential judge with no legal experience isn't likely to be confirmed by the Senate, so eliminate choice (A). Presidents want to nominate judges with similar political affiliations to their own to help support their policies, so eliminate choice (C). Presidents can use nominations of people with certain group identities (women, minorities) to improve their own public opinion ratings, so eliminate choice (D). Senatorial courtesy is a long-standing tradition of soliciting the advice of the senator whose state has the federal vacancy, so eliminate choice (E). The place a potential federal judge was born is generally not a consideration, so choice (B) is correct.

2. **B**   The press secretary is a member of the White House staff and is not subject to Senate confirmation. The White House staff is generally made up of the president's close friends and trusted acquaintances whom he or she hand picks. No further action is necessary to take the role than simple selection by the president. Accordingly, choice (B) is correct and all other choices can be eliminated.

3. **C**   The Warren Court and the Rehnquist Court are two well-known and much-studied courts, so both Warren and Rehnquist must have been confirmed. Eliminate choices (A) and (B). Sandra Day O'Connor was the first woman to serve on the Supreme Court, so eliminate choice (D). Although Clarence Thomas was a controversial nominee because of some of his beliefs and allegations of sexual harassment against him, he was ultimately confirmed by a vote of 52 to 48. Eliminate choice (E). Robert Bork, nominated by Ronald Reagan, was not confirmed.

4. **E**   The origination clause, found in Article I, Section 7 of the Constitution, states that all bills for raising revenue shall originate in the House of Representatives. Revenue bills originate in the House Ways and Means Committee and both that committee and the Senate Finance Committee research and debate the bills. The Senate Committee on Appropriations plays no role in that process. All other answers accurate describe the role of the Senate Committee on Appropriations and thus can be eliminated.

5. **A**   Executive privilege is the right of officials in the executive branch to refuse to disclose some information to other branches of government. This can interfere with the system of checks and balances because it limits the ability of Congress to obtain information that might be necessary for proper oversight of the executive agencies. Therefore, select (A) and eliminate (C) because oversight is a key component of the system of checks and balances. The exclusionary rule is not relevant because it is a legal rule that excludes from trial evidence obtained in an illegal search. Expressed powers are those explicitly given to the president and Congress by the Constitution and include powers related to checks and balances, so eliminate choice (D). A filibuster does not interfere with checks and balances because after the filibuster ends, the president could still veto the bill if it passes and the judiciary could strike it down as unconstitutional. Eliminate choice (E).

6. **B**   The question accurately defines pork barrel spending, so choice (B) is correct. Reapportionment is the process of reallocating representation in the House of Representatives after the census. Eliminate choice (A). Private goods are often the end goal of pork barrel projects, but the term does not describe the money itself, so eliminate choice (C). A progressive tax is one that increases as income increases. Eliminate choice (D). Public assistance, which is another term for welfare, comes in many forms (food stamps, housing assistance, tax credits, etc.) and benefits a large portion of the population. Eliminate choice (E).

7. **D**   Each Court of Appeals covers a geographic area, or circuit, that contains several district courts. For that reason, they are known as circuit courts. Courts of Appeals do not hold trials; they review the details of cases, so eliminate choice (C). The Court of Federal Claims is a type of trial court, so

eliminate choice (A). Judicial districts and agencies do not describe types of courts, so eliminate choices (B) and (E).

8. **D** A motion for cloture ends a filibuster in the Senate when 60 senators approve it. There are no filibusters in the House of Representatives and a simple majority is not sufficient. A filibuster does not directly affect the president. Accordingly, eliminate choices (A), (B), (C), and (E).

Free-Response Question 1

This question is scored on a scale of seven points. Students can earn one point for part (a), one point for part (b), three points for part (c), and two points for part (d).

Part (a) asks the student to define reapportionment. Reapportionment is the reallocation of the number of representatives each state has in the House of Representatives.

Part (b) asks the student to define redistricting. Redistricting is the redrawing of the boundaries of congressional districts.

In part (c), the student may earn one point for defining gerrymandering and one point for each reason why politicians might engage in gerrymandering. Gerrymandering is redistricting done for political motives. Politicians might gerrymander in order to reduce the strength of the opposition by splitting its members among multiple districts ("cracking"), make it easier for incumbents to get reelected, or to increase or decrease minority representation ("packing").

Part (d) asks what the Court has done in response to gerrymandering. The Court has required districts to have equal populations, to be contiguous in shape, to be not drawn solely based upon race, to not dilute minority voting strength, to not split communities, and to be compact (that is not overly "weirdly" shaped). The student may earn one point for each response described, up to a maximum of two points.

Drill 13

1. **C** The presentment clause (Article I, Section 7) establishes the process by which a bill becomes a law and it lays out the separate roles of the president and Congress in that process. Eliminate choice (A) because the elastic clause (Article I, Section 8) grants Congress the power to make laws that are necessary and proper for carrying out its duties, but it doesn't address the other branches of government. Eliminate choice (B) because the due process clause (Fifth Amendment) guarantees certain legal rights to people accused of crimes. Eliminate choice (D) because the equal protection clause (Fourteenth Amendment) guarantees all U.S. citizens the same rights. Eliminate choice (E) because the full faith and credit clause (Article I, Section 4) concerns relationships between states and does not address the branches of government.

2. **C** Cooperative federalism, also known as marble-cake federalism, is a system in which the roles of the federal and state governments are closely intertwined. Dual federalism and layer-cake federalism

both refer to a system in which the federal and state governments each have their own responsibilities and those responsibilities rarely overlap. Eliminate choices (A) and (B). New federalism is a push to return more power to the states and decrease the power held by the central government. Eliminate choice (D). Finally, fiscal federalism, in which the federal government gives the states money to help implement its programs, generally does occur under cooperative federalism, but the terms are not synonymous. Eliminate choice (E).

3. **E** A delegated power is a type of expressed power; powers that are outlined in the Constitution and formally granted by Congress. Eliminate choices (A) and (B). Inherent powers are those the president must exercise to properly serve in his or her role, but that aren't enumerated in the Constitution. Emergency powers are a type of those. Eliminate choices (C) and (D). There is no such thing as a formula power, so choice (E) is correct.

4. **E** According to Article II, Section 1 of the Constitution, if no presidential candidate has a majority (more than 50 percent) of electoral votes, the House of Representatives will select the president. In every other situation described, the president is still chosen through a general election. You can look at the 1992 or 1996 election to eliminate choice (A), the 2004 election to eliminate choice (B), the 1980 election to eliminate choice (C), and many other elections to eliminate choice (D).

5. **D** The Government Accountability Office evaluates how programs are administered, the Congressional Research Service reports on the performance of various governmental agencies, the Congressional Budget Office reports on budgetary requests and analyzes how agencies use their funding, and the Senate Committee on Appropriations approves funding for agencies on an annual basis. These are all oversight activities, so eliminate choices (A), (B), (C), and (E). The role of the Senate Committee on Finance is to deal with taxation, trade agreements, and public revenue sharing programs; this role is not directly linked to oversight.

6. **A** There are 94 federal district courts and 13 federal judicial circuits, each with a court of appeals, so eliminate choices (B) and (E). The Tax Court and Court of International Trade are two examples of specialty courts within the federal court system, so eliminate choices (C) and (D). Juvenile courts are state or county courts that deal with minors who have committed crimes. There are no specialized federal courts for juvenile cases.

7. **B** Congress oversees the federal bureaucracy in which there are 15 main departments and a large number of subordinate departments and agencies. The Department of Homeland Security is one of those main departments, so eliminate choice (A). The Office of Fair Housing and Equal Opportunity is part of the Department of Housing and Urban Development, the Veterans Health Administration is part of the Department of Veterans Affairs, and the National Renewable Energy Laboratory is run by the Department of Energy. Accordingly, eliminate choices (C), (D), and (E). The American Civil Liberties Union is an interest group, which is not directly subject to congressional oversight.

8.   C   The House Rules Committee can give a bill a closed rule, which means that amendments cannot be attached to it, so choice (C) is false. According to Article I, Section 2 of the Constitution, Representatives must live in the state they represent, so eliminate choice (A). The Apportionment Act of 1911 set the number of Representatives at 435, a number that can be altered with a new act, so eliminate choice (B). The members of the House of Representatives are all reelected together every two years to keep them more responsive to the people. Senators are only reelected every six years, so they are more secure in their jobs and therefore less susceptible to public pressure. Eliminate choice (D). Finally, you can eliminate choice (E) because the House leadership rewards members who vote with the party by giving them good assignments and likewise can punish those who stray from the party positions.

Free-Response Question 1

This question is scored on a scale of four points. Students can earn one point for part (a), two points for part (b), and one point for part (c).

Part (a) asks that the student define federalism. In the United States, federalism is the dividing of power between the federal and state governments.

Part (b) asks that the student select two and explain how each has been used to expand federal power. Students can receive one point for each.

- The interstate commerce clause gives the federal government the authority to regulate interstate commerce. It has been interpreted over time to allow the federal government to regulate even things that do not directly impact interstate commerce, such as racial discrimination in hotels and restaurants.
- Categorical grants allow the federal government to influence state actions by requiring them to cooperate with federal policy in order to receive federal money.
- Section 5 of the Fourteenth Amendment gives Congress the power to enforce the amendment's "due process" and "equal protection" clauses against the states. Examples include the incorporation of the Bill of Rights against the states, desegregation of public schools (*Brown v. Board*), and guarantees of federal civil rights such as the Civil Rights Act and the Voting Rights Act.

Part (c) asks that the student explain how one has been used to limit the power of the state governments.

- The Voting Rights Act requires that states with a demonstrated history of voting discrimination submit any changes to their voting procedures to the Department of Justice for approval before they can be implemented.
- The incorporation doctrine is the application of the Bill of Rights to the states. It has been used to limit states' abilities to enforce laws that conflict with the guarantees in the Bill of Rights. For example, in *Texas v. Johnson*, the Supreme Court held that Texas could not ban flag burning as it conflicted with the First Amendment.
- The Clean Air Act allows the federal government to set emissions standards that supersede any set by the states. For example, in *California v. EPA*, the Supreme Court held that California could not set more stringent emissions standards than the federal government did.

Drill 14

1. **D** The Federal Election Campaign Act of 1971 was passed to institute campaign finance disclosure requirements. It was amended in 1975 to create the Federal Election Commission which also enforces limits and prohibitions on contributions and oversees public funding of presidential elections. Accordingly, eliminate choices (A), (B), and (C). In 2002, the Bipartisan Campaign Reform Act, also known as the McCain-Feingold Act, enacted more regulations on where campaign financing could come from and what type of contributions could be used for what types of campaign activities. Eliminate choice (E). There was no Bipartisan Campaign Reform Act in 1994, so choice (D) is correct.

2. **D** Acting as a common-carrier describes the role of the media as an intermediary between the people and the government. A concurring opinion is issued by a judge who votes with the winning side but disagrees with the majority opinion. Eliminate choice (A). Eliminate choice (B) because a court may uphold the decision of the lower court, rather than overturn it. Eliminate choice (C) for the same reason because to cite *stare decisis* means to let a legal precedent stand. Finally, eliminate choice (E) because when the Supreme Court finds a law unconstitutional, it still remains on the books until Congress passes a law to repeal it.

3. **C** Divided government occurs when the executive branch is controlled by one political party and one or both houses of the legislative branch are controlled by another. This slows down the approval of presidential appointees because the political views of the executive branch and legislative branch differ. Dual federalism is a system in which the roles of the federal and the state government rarely overlap and horizontal federalism is the way in which state governments relate to each other. Eliminate choices (A) and (E). Hyperpluralism is the idea that there are too many different interest groups competing for resources and due process refers to receiving full legal consideration of your case. These are unrelated to the confirmation of presidential appointees, so eliminate choices (B) and (D).

4. **A** Article III, Section 2 of the Constitution gives the Supreme Court original jurisdiction over trials involving ambassadors. The number of justices has been established by statute and there are actually two fewer justices than there were initially, so eliminate choice (B). The Constitution is vague about the number of judicial circuits; it says "such inferior Courts as the Congress may from time to time ordain and establish." The number 13 is not in the Constitution, so eliminate choice (C). The Constitution states about trials of crime that "when not committed within any State, the Trial shall be at such Place or Places as the Congress may by Law have directed," so eliminate choice (D). Finally, the Supreme Court's decision to overturn an act of Congress in *Marbury v. Madison* established the precedent of judicial review, so eliminate choice (E).

5. **C** In a relatively rare parliamentary procedure, if a majority (218) of the representatives sign a discharge petition, the bill must leave its committee and come up for consideration in the House. This has been used when a committee has refused to submit a particular bill to the House. There are other parliamentary procedures for each of the remaining answer choices.

6. **A** One way the president could exert power over Congress was by refusing to spend money on programs that Congress created but the president felt were unnecessary. This practice would often effectively kill the program. The Budget and Impoundment Control Act of 1974 forces the president to spend all of the money Congress allocates for a given program, thus placing a check on the executive branch's power. The Hatch Act prevented federal employees from actively working on a campaign. This law, along with the Federal Election Campaigns Acts, limited power of both Congress and the president. Eliminate choices (B) and (D). Choice (C) is also incorrect, as the Freedom of Information Act attempts to make all participants in the federal government more accountable. The Gramm-Rudman-Hollings Bill aimed to limit federal spending. Eliminate choice (E).

7. **A** The Supreme Court ruled in *McCulloch v. Maryland* that the state of Maryland may not charge a tax on a federal institution. The legacy of this ruling was that the federal government trumps a state government when their statutes collide. This is the essence of the Supremacy Clause of the Constitution. The Equal Protection Clause is found in the Fourteenth Amendment, ratified nearly fifty years after the *McCulloch* decision: eliminate choice (B). The Free Exercise Clause and the Establishment Clause are both First Amendment clauses that deal with religion, so eliminate choices (C) and (E). Choice (D) is incorrect because the Commerce Clause, which establishes Congress's power to regulate interstate commerce, was not at issue in *McCulloch*.

8. **B** An engrossed bill is one that has been passed by both houses and is ready for the president's signature. Therefore, the conference committee would have already reconciled the differences between the House's bill and the Senate's bill before the final bill was voted upon. Eliminate choices (A) and (D). Both choices (C) and (E) are incorrect because they would occur during earlier steps in the legislative process.

Free-Response Question 1

This question is scored on a scale of seven points. Students can earn two points for part (a), one point for part (b), and four points for part (c).

Part (a) asks for the two ways the War Powers Resolution limits the president's war-making powers. Students can earn one point for each. First, the president may send U.S. armed forces abroad only if authorized by Congress or if there is "a national emergency created by attack upon the United States, its territories or possessions, or its armed forces." Second, the president must notify Congress within 48 hours of sending armed forces in combat and any military action may last no longer than 60 days (with a 30-day withdrawal window) without congressional authorization or a declaration of war.

Part (b) asks for the primary way that war-making power is balanced between Congress and the president. The War Making clause of Article I, Section 8 gives Congress the exclusive power to "declare war." On the other hand, the president is given power as commander-in-chief.

Part (c) asks what two other formal powers Congress has over the decision to go to war. Students can earn one point for each additional power Congress has for a maximum of two points. Possible answers include

- Appropriations (spending money)
- General law making
- Treaty ratification
- Congressional oversight through hearings or investigations
- Confirmation of nominees
- Impeachment

Students can also earn one point for explaining how each power works for a maximum of two points. Students must explain how each of these demonstrates Congress's power over war-making.

Drill 15

1. **B**   Only in 1978 and 1994 did Democrats control both the presidency and the House; in those elections, they lost 11 and 53 seats in Congress, respectively. Choice (A) is incorrect because the president's party had a majority in the House in 1978, 1994, 2002, and 2006, but only in 2002 did that party gain seats. Since the Republican president in 2002 saw a gain of 6 seats, choice (C) is incorrect. Choice (D) is incorrect because Congress had its lowest approval rating of 23 percent in 1994, and the Democratic majority lost 53 seats that year. Choice (E) is incorrect because Congress's highest approval rating of 50 percent was in 2002, a year in which Republicans held the House majority.

2. **D**   Midterm elections, with only some exceptions, have largely gone in favor of the opposition party. Many theorize that voters want balance in Washington, D.C., so they try to make the legislative branch act as a check against the president. The other effect in play could simply be weariness with the president, which would hurt those candidates associated with him or her. On the other hand, the "coattail" effect, the theory that presidential candidates help members of their parties in down-ballot races, has been observed to positively affect congressional candidates in general election years: eliminate choice (B). Choices (A), (C), and (E) all indicate advantageous situations for a candidate.

3. **C**   In 1977, 80 percent of the members of Congress had active duty military experience; in 2013, only 19 percent do. Meanwhile, the 113th Congress, elected in 2012, includes 98 women, 43 African Americans, 31 Hispanics, and 12 Asian Americans; all of these numbers are much higher than they were in the 1970s.

4. **B** While the Constitution offers two avenues for proposing amendments, the only method that has ever been used requires a two-thirds majority in each house. The other method, which involves a national convention called for by two-thirds of the states, has never been pursued. Eliminate choice (A). The Constitution also allows for two methods of ratification: by the state legislatures of three-fourths of the states or by conventions of three-fourths of the states. Every amendment except for the Twenty-first Amendment was ratified by three-fourths of the state legislatures, so eliminate choice (C). Choice (D) is not true, as most amendment processes begin as grass roots movements. Choice (E) is incorrect because several amendments do not affect individual rights (such as the Twenty-fifth Amendment) and in some cases restrict rights (such as the Eighteenth Amendment).

5. **A** Constitutional (or enumerated) powers are those which are specifically given to the president by the Constitution, so choice (B) is incorrect. A statutory power (such as the power to declare a national emergency) is given to the president by an act of Congress; therefore, choice (A) is correct. Expressed powers include constitutional and statutory constitutional powers, as both are expressly written down; therefore, choice (D) is incorrect. Inherent powers and emergency powers are not expressly written. They are assumed to be necessary for any national executive. Eliminate choices (C) and (E).

6. **E** Franking allows members of Congress to send mail material to their constituents without using a stamp. It is one if the privileges of being in Congress. Most congressional candidates, even those who are not incumbents, fund their campaigns with PAC money. Eliminate choice (A). Members of Congress cannot fly for free, so choice (B) is incorrect. While insider trading by members of Congress has been practiced, this is not the meaning of franking. Eliminate choice (C). Using aides for the purpose of running a political campaign is expressly prohibited. Eliminate choice (D).

7. **B** Similar bills passed by the House and Senate must go to a conference committee to iron out the differences between the two versions. Only when a bill is passed by both chambers in identical form can it be sent to the president. Standing committees are permanent, specialized committees (such as the House Ways and Means Committee or the Senate Finance Committee), while select committees are temporary and created for a specific purpose (such as writing legislation); therefore, choices (A) and (D) are incorrect. While a joint committee is composed of members of both chambers, its purpose is to conduct investigations or communicate to the public; therefore, you may eliminate choice (C). Only the House has a Rules Committee, which sets the rules by which a bill may be sent to the floor, debated, and voted upon; therefore, choice (E) is incorrect.

8. **B** To remand a case means that the Supreme Court sends it back to the lower court with specific instructions. Choice (A) is incorrect because it describes when the Court affirms a lower court's ruling. If the Court agrees to hear a case, it issues a writ of *certiorari* to request the lower court's transcript; therefore, choices (C) and (E) are incorrect. Choice (D) is incorrect because the Court may remand a case regardless of whether it affirms or reverses a lower court's ruling.

Free-Response Question 1

This question is scored on a scale of five points. Students can earn four points for part (a) and one point for part (b).

Part (a) asks that you explain how two of the three either expand or limit federal power relative to the states. For each answer, students can earn one point for describing it and one point for explaining how it has limited federal power. Possible answers are

- The Tenth Amendment reserves unenumerated powers to the states. The amendment has been interpreted to prevent the federal government from requiring that state governments enact federal policy. Examples include cases in which the federal government attempted to invade the states' police power, such as federal laws that attempted to regulate gun possession near schools (Gun Free School Zones Act 1995), mandatory background checks for gun purchases (the Brady Law 1997), and domestic violence (Violence Against Women Act 2000).
- The Eleventh Amendment provides states with immunity from prosecution in federal courts by citizens of other states or foreign countries. The Eleventh Amendment provides states with a kind of "sovereign immunity." Examples include cases in which a citizen of Utah attempted to sue Utah in federal court, a citizen of Utah attempted to sue Nevada in federal court, or a citizen of Canada attempted to sue New York in federal court.
- The Welfare Reform Act of 1996 gave states the funds and authority to design and run their own welfare programs consistent with the federal goal of transitioning welfare recipients to work.

Part (b) asks that students pick one piece of legislation and show how it has been used to encourage states to implement federal policy. All three are examples of cooperative federalism, in which the federal government uses its spending power to require that states implement a policy in order to received federal funds.

- The Children's Health Insurance Program provided states with matching funds if they expanded health care coverage to children.
- The National Minimum Drinking Age Act of 1984 required that states set the drinking age to 21 in order to receive federal highway funds.
- The No Child Left Behind Act of 2001 required that states implement a number of reforms, such as standardized testing requirements, in order to receive federal education funds.

Chapter 11
Public Policy

DRILL 1

1. What does it mean to say that the president has an informal power of the "bully pulpit"?

    (A) The president is required to attend a religious service once a week.
    (B) The Constitution grants the president the power to communicate with Congress and the American people.
    (C) The president is empowered to reprimand his or her policy advisors.
    (D) The president is empowered to build support for policies by communicating with the American people.
    (E) Presidential decrees automatically become law.

2. Which of the following accurately describes the chief justice of the United States?

    (A) The chief justice must side with the majority opinion.
    (B) The chief justice presides over the Supreme Court's oral arguments.
    (C) The chief justice presides over presidential impeachment proceedings in the House of Representatives.
    (D) The chief justice is always the deciding vote in split decision cases.
    (E) The Supreme Court justices vote to decide who becomes chief justice.

3. What is the term for an informal alliance made up of a congressional committee, industry lobbyists, and a government agency that regulates the industry at issue?

    (A) Steel square
    (B) Iron triangle
    (C) Copper parallelogram
    (D) Bronze octagon
    (E) Alloyed rectangle

4. Which of the following has the power to implement policy after Congress passes legislation?

    (A) Federal bureaucratic agencies
    (B) The U.S. Supreme Court
    (C) Political parties
    (D) Polling companies
    (E) Lobbyists

5. Which of the following accurately describes the connection between regulatory agencies and industries?

    (A) Industry leaders resent rules enforced by regulatory agencies.
    (B) Industry leaders and regulatory agencies do not work together to set regulations.
    (C) The regulations set by the agencies are generally easily applied by the industries.
    (D) While industries and regulatory agencies try to work together, they sometimes have serious disagreements.
    (E) Congress gives precise, detailed information to regulatory agencies and the agencies enforce those detailed instructions.

6. All of the following are current social insurance programs in the United States EXCEPT

    (A) Temporary Assistance for Needy Families (TANF)
    (B) Medicare
    (C) the Department of Education (DOE)
    (D) unemployment insurance
    (E) Social Security

7. States' rights supporters often prefer block grants to categorical grants because

    (A) block grants come with more restrictions on how states spend the money
    (B) block grants come with fewer restrictions on how states spend the money
    (C) block grants and categorical grants have the same restrictions on how states spend the money
    (D) economists agree that block grants are the best way to fund Medicare
    (E) block grants directly decrease the power of unions

8. Which of the following most accurately describes a balance of trade?

(A) Raising or lowering the interest banks pay to the Federal Reserve Bank for borrowing money
(B) Raising or lowering the amount of money banks are required to keep on hand
(C) Discretionary spending by the federal government
(D) Mandatory spending by the federal government
(E) A country's ratio of imported to exported products

Fiscal Year	Total Federal Grants (in billions)	Federal Grants as a Percentage of Gross Domestic Product
1980	100.3	4.1
1985	121.4	3.8
1990	138.2	3.5
1995	145.8	4.2
2000	150.4	4.1

9. The table above supports which of the following statements?

I. Total federal grants decreased every five years between 1980 and 2000
II. Federal grants as a percentage of gross domestic product did not vary by more than one percentage point in any five-year period between 1980 and 2000
III. The federal government gave more federal grants as a percentage of gross domestic product in 2000 than 1980
IV. The federal government gave more total federal grants in 2000 then 1980

(A) I and II only
(B) II and IV only
(C) I, II, and III only
(D) II, III, and IV only
(E) I, II, III, and IV

10. Which of the following is a Great Society program that originated during the Lyndon Johnson administration?

(A) Social Security
(B) The U.S. Army
(C) Don't Ask, Don't Tell
(D) Medicare
(E) Temporary Assistance for Needy Families (TANF)

11. Which member of government initiates the budget process by meeting with the president to discuss his or her policy initiatives?

(A) The committee chair of the House Ways and Means Committee
(B) Speaker of the House
(C) Senate majority leader
(D) Chief justice of the Supreme Court
(E) Director of the Office of Management and Budget (OMB)

12. A primary reason that the president will use an executive order to enforce a statute or treaty is that an executive order

(A) has the force of law without congressional approval
(B) generally concerns an issue that Congressmen are not interested in
(C) is a power only recently granted to the president by Congress
(D) cannot be challenged in the Supreme Court
(E) often will be unnoticed by the public

13. An "iron triangle" is

(A) the difficulty in finding a balance of power among the federal government, state governments, and local governments
(B) the influence that corporations exert on both members of Congress and the president
(C) the connection between the Department of Defense, the Department of Homeland Security, and the Department of State
(D) the relationship among congressional committees, the bureaucracy, and interest groups that influences policy-making decisions
(E) a series of three attempts to appeal a court decision to federal district courts

14. The National Minimum Drinking Age Act is an example of

(A) dual federalism
(B) judicial activism
(C) the elastic clause
(D) a federal mandate
(E) incorporation

15. A writ of *certiorari* is a legal document that

(A) orders a lower court to send a case to the Supreme Court for review
(B) explains the final ruling of a federal court of appeals
(C) is issued only when five justices want to hear a case
(D) indicates a violation of the Constitution has taken place
(E) pertains only to cases in which the United States government is one of the parties

16. The primary purpose of the National Voter Registration Act of 1993 was to

(A) increase minority representation among registered voters
(B) ensure that registered voters can travel to their polling locations on election day
(C) allow qualified voters to register to vote when applying for or renewing a driver's license
(D) reduce limitations to voter registration, such as poll taxes and literacy tests
(E) impose a fine on all citizens 18 years of age and older who did not register to vote

DRILL 2

1. Which of the following most accurately describes devolution?

   (A) The federal seizure of powers previously allocated to state or local governments
   (B) A sharing of power among various levels of government in all issues
   (C) A division of power between a central government and state or provincial governments
   (D) An effort to return power to state governments and slow the expansion of the federal government
   (E) The illusion of state sovereignty in a system actually dominated by a central government

2. Restricted federal money that is provided to the states for a specific purpose is known as

   (A) revenue sharing
   (B) a block grant
   (C) a categorical grant
   (D) an unfunded mandate
   (E) fiscal legislation

3. Funds that are allocated for individual benefits that have been established by legislation are known as

   (A) welfare mandates
   (B) pork barrel spending
   (C) charitable trusts
   (D) project grants
   (E) federal budget entitlements

4. Federal bureaucracies are given permission to operate through

   (A) an executive order
   (B) consensus in a congressional subcommittee
   (C) the elastic clause
   (D) enabling legislation
   (E) a consensus among cabinet members

5. Which of the following describes the phenomenon of "agency capture"?

   (A) A president stacks the agency full of his or her own party members.
   (B) An industry can longer operate successfully due to regulations imposed by the agency.
   (C) A regulatory agency settles a dispute between two private companies in the industry that it oversees.
   (D) An industry exerts influence over the members of its own oversight agency.
   (E) Congress takes over a regulatory agency after the discovery of malfeasance.

6. Which of the following dynamics is true of an "iron triangle"?

   (A) A congressional committee determines the budget for a federal agency.
   (B) An interest group provides industry information to a congressional committee.
   (C) A federal agency controls the subsidies given to an interest group.
   (D) An interest group refrains from the overt support of a congressional campaign.
   (E) A federal agency creates regulations for an industry.

7. In the Supreme Court, the "rule of four" refers to a procedure that

   (A) states that four justices must agree to grant a petition for review before the case is heard by the Court
   (B) allows only four justices to ask questions during oral argument
   (C) states that 50 percent, or four of the associate justices, must agree on the nomination for chief justice
   (D) limits the Supreme Court to hearing only four cases per session
   (E) limits the practice of "joining" on any majority, concurring, or dissenting opinion to four justices

8. How is entitlement spending different from military spending?

(A) Entitlement spending must be approved by Congress, whereas military spending is approved by the president.

(B) Entitlement spending is funded through a regular income tax, while military spending is funded through a payroll tax.

(C) Entitlement spending can change without congressional approval, but Congress must approve any changes to military spending.

(D) Entitlements cover health care, such as Medicare, Medicaid, and the Veterans Health Administration while military spending does not go toward any health care.

(E) Entitlements contributions go toward one's personal fund, while military spending goes toward a communal good.

Free Response

Time—25 minutes

1. The president and Congress are both responsible for setting fiscal policy, while the Federal Reserve Board sets monetary policy. Both of these policies influence the United States economy.

   (a) Define fiscal policy and monetary policy.

   (b) Explain the role the president plays in influencing fiscal policy and explain the role Congress plays in influencing fiscal policy.

   (c) Explain two reasons that Federal Reserve, rather than Congress or the president, is responsible for establishing monetary policy.

DRILL 3

1. The current office of the president is different from that of the nineteenth century in that the current presidency

    (A) is recognized as the leader of the party
    (B) appoints political supporters to public jobs
    (C) primarily affects change by addressing its message to the public, not Congress
    (D) is substantially weaker than Congress
    (E) seldom vetoes bills passed by Congress

2. Which of the following is NOT a reason for low voter turnout in the United States?

    (A) Similarity of the parties
    (B) Registration requirements
    (C) Alienation from the government
    (D) Lack of knowledge about candidates
    (E) Frequency of elections

3. How did the Unfunded Mandates Reform Act of 1995 help to address the burden of unfunded mandates?

    (A) It created the practice of granting waivers to individual states.
    (B) It placed a cap on total state government spending.
    (C) It doubled the availability of block grants.
    (D) It removed federal requirements placed on states that are burdened with an unfunded mandate.
    (E) It tasked the Congressional Budget Office with identifying mandates that presented a cost of more than $50 million for a state or local government.

4. The Obama Administration's "Race to the Top" program, which requires all states that accept federal money attached to the program to implement a national set of teaching standards, is an example of

    (A) a block grant
    (B) a federal mandate
    (C) a categorical grant
    (D) affirmative action
    (E) a devolutionary policy

5. Outside of the Supreme Court, the position that holds the most influence in recommending which cases receive a writ of *certiorari* is the

    (A) Speaker of the House
    (B) Attorney general
    (C) President *pro tempore*
    (D) Solicitor general
    (E) Secretary of State

6. If an appropriations bill is not passed by the start of the fiscal year, agencies must receive their funding through a

    (A) block grant
    (B) first budget resolution
    (C) second budget resolution
    (D) continuing resolution
    (E) categorical grant

7. Which of the following is NOT a protected status under federal hate crime legislation?

    (A) Race
    (B) Occupation
    (C) Religion
    (D) Sexual orientation
    (E) Disability

8. In what way did the terrorist attacks of September 11, 2001 impact the organization of federal agencies?

    (A) Agencies related to national security were pulled together with the creation of a new executive department.
    (B) Responsibility for the creation of new agencies was given exclusively to the executive department.
    (C) The government dissolved agencies that would slow down military response.
    (D) Each security oversight agency was given new leadership.
    (E) Agencies were beholden to new regulations due to the increased enforcement of Sunshine Laws.

Free Response

Time—25 minutes

1. Both the president and Congress are responsible for creating and enacting domestic policy. The president has certain tactics he or she can use to influence Congress to vote in favor of policies that support his or her agenda, but those tactics are limited.

   (a) Choose two of the following and explain how the president uses them to influence Congress.

   - Legislative powers
   - Appointment power
   - State of the Union address

   (b) Define each of the following and explain how they limit the president's influence over Congress.

   - Lame-duck period
   - Mandatory spending

DRILL 4

Federal Grants to State and Local Governments: 1960-2017

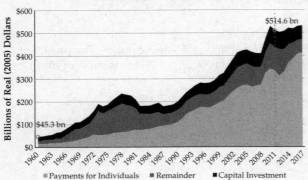

Source: OMB, Hisorial Tables, Table 12.1. Data estimates after 2011 are projected outlays. Produced by Veronique de Rugy, Mercatus Center at George Mason University

1. Which of the following statements is supported by information from the chart above?

   I. Federal grants to state and local governments will continue to rise after 2017.
   II. One significant change in recent years is that a majority of federal grant spending goes toward individuals.
   III. Federal grants experienced a sharp uptick during the early part of President Obama's presidency.
   IV. Federal grants to state and local governments were the largest federal spending category as a percent of GDP in 1978.

   (A) I and III only
   (B) I, II, and IV only
   (C) II and IV only
   (D) II and III only
   (E) II, III, and IV only

2. Which of the following contributes the LEAST to federal expenditures?

   (A) Social Security
   (B) Defense
   (C) Interest on the debt
   (D) Medicare
   (E) Social programs

3. Temporary Assistance to Needy Families (TANF), a federal welfare program that gives money to states and empowers those states to distribute the funds as they see fit, is

   (A) an interstate compact
   (B) a block grant
   (C) a categorical grant
   (D) an executive agreement
   (E) a federal mandate

4. Which of the following powers did President Obama use when he temporarily halted the practice of deporting undocumented young adults who were brought to the United States prior to the age of sixteen, had completed high school and were enrolled in post-secondary school, had enlisted in the military, or were gainfully employed?

   (A) Executive privilege
   (B) Amnesty
   (C) Emergency power
   (D) Pardon
   (E) Executive order

5. Which governing principle best characterizes the President Bill Clinton-era transfer of power over welfare implementation from the federal government to the individual states in the 1990s?

   (A) Devolution
   (B) Laissez-faire economics
   (C) Political socialization
   (D) Libertarianism
   (E) The Powell Doctrine

6. Which of the following best describes the members of a congressional committee?

   (A) Congresspersons who socialize outside of working hours
   (B) A formal group of legislators who focus on a specific issue
   (C) A fundraising group
   (D) An entire body of either the House or Senate
   (E) An informal group of legislators

7. Which of the following best describes why Social Security spending is considered a federal entitlement?

   (A) All citizens are entitled to it by executive order.
   (B) Legislation passed by Congress mandates the benefits to qualified individuals.
   (C) A Supreme Court majority opinion mandated the spending.
   (D) The Secretary of the Interior implements the spending.
   (E) Mass media campaigns are solely responsible for enacting the spending.

8. Which of the following actions would a special interest group NOT take to affect regulations for the industry it represents?

   (A) Fundraise for a Congressional candidate
   (B) Form a working group known as an "iron triangle"
   (C) Publish a letter in the media
   (D) Encourage the president to cast a vote in Congress
   (E) Lobby in Congress

Free Response

Time—25 minutes

1. After federal laws are written and enacted, federal bureaucratic agencies step in to execute those laws. Although the agencies do not play a role in writing the laws, they do have some discretion as to how those laws are carried out.

   (a) Identify two federal bureaucratic agencies and describe the types of laws they enact. For each agency, include one specific example of how it demonstrates its power of discretion as to how laws are carried out.

   (b) Explain one advantage of allowing federal bureaucratic agencies to have some discretion as to how federal laws are executed.

   (c) Describe one way in which Congress guarantees that federal bureaucratic agencies do not distort the intention of federal laws when using discretion in executing them.

Chapter 12
Public Policy:
Answers and
Explanations

ANSWER KEY

Multiple-Choice Questions

Drill 1
1. D
2. B
3. B
4. A
5. D
6. C
7. B
8. E
9. B
10. D
11. E
12. A
13. D
14. D
15. A
16. C

Drill 2
1. D
2. C
3. E
4. D
5. D
6. A
7. A
8. C

Drill 3
1. C
2. D
3. E
4. C
5. D
6. D
7. B
8. A

Drill 4
1. D
2. C
3. B
4. E
5. A
6. B
7. B
8. D

EXPLANATIONS

Drill 1

1. **D**   While it isn't written in the U.S. Constitution, the president has an informal power to communicate with Congress and the American people. Since the president is the most visible elected figure in the U.S. government, this is considered an important power, the power of the "bully pulpit." Franklin Delano Roosevelt took great advantage of this power with his "fireside chats" that were broadcast over the radio to Americans across the country. Since this power isn't written in the Constitution, choice (B) is incorrect. The president has representative democratic powers, not autocratic powers, so choice (E), which describes an autocratic power, is wrong. The "bully pulpit" refers neither to bullying nor religion in a literal sense, so choices (A) and (C) are incorrect. Choice (D) is the correct answer.

2. **B**   The chief justice presides at oral arguments before the Supreme Court. This means the chief justice has the option to speak first at oral arguments and thus frame the oral debate. The chief justice isn't necessarily the deciding vote, so eliminate choice (D). The president appoints the chief justice, who must then undergo Senate confirmation, so eliminate choice (E) as well. The Constitution states that the chief justice presides over a president's impeachment trial in the Senate, not the House of Representatives, so eliminate choice (C). The chief justice is sometimes in the majority and sometimes in the minority of court opinions, so you can eliminate choice (A). Choice (B) is the correct answer.

3. **B**   While all five choices describe a metal and a polygon, only "iron triangle" describes an actual relationship in government. Government regulatory agencies often make rules to regulate industries. Those rules should be well researched and informed so the rules don't unnecessarily harm an industry. Congressional committees, industry lobbyists, and governmental agencies (such as the Environmental Protection Agency), will often get together and share expertise to come up with proper regulations. Such a group is referred to as an "iron triangle."

4. **A**   After Congress passes legislation, federal bureaucratic agencies are in charge of implementing the policy that informs that legislation, making choice (A) the correct answer. The U.S. Supreme Court hears court cases, so choice (B) is wrong. Political parties are formal groups that attempt to influence elections and policy creation, but they don't have a formal role in implementing policy, so eliminate choice (C). Polling companies measure public opinion, so choice (D) is also incorrect. Lobbyists attempt to influence members of Congress and other politicians, so choice (E) is wrong.

5. **D**   It is not true that all industries resent rules enforced by regulatory agencies—for example, many food companies are happy to let the Food and Drug Administration set regulations for food safety because those rules increase public confidence in the companies' products. Regulatory agencies

consult with industries on a regular basis in order to work details of regulation. However, sometimes industries see regulations as unfair, spurious, or damaging while regulatory industries find industries flaunting regulations. The most accurate description of the relationship between regulatory agencies and the industries they regulate is that they sometimes work together, though the relationship is neither completely antagonistic nor completely harmonious. You can certainly eliminate choices (A), (B), and (C) in favor of the accurate description in choice (D). Finally, choice (E) is also incorrect because Congress provides general guidelines in its legislation. Regulatory agencies take the broad language and apply it to the smaller details of regulatory enforcement.

6. **C** Temporary Assistance for Needy Families (TANF) is a social insurance program passed in 1996 that aims to help the unemployed people get back to work, so eliminate choice (A). Medicare is a social insurance program that provides access to health insurance for Americans aged 65 and older, so eliminate choice (B). The Department of Education is an agency of the bureaucracy, not a social insurance program, making choice (C) the correct answer. Unemployment insurance is a current social insurance program that provides funds to unemployed Americans, so eliminate choice (D). Social Security is a social insurance program that pays money to Americans aged 65 and older, so eliminate choice (E).

7. **B** The federal government gives categorical grants of money to states that have restrictions on how the money may be spent. For example a categorical grant may require that states spend the money on Medicare or education. A block grant, on the other hand, is federal money given to the states with few restrictions on how the money should be spent. You can accept choice (B) and reject choices (A) and (C) on that basis. Economists have a wide variety of opinions on how to fund Medicare and there is no consensus that block grants are the best way, so eliminate choice (D). Block grants aren't directly related to unions, so eliminate choice (E) as well.

8. **E** Choice (A) describes the banking system's discount rate, so eliminate it. Choice (B) describes the banks' reserve requirement, so eliminate that one as well. Choices (C) and (D) are different types of spending by the federal government and don't describe a balance of trade, so eliminate them. That should leave you with (E), which is the correct answer since a balance of trade is a country's ratio of imported to exported products. More importing than exporting causes a deficit and more exporting than importing causes a surplus.

9. **B** The table shows that, while total federal grants increased between 1980 and 2000 from 100.3 to 150.4 billion, federal grants as a percentage of gross domestic product stayed fairly even, starting at 4.1% in 1980, dipping down to 3.5% in 1990, and returning to 4.1% in 2000. This information should lead you to reject choices I and III and accept choice IV. Federal grants as a percentage of gross domestic product never varied by more than 1% in any five year period as shown in the graph—the closest it got was a variation of 0.7% between 1990 and 1995. Therefore choice II is true. Choice (B), Numerals II and IV, is the correct answer.

10. **D** The U.S. Army predates Lyndon Johnson's administration (which followed JFK's assassination in the 1960s) by well more than a century, so eliminate choice (B) right away. The Social Security program was created as part of Franklin Delano Roosevelt's New Deal in the 1930s, so eliminate choice (A) too. Don't Ask, Don't Tell and Temporary Assistance for Needy Families both arose during the Clinton administration in the 1990s so eliminate choices (C) and (E). Medicare was created as a part of President Lyndon Johnson's Great Society, making choice (D) the correct answer.

11. **E** The Director of the Office of Management and Budget (OMB), a bureaucratic office, initiates the budget process by meeting with the president to discuss policy initiatives. The OMB then writes the president's budget and sends it to Congress. Choice (E) is the correct choice.

12. **A** An executive order is an order issued by the president that enforces statutes, the Constitution, or treaties, or sets rules around the way executive agencies operate. They have the same force of law as legislation passed by Congress but do not require congressional approval, which can take a long time. Therefore, the president often uses them for pressing matters, and not necessarily because Congress isn't interested in the issue. Eliminate choice (B). Executive orders have been used since the time of George Washington, so eliminate choice (C). They can be challenged through the system of checks and balances, so eliminate choice (D). Executive orders, like the Emancipation Proclamation, are publically recorded and often highly publicized, so eliminate choice (E).

13. **D** An "iron triangle" consists of members of a congressional committee focused on a particular issue, the bureaucratic agency that enforces laws related to that issue, and members of interest groups. Those three groups work together to create policy that benefits everyone. None of the remaining choices accurately describe an iron triangle and should all be eliminated.

14. **D** A federal mandate is an order from the federal government to the states requiring them to take certain actions. In this case, states were required to raise their legal drinking age to 21 and, if they did not, the federal government withheld highway funds. Dual federalism is a system in which the federal government and the state governments each have clearly defined powers and are allowed to operate without interference from the other. Eliminate choice (A). Eliminate choice (B) because judicial activism is the process of using court rulings to create new policies by overturning bad laws. The elastic clause states that Congress can pass all laws necessary to enforce the powers given to Congress by the Constitution. This is unrelated to the consumption of alcohol, so eliminate choice (C). Finally, incorporation refers to the requirement that the states uphold rights provided to citizens in the Bill of Rights. Eliminate choice (E).

15. **A** A writ of *certiorari* is issued when the Supreme Court agrees to review a case. It is the beginning of the process of a Supreme Court, not a final ruling, so eliminate choices (B) and (D). The Supreme Court tends to follow a rule of four when choosing cases to hear, but there is no formal regulation

about how many justices must agree to hear a case, so eliminate choice (C). While the Supreme Court is more likely to hear a case when the government is one of the parties, a writ of *certiorari* is issued for every case that is reviewed. Eliminate choice (E).

16. C The National Voter Registration Act, or Motor Voter Act, was passed to reduce the cost of voter registration by giving people a chance to register while they were registering for other government programs, such as a driver's license or federal assistance. The Act may have increased the number of minorities who registered to vote by simplifying the process of registration, but that was not the primary purpose of the Act. Eliminate choice (A). The Act relates to registration, not voting, so eliminate choice (B). Choice (D) describes the Voting Rights Act of 1965, so that choice can be eliminated. There is no fine for failing to register in the United States, so eliminate choice (E).

Drill 2

1. D Choice (D) is an accurate description of devolution. Choice (B) describes marble-cake federalism, choice (C) describes the overall concept of federalism, and choice (E) describes permissive federalism. All of those answer choices should be eliminated. Also eliminate choice (A) because it is the opposite of devolution.

2. C Choice (C) is the correct term for restricted federal funds designated for a specific purpose. Revenue sharing and block grants refer to unrestricted funds, so eliminate choices (A) and (B). An unfunded mandate is a requirement the federal government places on the states without providing funds to help the states meet that requirement. Eliminate choice (D). Finally, choice (E) can be eliminated because it is just a general concept that could refer to any of the above choices.

3. E Federal budget entitlements are funds for individuals who qualify for programs such as Medicare. Mandates are the orders, not the funds, so choice (A) is incorrect. Pork barrel spending and project grants are funds for state or local projects, but not at the individual level, so eliminate choices (B) and (D). Charitable trusts are not established by legislation, so eliminate choice (C).

4. D Since Congress cannot actively enforce the regulations that they create, they form bureaucratic agencies to carry out these duties. Bureaucracies are able to set their own rules and operate quasi-independently once they are formed by Congress through enabling legislation. Even though bureaucracies are part of the executive branch, they are created through the legislature, so eliminate choice (A). While congressional subcommittees can be credited with the idea for a particular agency, the agency must be approved by both chambers of Congress. Eliminate choice (B). The elastic clause is just another name for the necessary and proper clause, which gives Congress the ability to make all laws necessary to carry out its duties. This clause is irrelevant to the question, making choice (C) incorrect. The cabinet members lead but do not create the federal bureaucracies, so choice (E) is wrong.

5. **D**   Agency capture occurs when the federal agency is no longer effective due to the influence the regulated industry has over it. It is akin to "inmates running the asylum." It is law for a federal agency to be represented by both parties, so choice (A) is incorrect. The situations described in choices (B) and (E) are wrong because they represent the opposite of agency capture—in this case the agency has more than enough power over the industry. Settling disputes between companies in an industry is part of an agency's job and an indication that the agency is operating correctly. Eliminate choice (C).

6. **A**   The "iron triangle" is the cooperative relationship between a federal agency, an interest group, and Congress. One component of this give-and-take relationship is that Congress sets the regulatory agency's budget. An interest group's role in this relationship is to offer information to the agency and to fund congressional campaigns, so choices (B) and (D) are incorrect. Congress gets to determine subsidies offered to interest groups as well as create the regulations over that industry, so choices (C) and (E) are wrong.

7. **A**   The "rule of four" refers to the process typically used to decide which cases the Supreme Court should hear in the upcoming session. To prevent case overload, a case will generally only appear on the Court's docket if at least four justices have agreed to hear it. All justices may ask as many questions as they wish during oral arguments, so choice (B) is incorrect. Choice (C) is wrong because the chief justice is appointed by the president and confirmed by the Senate. The Supreme Court may hear as many cases as it sees fit, so eliminate choice (D). There is no limit on how many justices may join on an opinion, so choice (E) is incorrect.

8. **C**   Entitlement spending does not follow normal budgetary procedure and can rise or fall with inflation and the changing cost of living. Military spending, on the other hand, falls under the traditional budgetary scope of Congress, so choice (A) is wrong. Choice (B) is incorrect because military spending is funded with regular income tax, while entitlement spending comes through a payroll tax. The military covers certain health care needs, for instance through the Department of Veterans Affairs. Eliminate choice (D). It is a misconception that the payroll taxes deducted from one's paycheck go toward an individual pension fund. Social Security and other entitlements are actually "pay as you go" programs, in which current payees fund current beneficiaries. This would make choice (E) incorrect.

Free-Response Question 1

Students may earn a total of six points on this question. Two points are available for part (a), two for part (b), and two for part (c).

Part (a) asks for the definition of fiscal policy and monetary policy. You will receive one point for each definition. To receive credit, you must state that fiscal policy involves establishing the federal budget through decisions about taxing and spending. To earn the second point, you can identify some or all of the following points related to monetary policy: controlling interest rates, setting requirements for bank reserves, regulating the supply of money, controlling market operations, or controlling inflation and deflation.

Part (b) asks for the role of both the president and Congress in influencing fiscal policy. You will receive one point for each explanation. To earn the first point, you should state that the president prepares and proposes the federal budget and he or she either signs into law or vetoes legislation concerning taxes, expenditures, and borrowing money. To earn the second point, you must state that Congress approves the federal budget, as well as drafts and votes on legislation concerning taxing and spending, or that the Congressional Budget Office (CBO) advises Congress on issues that affect fiscal policy.

Part (c) asks for two reasons that the Federal Reserve is responsible for establishing monetary policy. You will receive one point for each explanation. To earn credit for this answer, you can offer any of the following explanations: monetary policy remains independent from political pressure; the level of expertise required to set good monetary policy is beyond that of most members of Congress; Congress and the president have many other laws and policies to create, which makes them less efficient; or, members of Congress can be free from blame for difficult or bad monetary policy decisions.

Drill 3

1. **C** The president's relationship with the public has evolved for a few reasons. For one, the rise of the media has created regular outlets for the president to communicate with the public. This is a strategy employed by nearly every president of the past one hundred years as they try to pit the public on their side of an issue, which in turn puts pressure on Congress to act in the president's interest. Further, the presidency of Theodore Roosevelt created the "bully pulpit," which has empowered presidents to take a message to the people and demand action from Congress. Presidents were seen as top members of their parties in the nineteenth century, so choice (A) is incorrect. The spoils system is far more characteristic of the 1800s than it is of today, so eliminate choice (B). The presidency, which was weaker than Congress in the nineteenth century, has strengthened greatly beginning with Theodore Roosevelt. Now, the executive office is seen as an equally powerful as the legislature. Eliminate choice (D). Choice (E) is incorrect because vetoes have become more common in the twentieth and twenty-first century than they were during the nineteenth century.

2. **D** Internet, television, radio, and print give citizens a large amount of information about candidates running for office. In addition, the majority of people vote on a single-party ticket, so a lack of knowledge is not a main cause of low voter turnout. All of the remaining choices accurately describe reasons that people choose not to vote in the United States, and thus can all be eliminated.

3. **E** The purpose of the Unfunded Mandates Reform Act of 1995 was to limit the larger financial burdens placed on states through mandates. One way this was done was by having the Congressional Budget Office report on those mandates in excess of $50 million. Waivers had been offered to states since before this law, so choice (A) is incorrect. The federal government cannot determine how much a state may spend, so choice (B) is wrong. Block grants are not tied to all federal

mandates, so choice (C) is neither true nor necessarily relevant to mandates. The federal government can issue a waiver for a state to opt out of a mandate, but it needs to be requested from the states, so eliminate choice (D).

4. **C** Categorical grants demand that a state comply with specific policies outline by the federal government if the state is to accept the money. "Race to the Top" is therefore a categorical grant because there are stipulations tied to the available money. Block grants leave much of the specific policy formation up to the states, so choice (A) is incorrect. A federal mandate requires all states to comply, whereas the situation described in this question applies only to those states that choose to accept federal money. Eliminate choice (B). The example provided is not devolutionary because devolution refers to power going from the federal government to a state or local government. Since the federal government retains the upper hand in "Race to the Top," choice (E) would not be correct. Finally, choice (D) is incorrect as affirmative action policy deals with diversity initiatives.

5. **D** The solicitor general is a justice department official who represents the federal government in Supreme Court cases. One of the jobs of the solicitor general is to put pressure on the Court to hear the cases that the White House would like argued, making choice (D) the correct answer. The answer is not the attorney general because, even though he or she is the head of the justice department, it is not the attorney general's job to argue presidential policy before the court. Eliminate choice (B). The Speaker of the House presides over the House of Representatives. The president *pro tempore* presides over the Senate whenever the vice president is not present. Neither position holds significant influence over the Supreme Court, so choices (A) and (C) are incorrect. The Secretary of State handles foreign policy matters for the White House. Choice (E) is incorrect.

6. **D** In recent years, Congress has failed to pass a budget. When this occurs and no money is appropriated to federal agencies, the agencies will continue to receive the funds they received in the previous fiscal year through a continuing resolution. The first budget resolution and the second budget resolution are earlier stages in the budgetary process that set goals and limits for the upcoming fiscal year, so choices (B) and (C) are incorrect. Block grants and categorical grants are federal money allocated to states, not agencies. Eliminate choices (A) and (E).

7. **B** A 1969 hate crime law allowed federal prosecution of those who harm a person or damage property while motivated by a bias against the target's race, color, ethnicity, national origin, sex, age, and/or religion. Therefore choices (A) and (C) are incorrect. The 2009 Matthew Shepard Act added gender identity/expression, sexual orientation, and disability to the list. Eliminate choices (D) and (E).

8. **A** The Department of Homeland Security was created to centralize the information collected by a variety of federal agencies. The lack of communication among these agencies was seen as contributing to the security lapse that led to the events of September 11, 2001. The legislative branch retains the power to create federal agencies, so choice (B) is wrong. Choices (C) and (D) are incorrect because no agencies were shut down as a result of the September 11 attacks nor were there any significant

leadership changes in the those agencies due to the events. Due to security measures, the trend toward "government in the sunshine" (the ability for the public to know the inner workings of federal agencies) has actually decreased following September 11, making choice (E) incorrect.

Free-Response Question 1

Students may earn a total of six points on this question. Two points are available for part (a) and four for part (b).

Part (a) asks you to select and explain two of the tactics that the president can use to influence Congress. You will earn one point for each tactic you explain. To earn credit, your answer can include

- Legislative powers: the president has the power to veto legislation or sign it into law. The president can also use the pocket veto to passively express disagreement with legislation.
- Appointment power: the president can appoint members to his or her cabinet who agree with his or her agenda. He or she also appoints, and fires, heads of agencies, who are responsible for executing legislation, and appoints federal judges, who interpret legislation.
- State of the Union Address: the president can use the State of the Union Address to appeal to the American public who can pressure their legislators to vote a certain way. The State of the Union Address can also increase the president's popularity, which plays a role in how much members of Congress are willing to cooperate with him or her on legislative issues.

Part (b) asks you to define and explain two of the limitations on the president's ability to influence Congress. You will earn one point for each correct definition and one for each correct explanation. To earn the first two points, you must explain that the lame-duck period is the period between the election of a new president and the time when that president actually takes over the office. Mandatory spending is spending that is automatic or not related to annual budgetary decisions. Your explanation of how the lame-duck period limits the president's influence should mention either a perception of the president as having diminished power or that members of Congress don't need to be responsive to him or her during this time. Your explanation of mandatory spending should mention that funds allocated for mandatory spending can create difficulties in coming up with the funds for discretionary policy goals or that mandatory spending limits the type of budget cuts that can be made.

Drill 4

1. **D** Since we do not have data projecting beyond 2017, we can eliminate any answer choice with Numeral I included, such as choices (A) and (B). Numeral II is found in all of the remaining answer choices, so there is no need to check it any further. Further, the lighter shaded region, which represents spending on individuals, comprises the vast majority of the grants in recent years. Numeral III is supported by the graph because we can see a steep increase in grant spending around the time of President Obama's inauguration (2009). This is largely due to the stimulus package that addressed the recession of 2008. You should eliminate choice (C) because it does not contain Numeral III. Since we do not have any information on GDP, we know that Numeral IV is not supported. Eliminate choice (E).

2.   **C**   Interest on the debt represents about 5% of federal expenditures. The budget is dominated by entitlements, which make up approximately one-third of all spending. Therefore, you can eliminate any answer choices that are entitlements, such as choices (A) and (D). Social programs and defense each represent about 20% of the budget, so eliminate choices (B) and (E).

3.   **B**   Block grants give money to states. Those states get to decide how to best implement the policy in their locale. This is the situation described in the TANF example, making (B) the correct answer. Categorical grants and federal mandates do not give states much leeway in matters of implementation, so choices (C) and (E) are incorrect. An interstate compact is an agreement made between states that does not involve Congress, so eliminate choice (A). Choice (D) is incorrect because an executive agreement is a foreign policy decision made between the president and another head of state.

4.   **E**   President Obama issued an executive order (a rule issued by the president that has the effect of law) when he suspended the deportation of these young adults. Executive privilege is the right of the president to withhold information from a legislative committee, so eliminate choice (A). These orders did not give citizenship or refrain from administering future legal consequences, so the president offered neither a pardon nor amnesty. Eliminate choices (B) and (D). Emergency powers are rare and only utilized by the president during a time of crisis, which was not the case in the immigration example. Choice (C) is incorrect.

5.   **A**   "Devolution" occurs when a large governmental entity gives a power it would normally exercise to a smaller governmental entity. When President Clinton and Congress passed welfare reform in the 1990s, it "devolved" the power to implement the policy to the states. This means that the states had the power and responsibility to implement welfare reform, making choice (A) the correct answer. Laissez-faire economics is the idea that business functions best without governmental interference, so eliminate choice (B). Political socialization is the process by which people develop political views, so eliminate choice (C). While Libertarians might have supported the policy of devolving welfare reform to the states, Libertarian focus is generally on the liberty of individuals, not the devolution of power from the federal to the state government, so choice (D) is not as good of a response as choice (A). The Powell Doctrine is a military doctrine coined by General Colin Powell that iterates certain conditions that should be met before the United States takes military action.

6.   **B**   A congressional committee is a formal group of legislators in either the House of Representatives or the Senate that focus on a specific issue, making choice (B) the correct answer. Since the group is formal, eliminate choices (A) and (E), which describe social and informal groups. Since the groups are chosen from the entire congressional body, but are much smaller than a congressional body, eliminate choice (D). Congressional committees are formed to legislate, not fundraise, so eliminate choice (C).

7. **B** The Social Security program was enacted through legislation during the New Deal era. Although the legislation has been altered by amendments since that time, it directs that money be given to qualified individuals and is thusly considered a federal entitlement. Since choices (A), (C), (D), and (E) all inaccurately describe the Social Security program's inception, you can eliminate them.

8. **D** There are many strategies used by special interests groups to shape government regulations, including fundraising; forming "iron triangles" of bureaucratic agencies, congressional committees, and industry groups; publishing facts and opinions in the media; and lobbying in Congress, among many other options. However, special interest groups would not encourage the president to cast a vote in Congress because the Constitution's separation of powers denies the president this power.

Free Response Question 1

Students may earn a total of six points on this question. Four points are available for part (a), one for part (b), and one for part (c).

Part (a) asks you to explain, using specific details, how federal bureaucratic agencies use discretion in executing federal laws. You will receive one point for each accurate description of the laws over which the agencies have discretion and one point for each specific example you give. There are well over 100 different agencies you can select from to answer this question. Be sure to select two agencies for which you can come up with specific examples. Some examples are

- The Occupational Safety and Health Administration assures safe working conditions and also enforces a variety of whistleblower regulations.
- The Drug Enforcement Administration combats drug smuggling and use within the United States and pursues drug investigations abroad.
- The Bureau of Land Management preserves public land for a variety of uses and enjoyment.
- The National Endowment for the Arts supports and funds artistic projects.

Part (b) asks you to describe one advantage of giving federal bureaucratic agencies discretion. You will receive one point for your answer. Your answer can include any of the following: members of Congress are not always highly knowledgeable about every law they pass, so they don't necessarily understand the best way to implement them; members of Congress don't want to be held responsible for bad policy decisions; or, executing laws requires a good deal of time and effort, which means that specialized agencies and workers can be more efficient.

Part (c) asks you to describe one way in which federal bureaucratic agencies are limited in using their own discretion. You will receive one point for your description. Your answer can include any of the following: congressional oversight (includes hearings and investigations); allocation of funding to agencies; reviews conducted by the Government Accountability Office (GAO); creation of new laws to supersede the old ones; or, the dissolution of agencies and the creation of new ones.

Chapter 13
Civil Rights and
Civil Liberties

DRILL 1

1. In which of the following cases did the Supreme Court order schools to desegregate "with all due and deliberate speed"?

   (A) *Plessy v. Ferguson*
   (B) *Katzenbach v. McClung*
   (C) *Regents of the University of California v. Bakke*
   (D) *Lawrence v. Texas*
   (E) *Brown v. Board 2nd*

2. *Schenck v. United States* (1919) established that

   (A) students do not "shed their constitutional rights at the schoolhouse door"
   (B) burning the American flag is an example of permissible free speech
   (C) school officials could suspend students for lewd or indecent speech
   (D) speech which evokes "a clear and present danger" is not permissible
   (E) speech could be restricted even if it only had a tendency to lead to illegal action

3. The Civil Rights Act of 1964

   (A) banned racial discrimination in housing
   (B) outlawed poll taxes that had been used to prevent African Americans from voting
   (C) banned discrimination in public accommodations and all federally funded programs
   (D) allowed "separate but equal" facilities based on race
   (E) banned discrimination in hotels, restaurants, and railroad cars

4. The Fourteenth Amendment establishes that

   (A) slavery or involuntary servitude shall not exist in the United States
   (B) Congress has the power to lay and collect taxes on income
   (C) the manufacture, sale, or transportation of intoxicating liquors in the United States is prohibited
   (D) no state shall deprive any person of life, liberty, or property, without due process of law
   (E) no individual can be elected to the office of the president more than two times

5. The Warren Court ruled in all of the following Supreme Court cases EXCEPT

   (A) *Gideon v. Wainwright*
   (B) *Betts v. Brady*
   (C) *Brown v. Board of Education of Topeka*
   (D) *Miranda v. Arizona*
   (E) *Escobedo v. Illinois*

6. In *Miranda v. Arizona*, the court

   (A) ruled that suspects must be informed of the right to remain silent and the right to a lawyer upon arrest
   (B) ruled that illegally obtained evidence could not be used in federal court
   (C) ruled that state governments must provide counsel to individuals who cannot afford legal representation if a case involves the death penalty
   (D) established judicial review
   (E) prohibited state-sponsored recitation of prayer in public schools

7. Two related cases that focused on the right to privacy for all American citizens were

   (A) *Near v. Minnesota* and *New York Times v. Sullivan*
   (B) *Texas v. Johnson* and *Morse v. Frederick*
   (C) *Thornhill v. Alabama* and *Cox v. New Hampshire*
   (D) *Epperson v. Arkansas* and *Lemon v. Kurtzman*
   (E) *Griswold v. Connecticut* and *Roe v. Wade.*

8. The doctrine of "separate but equal" was ruled unconstitutional in

   (A) *Plessy v. Ferguson*
   (B) *Brown v. Board 2nd*
   (C) *Gratz v. Bollinger*
   (D) *Brown v. Board of Education of Topeka*
   (E) *Heart of Atlanta Motel, Inc. v. United States*

9. The Fourteenth Amendment reversed the decision from which Supreme Court case that ruled slaves or descendents of slaves could not be citizens?

   (A) *McCulloch v. Maryland*
   (B) *Sweatt v. Painter*
   (C) *Dred Scott v. Sandford*
   (D) *Plessy v. Ferguson*
   (E) *Missouri ex el Gaines v. Canada*

10. While best known for protecting freedom of speech and religion, the First Amendment also protects Americans' right to

(A) due process of the law in any criminal case
(B) retain personal property unless justly compensated by the government
(C) not be subjected to excessive fines or unusual punishment
(D) petition the government for a redress of grievances
(E) not be searched without probable cause

11. Which of the following best explains why only 5 percent of African Americans living in Mississippi in 1956 were registered to vote but by 1971 that amount had increased to 59 percent?

(A) The Civil Rights Act of 1964 was passed.
(B) The assassination of Martin Luther King, Jr. inspired more African Americans to become involved in politics.
(C) African American candidates were seen more often on ballots for state and national offices.
(D) Equal opportunity efforts had given African Americans access to higher-paying jobs, so more of them were able to afford the poll tax.
(E) The Voting Rights Act of 1965 was passed.

12. Which of the following is the primary result of *Miranda v. Arizona* (1966)?

(A) The warrantless seizure of items from a private residence is considered a violation of constitutional rights.
(B) Prior to interrogation, criminal suspects must be made aware of their constitutional rights to consult with an attorney and to not self-incriminate.
(C) Civilians cannot be tried in a military court when a civilian court is accessible.
(D) All criminal defendants must be given access to an attorney, regardless of ability to pay for such a service.
(E) Sitting presidents do not have immunity against lawsuits related to unofficial matters.

13. When the Voting Rights Act of 1965 was renewed in 1975, it included the provision that

(A) members of the military be automatically registered to vote
(B) federal funds must be used to run local and state elections whenever those municipalities lack their own funds
(C) convicted felons be prohibited from voting
(D) districts that contain sizeable linguistic minorities must provide voting materials in the native languages of those populations
(E) no person be denied from voting in a primary election

14. The right to privacy, as implied in the Fourteenth Amendment, was used as a legal basis for the decision in which of the following cases?

(A) *Bakke v. Regents of the University of California* (1978)
(B) *Roe v. Wade* (1973)
(C) *Gideon v. Wainwright* (1963)
(D) *Muller v. Oregon* (1908)
(E) *Marbury v. Madison* (1803)

15. The Supreme Court has interpreted which of the following to protect religious beliefs but not necessarily all religious practices?

(A) The Establishment Clause
(B) The Elastic Clause
(C) The Free Exercise Clause
(D) The Full Faith and Credit Clause
(E) The Supremacy Clause

16. The "separate but equal" doctrine, as interpreted in *Plessy v. Ferguson*, was used to justify

(A) the continued practice of slave ownership in the territories that became Kansas and Nebraska
(B) the abolition of separate schools for blacks and whites in the south
(C) differences in salaries between men and women holding the same positions
(D) the practice of imposing poll taxes and literacy tests for the right to vote
(E) refusing service to African Americans or persons of mixed heritage

DRILL 2

1. All of the following cases were decided based on rights enumerated in the First Amendment EXCEPT

   (A) *Gitlow v. New York*
   (B) *Schenck v. United States*
   (C) *Engel v. Vitale*
   (D) *Brandenburg v. Ohio*
   (E) *Mapp v. Ohio*

2. The doctrine of incorporation is

   (A) the decision of a court to apply precedent when making a ruling
   (B) the division of power between a central government and the states
   (C) an order that requires a lower court to send a case to the Supreme Court for review
   (D) a legal requirement for states to provide their citizens with the same rights guaranteed by the Constitution
   (E) a principle which states that evidence collected in violation of one's constitutional rights may be inadmissible in court

3. Which of the statements about Supreme Court rulings concerning the death penalty is false?

   (A) Electrocution constitutes cruel and unusual punishment.
   (B) Lethal injection is not cruel and unusual punishment.
   (C) Persons with mental retardation cannot be sentenced to death.
   (D) The death penalty cannot be applied in cases in which the crime committed did not result in the death of the victim.
   (E) Persons under 18 years of age at the time of their crime cannot be sentenced to death.

4. All of the following are true about the Voting Rights Act of 1965 EXCEPT:

   (A) It bans poll taxes and literacy tests.
   (B) It is a permanent piece of legislation.
   (C) It prohibits intimidation and coercion of voters.
   (D) It limits the advance voter registration period to 30 days before a presidential election.
   (E) Its passage greatly increased the number of African Americans who registered to vote.

5. The equal protection clause of the Fourteenth Amendment was the basis for the decision in which of the following cases?

   (A) *Planned Parenthood v. Casey*
   (B) *Gideon v. Wainwright*
   (C) *Brown v. Board of Education of Topeka*
   (D) *Tinker v. Des Moines*
   (E) *Lemon v. Kurtzman*

6. The right to privacy was a principle most defined by the

   (A) Rehnquist Court
   (B) Taney Court
   (C) Taft Court
   (D) Warren Court
   (E) Marshall Court

7. All of the following cases expanded the rights of the accused EXCEPT

   (A) *Texas v. Johnson*
   (B) *Mapp v. Ohio*
   (C) *Griffin v. California*
   (D) *Miranda v. Arizona*
   (E) *Gideon v. Wainwright*

8. Which of the following courts represents the most radical change from the decisions of the Warren Court?

   (A) The Burger Court
   (B) The Rehnquist Court
   (C) The Taft Court
   (D) The White Court
   (E) The Vinson Court

Free Response

Time—25 minutes

African American and Hispanic Members of Congress

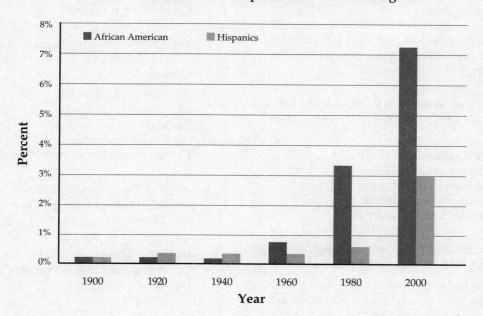

1.   (a)   Using the chart above, describe how the percentage of African American and Hispanic members of Congress has changed over time.

(b)   Describe two barriers that currently prevent African Americans, Hispanics, or other minorities from holding a larger percentage of the seats in Congress.

(c)   Explain how the implementation of each of the following was effective in increasing the number of minority voters.

   •   Voting Rights Act of 1965
   •   Twenty-fourth Amendment

DRILL 3

1. Which of the following was NOT a result of the Fourteenth Amendment?

   (A) All individuals born in the United States were recognized as legal citizens.
   (B) Jim Crow Laws were banned.
   (C) The United States was declared responsible for its debts.
   (D) The protections of the Bill of Rights were applied to state and local governments.
   (E) The protections of the Constitution were applied to all citizens.

2. The authority of the Civil Rights Act of 1964 over the private sector was primarily justified under the

   (A) First Amendment
   (B) Citizenship Clause
   (C) Commerce Clause
   (D) Fourteenth Amendment
   (E) Power of Executive Order

3. The primary difference between *Schenck v. United States* and *Brandenburg v. Ohio* was that

   (A) Brandenburg's speech was unprotected hate speech, while Schenck's was protected
   (B) Schenck's case involved the freedom of assembly, while Brandenburg's concerned freedom of the press
   (C) the court protected Brandenburg's actions because they did not provoke a riot, while Schenck's did
   (D) the court ruled that Schenck's speech created a clear and present danger while Brandenburg's speech did not provoke an imminent lawless action
   (E) the Court used Brandenburg's case to create a doctrine of "hate speech," while Schenck's speech was protected under the First Amendment

4. The doctrine set forth in *Plessy v. Ferguson* was overturned through the

   (A) Civil Rights Act of 1964
   (B) Voting Rights Act of 1965
   (C) Fourteenth Amendment
   (D) *Katzenbach v. McClung* decision
   (E) *Brown v. Board of Education* decision

5. The separation of students by race was deemed an unconstitutional act in

   (A) *Bethel School District v. Fraser*
   (B) *Morse v. Frederick*
   (C) *Abington School District v. Schempp*
   (D) *Brown v. Board of Education of Topeka*
   (E) *Epperson v. Arkansas*

6. Which of the following Supreme Court cases resulted in a majority opinion based on the right to privacy?

   (A) *Lemon v. Kurtzman*
   (B) *Furman v. Georgia*
   (C) *Mapp v. Ohio*
   (D) *Escobedo v. Illinois*
   (E) *Griswold v. Connecticut*

7. Which of the following Supreme Court rulings found that states must provide attorneys to indigent defendants?

   (A) *Gideon v. Wainwright*
   (B) *Roper v. Simmons*
   (C) *Brown v. Board of Education of Topeka*
   (D) *Mapp v. Ohio*
   (E) *Miranda v. Arizona*

8. Which amendment protects "the right of the people peaceably to assemble"?

   (A) First Amendment
   (B) Second Amendment
   (C) Third Amendment
   (D) Fourth Amendment
   (E) Fifth Amendment

1. The Fifteenth Amendment, ratified in 1870, prohibits the denial of voting rights on account of race. However, for a long time after 1870 very few African Americans voted. Not until the 1960s was there a noticeable increase in voter turnout among African Americans.

    (a)   Select two of the following methods and explain how they were used to discourage African Americans from voting.

- Poll taxes
- White primaries
- Grandfather clause

    (b)   Even though they were often barred from voting, African Americans engaged in politics in a variety of other ways. Explain how three of the methods of political participation listed below were used by African Americans to help bring about changes in civil rights.

- Civil disobedience
- Litigation
- Protests or boycotts
- Participation in special interest groups
- Participating in elections in ways other than voting

DRILL 4

1. Which of the following best characterizes the Supreme Court holding in *Plessy v. Ferguson*?

   (A) Separate but equal institutions (such as schools) are inherently unequal.
   (B) The Civil Rights Act of 1964 prohibited racial discrimination in public places (such as libraries).
   (C) Race-based affirmative action is acceptable at universities.
   (D) Institutions (such as schools) can have separate but equal facilities based on race.
   (E) The Civil Rights Act of 1964 prohibited racial discrimination in private places (such as businesses).

2. Which of the following Constitutional clauses would be violated by state-sponsored prayer in a public school?

   (A) The equal protection clause
   (B) The necessary and proper clause
   (C) The establishment clause
   (D) The interstate commerce clause
   (E) The free exercise clause

3. The Twenty-fourth Amendment prohibited which of the following?

   (A) Slavery
   (B) Alcohol sales
   (C) Immediate congressional pay increases
   (D) More than two full presidential terms served by one person
   (E) Poll taxes

4. A major provision of the Voting Rights Act, as it was written in 1965, was that

   (A) poll taxes would be banned from all federal elections
   (B) states with a history of disenfranchisement were required to obtain federal approval before changing voting procedures or election laws
   (C) voter identification cards need not be requested at polling locations
   (D) most substantial changes to voting procedures would have to come from the states
   (E) African Americans were allowed to run for federal office

5. Which of the following rules concerning the death penalty has been established by the Supreme Court?

   (A) A state's use of the death penalty cannot be infringed upon by the federal government.
   (B) The lethal injection is the only allowable method for execution.
   (C) The bifurcation process determines a defendant's guilt and sentence simultaneously.
   (D) Judges may not decide on the death penalty as a punishment.
   (E) Capital punishment may not be used, as it is considered cruel and unusual.

6. The Supreme Court revisited the issue of freedom of speech in *Gitlow v. New York* (1925) and for the first time noted that the Fourteenth Amendment

   (A) guarantees equal protection
   (B) requests states to pay legal fees for both plaintiff and defendant
   (C) was unconstitutional
   (D) does not apply to naturalized citizens
   (E) applies most of the protections of the Bill of Rights to state governments

7. *Gideon v. Wainwright* was similar to *Powell v. Alabama* in that both cases

   (A) were landmark decisions on capital punishment
   (B) were denied a writ of *certiorari*
   (C) involved the accused's right to a lawyer
   (D) were argued in front of the Warren Court
   (E) expanded the scope of the free exercise clause

8. The precedent created by *Plessy v. Ferguson* allowed for

   (A) incorporation to take effect
   (B) the racial integration of public schools
   (C) African Americans to become enfranchised citizens
   (D) hate groups to speak out publicly
   (E) Jim Crow laws to proliferate

Free Response

Time—25 minutes

1. The First Amendment protects an array of freedoms; the freedom of religion is one of those.

    (a)   Identify and define the two clauses in the First Amendment that are related to the freedom of religion.

    (b)   For each clause identified in part (a), select from the list below a case in which that clause was at issue. Describe the Supreme Court's decision for each.
- *Reynolds v. United States* (1879)
- *Engel v. Vitale* (1962)
- *Lemon v. Kurtzman* (1971)
- *Employment Division, State of Oregon v. Smith* (1990)
- *Church of the Lukumi Babalu Aye v. Hialeah* (1993)
- *McCreary v. ACLU of KY* (2005)

    (c)   While the Supreme Court is the highest court to which a decision can be appealed, there are other political institutions that can alter or influence rulings of the Supreme Court. Describe two methods used by political institutions to do so.

Chapter 14
Civil Rights and Civil Liberties: Answers and Explanations

ANSWER KEY

Multiple-Choice Questions

Drill 1
1. E
2. D
3. C
4. D
5. B
6. A
7. E
8. D
9. C
10. D
11. E
12. B
13. D
14. B
15. C
16. E

Drill 2
1. E
2. D
3. A
4. B
5. C
6. D
7. A
8. B

Drill 3
1. B
2. C
3. D
4. E
5. D
6. E
7. A
8. A

Drill 4
1. D
2. C
3. E
4. B
5. D
6. E
7. C
8. E

EXPLANATIONS

Drill 1

1. **E** *Brown v. Board 2nd* was a follow-up case to *Brown v. Board of Education of Topeka,* in which the Supreme Court ordered schools to desegregate "with all due and deliberate speed." Eliminate choice (A) because *Plessy v. Ferguson* allowed separate but equal facilities based on race. Choice (B) can be eliminated because the Supreme Court ruled that the Civil Rights Act of 1964 applied to almost all businesses in *Katzenbach v. McClung.* In the case of *Regents of the University of California v. Bakke,* the court ruled that race-based affirmative action was permissible so long as it was utilized for diversification purposes; eliminate choice (C). Finally, choice (D) can be eliminated because in *Lawrence v. Texas* the court ruled that the prohibition of homosexuals from privately engaging in sodomy was an unreasonable invasion of privacy.

2. **D** In *Schenck v. United States*, Chief Justice Oliver Wendell Holmes established that speech evoking "a clear and present danger" is not permissible. Perhaps the most famous example of prohibited speech would be an individual falsely yelling "Fire!" in a packed theater. Choice (A) can be eliminated because *Tinker v. Des Moines* established that students do not "shed their constitutional rights at the schoolhouse door." Choice (B) can be eliminated because *Texas v. Johnson* established that burning the American flag is an example of permissible free speech. Eliminate choice (C) because *Bethel School District v. Fraser* gave school officials the authority to suspend students for speech considered lewd or indecent. Finally, choice (E) can be eliminated because *Gitlow v. New York* established the "Bad Tendency Doctrine," which stated that speech could be restricted even if it only had a tendency to lead to illegal action.

3. **C** The Civil Rights Act of 1964 increased the rights of blacks and minorities, gave the federal government more power to enforce the law, banned discrimination in public accommodations and federally funded programs, prohibited racial and gender discrimination in the workplace, and required the government to cut off all funding to programs that failed to comply with all of aforementioned regulations. Choice (A) can be eliminated because the Civil Rights Act, Title VIII (1968) banned racial discrimination in housing. Choice (B) can be eliminated because the Twenty-fourth Amendment outlawed poll taxes that had been used to prevent African Americans from voting. Eliminate choice (D) because in the case of *Plessy v. Ferguson*, the Supreme Court ruled that separate but equal facilities based on race were allowable. Eliminate choice (E) because the Civil Rights Act of 1875, which was declared unconstitutional in 1883, banned discrimination in hotels, restaurants, and railroad cars.

4. **D** In Section 1 of the Fourteenth Amendment, it is established that all individuals born or naturalized in the United States are citizens and subject to its jurisdiction; states cannot make or enforce

laws that abridge the privileges or immunities of citizens, states cannot deprive citizens of life, liberty, or property, without due process of law, and no citizen can be denied equal protection of the laws. Eliminate choice (A) because the Thirteenth Amendment establishes that slavery or involuntary servitude shall not exist in the United States. Choice (B) can be eliminated because the Sixteenth Amendment states that Congress has the power to lay and collect taxes on incomes from whatever source derived. Eliminate choice (C) because the Eighteenth Amendment prohibited the manufacture, sale, or transportation of intoxicating liquors in the United States. Finally, choice (E) can be eliminated because it is the Twenty-second Amendment that states no person can be elected as president more than two times.

5. **B** The Warren Court reached a number of dramatic decisions regarding the rights of the people between 1953 and 1969. However, *Betts v. Brady* was not decided under the leadership of Chief Justice Earl Warren, and the decision established that state governments did not have to provide lawyers to indigent defendants in capital cases. Eliminate choice (A) because *Gideon v. Wainwright* overturned the ruling made in *Betts v. Brady*; the Warren Court established that all state governments must provide an attorney in all cases for those who cannot afford one. Choice (C) can be eliminated because the court, led by Earl Warren, ruled the doctrine of "separate but equal" to be unconstitutional. Choice (D), *Miranda v. Arizona*, is the most well-known of the Warren Court decisions that mandated that all defendants be informed of their legal rights prior to arrest. Eliminate choice (E) because in *Escobedo v. Illinois*, the Warren Court ruled that a lawyer be granted to any defendant who asks—failure to do so means that any confession is inadmissible in court.

6. **A** In *Miranda v. Arizona* (1966), the Warren Court ruled that all defendants must be informed of all their legal rights prior to being arrested. Choice (B) can be eliminated because it was the case of *Weeks v. U.S.* that ruled that illegally obtained evidence could not be used in federal court. Eliminate choice (C) because in *Powell v. Alabama* the court ruled that, in cases involving the death penalty, state governments must provide counsel to those who cannot afford it. Choice (D) can be eliminated because *Marbury v. Madison* established judicial review. Eliminate choice (E) because the prohibition of state-sponsored prayer in public schools was established in *Engel v. Vitale*.

7. **E** While the right to privacy is not explicitly mentioned in the Constitution, in *Griswold v. Connecticut* the Warren Court ruled that the Bill of Rights contained an implied right to privacy. In the case of *Roe v. Wade*, the Court established national abortion guidelines by extending the inferred right of privacy from *Griswold v. Connecticut*. Eliminate choice (A) because *Near v. Minnesota* and *New York Times v. Sullivan* focused on freedom of the press. Choice (B) can be eliminated because the cases of *Texas v. Johnson* and *Morse v. Frederick* were rulings regarding freedom of speech. Eliminate choice (C) because cases *Thornhill v. Alabama* and *Cox v. New Hampshire* were related to the freedom of assembly and association. Choice (D) can be eliminated because the cases of *Epperson v. Arkansas* and *Lemon v. Kurtzman* were related to freedom of religion.

8.   **D**   In one of the Warren Court's more dramatic cases, the court unanimously ruled that the doctrine of "separate but equal" was unconstitutional. Eliminate choice (A) because *Plessy v. Ferguson* allowed Southern states to manipulate the Equal Protection Clause and establish "separate but equal" facilities based on race. Choice (B) can be eliminated because, recognizing that segregation still existed, the Court ruled that schools desegregate "with all due and deliberate speed" in *Brown v. Board 2nd*. In *Gratz v. Bollinger,* the court ruled that giving undergraduate minority applicants score boosts in the admission process was unconstitutional; eliminate choice (C). In *Heart of Atlanta Motel, Inc. v. United States,* the court ruled that the Constitution's Commerce Clause could be used to force private businesses to abide by the Federal Civil Rights Act of 1964; thus, eliminate choice (E).

9.   **C**   In *Dred Scott v. Sandford,* the Supreme Court ruled that African Americans, slaves or free, were not citizens and could not sue someone in federal court. The Fourteenth Amendment states that all persons born or naturalized in the United States are citizens. *McCulloch v. Maryland* was about implied powers of the federal government in relation to states' powers; eliminate choice (A). *Sweatt v. Painter* and *Missouri ex el Gaines v. Canada* were challenges to the "separate by equal" doctrine, which was established in *Plessy v. Ferguson.* Eliminate choices (B), (D), and (E) accordingly.

10. **D**   The First Amendment states that "Congress shall make no law…abridging…the right of the people…to petition the Government for a redress of grievances." Choices (A) and (B) are in the Fifth Amendment, choice (C) is in the Eighth Amendment, and choice (E) is in the Fourth Amendment. Accordingly, they can all be eliminated.

11. **E**   The Voting Rights Act prohibited poll taxes and literacy tests, which had been major impediments for African American voters. The Civil Rights Act prohibited discrimination but was not as directly linked to voting as the Voting Rights Act was, so eliminate choice (A). Martin Luther King, Jr. was an inspirational figure but alone could not have accounted for such a dramatic increase in registered, African American voters. Eliminate choice (B). Choice (C) is true, but also alone could not have accounted for such a dramatic increase in registered, African American voters, so eliminate choice (C). The poll tax was eliminated during the period of time in question, so eliminate choice (D).

12. **B**   In *Miranda v. Arizona,* the Court established that criminal suspects must be made aware of their constitutional rights to consult with an attorney and to not self-incriminate. Choice (A) describes *Mapp v. Ohio,* choice (C) describes *Ex parte Milligan,* choice (D) describes *Gideon v. Wainwright,* and choice (E) describes *Clinton v. Jones.* Accordingly, all of those choices should be eliminated.

13. **D**   Members of the military must register to vote; the process is not automatic, so eliminate choice (A). The Voting Rights Act does not address election funding, so eliminate choice (B). Felony disenfranchisement does exist in the United States, but was not established by the Voting Rights Act; eliminate choice (C). In closed primaries, only members of that party can vote, so choice (E) is not accurate.

14. **B** In *Roe v. Wade*, the Court ruled that a woman's right to have an abortion is protected under the due process clause, which protects one's right to liberty. The right to liberty was interpreted to include privacy in the decision to abort a fetus. *Bakke v. Regents of the University of California* was an affirmative action case, *Gideon v. Wainwright* was a criminal defense case, *Muller v. Oregon* was a discrimination and labor law case, and *Marbury v. Madison* was a judicial review case. Accordingly, all choices except choice (B) can be eliminated.

15. **C** The Free Exercise Clause states that "Congress shall make no law...prohibiting the free exercise thereof." In cases such as *Reynolds v. United States*, the court ruled that polygamy was not permissible, even though it was a Mormon religious practice. The establishment clause prevents the government from establishing a state religion. The elastic clause gives Congress the power to make laws necessary to carry out its duties and enforce its powers. The full faith and credit clause states that judicial proceedings of one state must be respected by other states. The supremacy clause establishes the Constitution and federal statutes as the supreme law of the United States. Accordingly, all choices except choice (C) can be eliminated.

16. **E** *Plessy v. Ferguson* was a case involving a man of mixed-race heritage to leave the "whites only" car of a train and sit in the "colored" car. The court upheld this form of segregation and stated that as long as there was an equal option available, refusal to allow someone of mixed-race to be served in a "white only" establishment was permissible. Choice (B) describes *Brown v. Board of Education*, which overturned *Plessy v. Ferguson*, so it can be eliminated. Choices (A), (C), and (D) are all unrelated to "separate but equal" and should be eliminated.

Drill 2

1. **E** *Mapp v. Ohio* was a Fourth Amendment case involving the collection of evidence in a way that violates constitutional rights. *Gitlow v. New York, Schenck v. United States,* and *Brandenburg v. Ohio* were all freedom of speech cases. *Engel v. Vitale* was a case concerning the establishment clause and prayer in public schools. Accordingly, eliminate all choices except choice (E).

2. **D** Choice (A) describes *stare decisis*, choice (B) describes federalism, choice (C) describes a writ of *certiorari*, and choice (E) describes the exclusionary rule. Accordingly, all choices except choice (D) can be eliminated.

3. **A** In *Glass v. Louisiana* (1985), the Court ruled that electrocution does not violate the prohibition on cruel and unusual punishment stated in the Eight Amendment. Choice (B) was ruled in *Baze v. Rees* (2008), choice (C) was ruled in *Atkins v. Virginia* (2002), choice (D) was ruled in *Kennedy v. Louisiana* (2008), and choice (E) was ruled in *Roper v. Simmons* (2005). All of those choices can be eliminated.

4. **B.** The Voting Rights Act of 1965 must be renewed. Most recently in 2006, George W. Bush extended it for 25 years. Every other answer choice accurately describes the Act.

5. **C** In *Brown v. Board of Education of Topeka*, the Court ruled that the doctrine of "separate but equal" violated the equal protection clause of the Fourteenth Amendment, overturning *Plessy v. Ferguson*. *Planned Parenthood v. Casey* was a case that challenged abortion regulations, *Gideon v. Wainwright* was a case concerning the right to an attorney, *Tinker v. Des Moines* was a case concerning the First Amendment rights of students in public schools, and *Lemon v. Kurtzman* dealt with the establishment clause. Accordingly, all choices except choice (C) can be eliminated.

6. **D** Earl Warren's tenure as chief justice of the Supreme Court is best characterized as a broad expansion of the civil liberties outline in the Bill of Rights. The Warren Court saw the right to privacy as a recurring trend in the Constitution. The right to privacy was cited in the Warren Court's decision against bans on contraception (*Griswold v. Connecticut*). The Rehnquist Court is known for a more conservative and narrow interpretation of these rights, so choice (A) is incorrect. The Taney Court is most remembered for denying citizenship rights to free blacks in the *Dred Scott* case, so choice (C) is not true. Choice (C) is incorrect because not only did the Taft Court largely focus on business issues, but the few cases they decided on privacy actually restricted privacy rights (*Carroll v. United States* allowed police probable cause searches in automobiles). The Marshall Court was best known for *Marbury v. Madison*, a judicial review, not privacy rights, case. Choice (E) is incorrect.

7. **A** *Texas v. Johnson* is a landmark First Amendment case that upholds flag-burning as a constitutionally protected act. Much of our understanding of the rights of the accused can be attributed to Earl Warren's term as chief justice. The Warren Court ruled that one must be read his or her rights upon arrest (*Miranda v. Arizona*), one has the right to be provided with legal counsel following arrest (*Gideon v. Wainwright*), one's refusal to testify in his or her own trial may not be used as evidence toward his or her guilt (*Griffin v. California*), and that evidence gathered illegally cannot be used in trial (*Mapp v. Ohio*), making choices (B), (C), (D), and (E) incorrect.

8. **B** The Warren Court was seen as having a more liberal view of civil liberties and civil rights. By contrast, the Rehnquist Court had a more narrow view. The Warren Court decided to integrate schools (*Brown v. Board of Education*) and expand the rights of the accused (*Miranda v. Arizona*), while the Rehnquist Court limited the scope of the Civil Rights Act (*Alexander v. Sandoval*) and the rights of the accused (*Minnesota v. Dickerson*). The Burger Court, much to the surprise of the Nixon Administration that nominated Warren Burger to reverse the decisions of the Warren Court, actually furthered many of the Warren Court's precedents. Eliminate choice (A). The Taft, White, and Vinson Courts were all previous to the Warren Court, so choices (C), (D), and (E) are incorrect.

Free-Response Question 1

Students may earn a total of five points on this question. One point is available for part (a), two for part (b), and two for part (c).

Part (a) asks you describe the trend shown in the chart. You will earn one point for indicating that the percentage of African Americans and Hispanics has been increasing over time. You could also indicate that the representation of these minority groups increased exponentially over time or that African American representation has grown faster than Hispanic representation.

Part (b) asks for descriptions of two barriers that limit the percent of members of Congress who belong to minority groups. Among the options you can discuss are

- Incumbency advantage
- Resources needed to run a successful campaign
- Gerrymandering
- Electoral qualifications
- Winner-take-all districts
- English language ballots
- ID requirements for voters
- Voter intimidation or illegal disenfranchisement

Be sure to describe the connection of the barriers you choose to the number of minorities in Congress. You will not receive credit if you only identify the barrier.

Part (c) asks you to explain the impact of two pieces of legislation on the number of minority voters. To earn credit for the first, you must state that the Voting Rights Act eliminated many of the voter registration requirements, such as literacy tests, and established federal oversight of elections to help abolish voter discrimination. To earn credit for the second, you must state that the Twenty-fourth Amendment abolished the poll tax. The poll tax was a barrier to voting among lower income populations, and minority populations make up a disproportionate amount of lower income populations.

Drill 3

1. **B**   The Fourteenth Amendment was adopted in 1868, yet Jim Crow Laws were in existence until the Civil Rights Act of 1964. The Fourteenth Amendment is a relatively long document covering many seemingly unrelated post-Civil War issues. The citizenship and equal protection clauses recognized that all people born in the United States were to be granted the rights and protections of the Constitution, so eliminate choices (A) and (E). Because of the enormous financial debt following the Civil War, the United States included a validity of public debt clause in the Fourteenth Amendment, making the country responsible to pay all of its debts. Eliminate choice (C). The due process clause led to the incorporation of the Bill of Rights—a process that began to require individual states to protect those rights. Eliminate choice (E).

2. **C**   Almost immediately following the passage of the Civil Rights Act in 1964, challenges to the law reached the Supreme Court. In both 1964, the Supreme Court ruled in both *Heart of Atlanta Motel v. United States* and *Katzenbach v. McClung*, that Congress passed the Civil Rights Act within its jurisdiction of the Commerce Clause (Article II, Section 8). The earlier Civil Rights Act of 1875 was struck down in 1883. Since the Fourteenth Amendment was not an adequate defense of that previous law in relation to privately owned businesses, lawmakers decided to utilize the Commerce Clause in the 1964 Civil Rights Act. Eliminate choice (D). Choice (A) is incorrect because the Civil Rights Act was not a case of free speech. Choice (C) is wrong because the citizenship clause is part of the Fourteenth Amendment and not a justification for the Civil Rights Act. Choice (E) is incorrect, because the Act came from Congress, not the president.

3. **D**   Both *Schenck* and *Brandenburg* dealt with the limits of free speech in potentially dangerous situations, so choice (B) is wrong. In *Schenck*, the court used the doctrine of "clear and present danger" to demonstrate that Mr. Schenck's speech was not protected. The Court further defined this doctrine with the concept of "imminent lawless action" in the *Brandenburg* case, allowing Mr. Brandenburg First Amendment protection. *Brandenburg* was not a case of hate speech, even though Mr. Brandenburg was a member of the Ku Klux Klan. Eliminate choices (A) and (E). Neither party created a riot, so choice (C) is incorrect.

4. **E**   *Plessy v. Ferguson* interpreted the Fourteenth Amendment with a doctrine of "separate but equal," so choice (C) is incorrect. This doctrine was overturned in 1954 when *Brown v. Board of Education* mandated that separate schools are not equal. The Civil Rights Act and Voting Rights Acts were passed ten years after the *Brown* decision, and likely were only possible with the Court protection of the *Brown* decision, so choices (A) and (B) are incorrect. *Katzenbach v. McClung* was one of the first challenges to the Civil Rights Act of 1964. The Supreme Court upheld the law. Eliminate choice (D).

5. **D**   *Brown v. the Board of Education* was a landmark case that rejected the application of the doctrine of "separate but equal." *Bethel v. Fraser* and *Morse v. Frederick* were cases dealing with the freedom of speech in school, so choices (A) and (B) are incorrect. *Abington School District v. Schempp* dealt with prayer in public schools, so eliminate choice (C). *Epperson v. Arkansas* decided that the teaching of human evolution could not be banned in schools, so choice (E) is incorrect.

6. **E**   In *Griswold v. Connecticut*, the Supreme Court struck down a Connecticut law banning the use of contraceptives based on a right to marital privacy, making choice (E) the correct answer. *Lemon v. Kurtzman* created a three-part test to determine a potential violation of the establishment clause (which bans the establishment of a state religion). *Furman v. Georgia* (temporarily) put a stop to all death penalty punishments. *Mapp v. Ohio* extended the exclusionary rule, which bars improperly obtained evidence from being presented in a criminal trial, from federal-level courts to state-level

courts. *Escobedo v. Illinois* affirmed a criminal defendant's right to a lawyer. None of choices (A), (B), (C), or (D) is based on the right to privacy.

7. **A** There is some vocabulary in this question: an "indigent defendant" is one who cannot afford an attorney. In 1963, the Warren Court (so-called because Earl Warren was the chief justice) held that states must provide attorneys to indigent defendants in the case of *Gideon v. Wainwright*, making choice (A) the correct answer. Choice (B) is incorrect because *Roper v. Simmons* was a 2005 case that held the death penalty unconstitutional for crimes committed by minors. Choice (C) is incorrect because the Court ruled against racial segregation in schools in *Brown v. Board of Education*. Choice (D) is incorrect because the Court found in *Mapp v. Ohio* that state courts must abide by the exclusionary rule and disallow improperly obtained evidence. Choice (E) is incorrect because the Court found in *Miranda v. Arizona* that defendants must be informed of their legal rights before they are arrested.

8. **A** The quote from the question comes right from the First Amendment, making choice (A) correct. The text of the First Amendment prohibits Congress from making laws establishing a state religion or prohibiting the exercise of religion. It also prohibits laws restricting speech or the press. The First Amendment protects the right of assembly and the right to "petition the government for a redress of grievances."

Free-Response Question 1

Students may earn a total of five points on this question. Two points are available for part (a) and three for part (b).

Part (a) asks you two explain two methods that were used to discourage African Americans from voting. To earn credit, your answer must mention two of the following:

- Poll taxes—a fee that had to be paid in order to vote. Many African Americans could not afford this fee.
- White primaries—allowing only whites to vote in primary elections, thus discouraging African Americans from voting in the general election and not allowing them to have a say in the candidates.
- Grandfather clause—If someone's grandfather was eligible to vote before 1867, that person could vote without taking the literacy test. This clause enabled illiterate whites to vote and ensured that blacks could not vote.

Part (b) asks you to describe other ways that African Americans participated in politics. You must link those methods to changes in civil rights. To earn credit, your answer must mention three of the following:

- Civil disobedience—refusing to follow a law (e.g. Rosa Parks)
- Litigation—court cases to stop discrimination (e.g. *Brown v. Board of Education*)
- Protests and boycotts—staging a rally in order to promote a cause or refusing to by a product of service (e.g. the Montgomery bus boycott)
- Participation in special interest groups—joining together to promote a cause (e.g., the NAACP or ACLU)
- Participating in elections in ways other than voting—donating funds or campaigning for a candidate (e.g., Martin Luther King Jr.'s civil rights campaigns)

Drill 4

1. **D**   Decided in 1896, *Plessy v. Ferguson* found that the Fourteenth Amendment's Equal Protection Clause permitted institutions such as schools to have separate, but equal, facilities. Choice (A) is incorrect because it describes the Court's ruling in *Brown v. Board of Education* (1954), which overturned *Plessy*. Choice (B) is incorrect because it articulates the Court's finding in *Heart of Atlanta Motel, Inc. v. United States* (1964). Choice (E) is incorrect because it expresses the Court's ruling in *Katzenbach v. McClung* (1964). Choice (C) is incorrect because the Court hasn't issued an affirmative action ruling as clearly stated as in choice (C): instead, the Court has focused on the rationale and motivation behind affirmative action plans.

2. **C**   State-sponsored prayer in a public school would directly violate the First Amendment's establishment clause, which prohibits the government from establishing an official religion. The free exercise clause gives people the freedom to practice their religions without government interference, so eliminate choice (E). The equal protection clause refers to the Fourteenth Amendment's protection of equality among races, so eliminate choice (A). The necessary and proper clause gives Congress the power to execute its Constitutional duties, so eliminate choice (B). Finally, the interstate commerce clause gives Congress the power to regulate interstate trade, so eliminate choice (D).

3. **E**   The Twenty-fourth Amendment (1964) eliminated poll taxes, which had prevented many minority individuals from voting. Choice (A) is incorrect because slavery was prohibited by the Thirteenth Amendment (1865). Choice (B) is incorrect because the sale of alcohol was banned by the Eighteenth Amendment (1919), which was repealed by the Twenty-first Amendment (1933). Choice (C) is incorrect because immediate congressional pay increases were prohibited by the Twenty-seventh Amendment (1992), which is the most recent amendment to the Constitution. Choice (D) is incorrect because the Twenty-second Amendment (1951) established the two-term limit for presidents, in response to Franklin Roosevelt's four terms in office in during the 1930s and 1940s.

4. **B**   Section 5 of the Voting Rights Act (VRA) requires that states with a history of disenfranchising voters obtain authorization from the Department of Justice or a panel of federal judges before making changes to election laws or procedures: this is known as the "preclearance" requirement of the

VRA. Section 4(b) of the VRA determined which states were subject to the preclearance requirement. However, the future of the VRA has been place in doubt: the Supreme Court's 2013 ruling in *Shelby County v. Holder* struck down the Section 4(b) formula as outdated. Without Section 4(b) in effect, no states are subject to the preclearance requirement; only if Congress revises Section 4(b) will any states require preclearance of changes to voting procedures. The Twenty-fourth Amendment, which was enacted a year before the VRA, prohibited poll taxes, so eliminate choice (A). The practice of requesting voter identification cards is still allowed under federal law, so choice (C) is incorrect. The federal government oversees the enforcement of the VRA, making choice (D) wrong. Choice (E) is wrong because African Americans have won elections to the House and Senate since Reconstruction.

5. **D** In *Ring v. Arizona* (2002), the Supreme Court ruled that only juries were allowed to decide death sentences. The Supreme Court has made quite a few decisions regarding capital punishment, so choice (A) is incorrect. States may execute convicts by means other than lethal injection, so eliminate choice (B). When the national moratorium on the death penalty was lifted in 1976, states were allowed to resume executions only if they established a bifurcation process. In such a process, a capital case was split into two parts: the first to determine guilt and the second to determine the sentence. Therefore, choice (C) is incorrect. Choice (E) is incorrect since the Supreme Court has upheld states' use of the death penalty at various times (e.g. *Gregg v. Georgia*).

6. **E** Starting in the 1920s, and continuing for decades, the Supreme Court revisited many protections that are covered by the Bill of Rights. The Supreme Court ruled that the Due Process Clause of the Fourteenth Amendment applies federal protections to state laws. The Equal Protection Clause of the Fourteenth Amendment had been visited by the Court on a variety of occasions prior to this case, so eliminate choice (A). Choice (B) is irrelevant to this case. The Supreme Court cannot overturn constitutional amendments, so choice (C) is incorrect. The text of the Fourteenth Amendment clearly states that naturalized citizens receive the protections of the Constitution, so eliminate choice (E).

7. **C** *Powell v. Alabama* established that a defendant has the right to a lawyer in death penalty cases and *Gideon v. Wainwright* established that defendants have the right to a lawyer in all felony cases. Only one dealt with capital punishment, so choice (A) is incorrect. Choice (B) is wrong because the Supreme Court issues a writ of *certiorari* for each appeal it hears. Only *Gideon* was argued in front of the Warren Court, so choice (D) is incorrect. Neither case dealt with the First Amendment, so eliminate choice (E).

8. **E** The doctrine set forth in *Plessy* was that separate facilities based on racial segregation (in this case a train car) did not violate the Equal Protection Clause of the Fourteenth Amendment: hence the lasting phrase from this case, "separate but equal." This doctrine led to a series of statutes, known as Jim Crow laws, to pop up around the country, particularly in the South. These laws prohibited interaction between whites and blacks in public accommodations. Choice (A) is incorrect because incorporation first took effect with *Gitlow v. New York* (1925). The racial integration of public

schools was the result of *Brown v. Board of Education*, which effectively overturned "separate but equal." Eliminate choice (B). Choice (C) is incorrect because African Americans became enfranchised with the ratification of the Fifteenth Amendment. Choice (D) is incorrect as *Plessy* did not address any issue relating to hate speech.

Free Response Question 1

Students may earn a total of six points on this question. Two points are available for part (a), two for part (b), and two for part (c).

Part (a) asks for the clauses in the First Amendment related to freedom of religion. To earn the first point, you must state that the Establishment Clause is the part of the First Amendment that forbids the government to establish religion. To earn the second point, you must state that the Free Exercise Clause is the part of the First Amendment that ensures people the right to practice their religion.

Part (b) asks you to describe one court case related to the Establishment clause and one related to the Free Exercise clause. To earn the first point, you must write about one of the following:

Establishment:

- *Engel v. Vitale* (1962) struck down mandatory school prayer.
- *Lemon v. Kurtzman* (1971) ruled that the state could not subsidize part of the salaries of teachers in religious schools, even of those teachers instructing in secular subjects.
- *McCreary v. ACLU of KY* (2005) upheld right to display 10 Commandments in a public school because they also have secular importance.

To earn the second point, you must write about one of the following:

Free Exercise:

- *Reynold v. United States* (1879) rejected the right to practice polygamy.
- *Employment Division, State of Oregon v. Smith* (1990) ruled that a ban on peyote did not violate the First Amendment.
- *Church of the Lukumi Babalu Aye v. Hialeah* (1993) ruled that banning ritual slaughters among practitioners of Santeria did not violate the First Amendment.

Part (c) asks for two methods through which political institutions can influence the rulings of the Supreme Court. Your answer does not have to be limited to rulings concerning religion, and you do not need to specify which institutions take which action. To earn credit, you can describe any of the following:

- The president's ability to appoint judges whose beliefs align with his or her party's agenda
- Passing a constitutional amendment that supersedes Supreme Court rulings
- Refusing to enforce a Supreme Court decision within a local or state judiciary
- Passing local or state legislation that contradicts a ruling of the Supreme Court
- Altering appellate jurisdiction so cases are reviewed by judges that are more aligned with one's beliefs

Part V
Practice Exam

Chapter 15
Practice Test

AP® U.S. Government and Politics Exam

SECTION I: Multiple-Choice Questions

DO NOT OPEN THIS BOOKLET UNTIL YOU ARE TOLD TO DO SO.

At a Glance

Total Time
45 minutes
Number of Questions
60
Percent of Total Grade
50%
Writing Instrument
Pencil required

Instructions

Section I of this examination contains 60 multiple-choice questions. Fill in only the ovals for numbers 1 through 60 on your answer sheet.

Indicate all of your answers to the multiple-choice questions on the answer sheet. No credit will be given for anything written in this exam booklet, but you may use the booklet for notes or scratch work. After you have decided which of the suggested answers is best, completely fill in the corresponding oval on the answer sheet. Give only one answer to each question. If you change an answer, be sure that the previous mark is erased completely. Here is a sample question and answer.

Sample Question Sample Answer

Chicago is a   Ⓐ ● Ⓒ Ⓓ Ⓔ
(A) state
(B) city
(C) country
(D) continent
(E) village

Use your time effectively, working as quickly as you can without losing accuracy. Do not spend too much time on any one question. Go on to other questions and come back to the ones you have not answered if you have time. It is not expected that everyone will know the answers to all the multiple-choice questions.

About Guessing

Many candidates wonder whether or not to guess the answers to questions about which they are not certain. Multiple choice scores are based on the number of questions answered correctly. Points are not deducted for incorrect answers, and no points are awarded for unanswered questions. Because points are not deducted for incorrect answer, you are encouraged to answer all multiple-choice questions. On any questions you do not know the answer to, you should eliminate as many choices as you can, and then select the best answer among the remaining choices.

This page intentionally left blank.

UNITED STATES GOVERNMENT AND POLITICS

Section I

Time—45 minutes

60 Questions

Directions: Each of the questions of incomplete statements below is followed by five suggested answers or completions. Select the one that is best in each case and then fill in the corresponding oval on the answer sheet.

1. The primary point of disagreement between Federalists and Anti-Federalists was over

    (A) whether representation in Congress should be equal among states or proportional to population
    (B) the strength of the federal government relative to the states
    (C) the future of the slave trade
    (D) whether people had inalienable rights
    (E) the future location of the nation's capital

2. All of the following statements about gerrymandering are true EXCEPT that it

    (A) favors incumbent candidates over challengers
    (B) can divide like-minded voters into several districts to reduce their influence
    (C) has been allowed by the Supreme Court in some instances
    (D) increases the control voters have over their elected officials
    (E) can group members of a racial minority into a single district

3. Federalism is a principle of government in which

    (A) power is shared between the national government and state governments
    (B) states have equal representation in the national government
    (C) individual liberties are guaranteed by a Bill of Rights
    (D) legislative, executive, and judicial powers are separated
    (E) states give their law-making powers over to the national government

4. Which of the following is the best illustration of "pork barrel" legislation?

    (A) A federal agency is created to ensure the safety of food and animal products.
    (B) A bill can be passed only if a majority of Congresspersons from rural districts approve of it.
    (C) A senator refuses to vote for a tax increase without a corresponding decrease in spending.
    (D) A federal program provides free lunches to schoolchildren of low-income families.
    (E) A member of Congress inserts a provision into a bill to secure funding for a project in his or her district.

5. An appointment to which of the following offices is NOT subject to confirmation by the U.S. Senate?

    (A) Securities and Exchange commissioner
    (B) Secretary of the Interior
    (C) White House Chief of Staff
    (D) Administrator of the Environmental Protection Agency
    (E) Chair of the Federal Deposit Insurance Corporation

6. The opposition of the American Civil Liberties Union (ACLU), the National Association of Women Lawyers (NAWL), and the American Federation of Labor and Congress of Industrial Organizations (AFL-CIO) to Samuel Alito's 2006 nomination to the Supreme Court is an example of

    (A) realignment
    (B) coalition building
    (C) impeachment
    (D) a recall election
    (E) a voter drive

GO ON TO THE NEXT PAGE.

7. Which of the following does the Supreme Court NOT have the power to override?

   (A) Constitutional amendments
   (B) Presidential executive orders
   (C) Laws passed by Congress
   (D) Laws passed by state legislatures
   (E) Decisions of state courts

8. Which of the following does NOT appear in the Constitution?

   (A) The Electoral College
   (B) Political parties
   (C) Separation of powers
   (D) The term length for members of Congress
   (E) Supremacy of the federal law over state law

9. Which of the following best describes the balance the Supreme Court has struck between the establishment clause and the free-exercise clause?

   (A) Freedom of speech is protected except in certain situations, such as yelling "fire" in a crowded theater.
   (B) Once a church has been recognized by the federal government, its tax-exempt status can never be revoked.
   (C) Once Congress has created an administrative agency, that agency can be dissolved only by a constitutional amendment.
   (D) State-sponsored prayer during school hours is prohibited, but voluntary prayer by student groups before school is allowed.
   (E) Religious freedom allows people to avoid paying taxes.

10. Which principle was established by the Supreme Court's decision in *Marbury v. Madison*?

    (A) One man, one vote
    (B) Separate but equal
    (C) Judicial review
    (D) Right to privacy
    (E) Freedom of expression

11. Divided government frequently results in

    (A) reapportionment of voting districts
    (B) amendments to the Constitution
    (C) conflict between states and the federal government
    (D) an expansion of executive power
    (E) delays in the confirmation of those nominated to be ambassadors

12. In which of the following cases did the Supreme Court decision establish the "separate but equal" doctrine of state-sponsored racial segregation?

    (A) *Plessy v. Ferguson*
    (B) *McCulloch v. Maryland*
    (C) *Gibbons v. Ogden*
    (D) *Brown v. Board of Education*
    (E) *Gideon v. Wainwright*

13. Which of the following describes a core principle of the Constitution as it was written in 1787?

    (A) Direct democracy
    (B) Checks and balances
    (C) Equal representation
    (D) Unitary government
    (E) Universal suffrage

14. The legal principle that instructs judges to follow established precedent when deciding cases is commonly referred to as

    (A) *certiorari*
    (B) *de jure*
    (C) *ex post facto*
    (D) *stare decisis*
    (E) *de facto*

15. Federal election laws are designed to achieve all of the following EXCEPT

    (A) require disclosure of campaign donations
    (B) prevent campaigns from issuing "attack" ads
    (C) limit campaign contributions
    (D) require disclosure of campaign expenditures
    (E) provide public financing of presidential campaigns

16. Which of the following statements about the House of Representatives is true?

    (A) All revenue bills must originate in the Senate before moving to the House.
    (B) Representation in the House is allocated equally among the states, while representation in the Senate is allocated proportional to population.
    (C) The Speaker of the House wields less power than the president *pro tempore* of the Senate.
    (D) The House allows for unlimited debate, while the Senate does not.
    (E) The House has a Committee on Ways and Means, while the Senate does not.

GO ON TO THE NEXT PAGE.

17. According to the Constitution, who determines voter eligibility requirements?

    (A) The president
    (B) Congress
    (C) State legislatures
    (D) Federal administrative agencies
    (E) The Supreme Court

18. Which of the following is NOT part of the "iron triangles" that influence public policy-making?

    (A) House committees
    (B) Senate committees
    (C) The courts
    (D) Bureaucratic agencies
    (E) Interest groups

19. Which of the following is the most direct result of an electoral system with single-member districts?

    (A) Proliferation of many small parties
    (B) A balance of power that favors the president over Congress
    (C) A persistent third-party presence
    (D) Development of a two-party system
    (E) Elected officials who are more responsive to voter demands

20. Which of the following court decisions did NOT deal with the First Amendment?

    (A) *Roe v. Wade*
    (B) *New York Times v. United States*
    (C) *DeJonge v. Oregon*
    (D) *Dennis v. United States*
    (E) *Engel v. Vitale*

21. Which of the following statements about political action committees (PACs) is most accurate?

    (A) They may only campaign for issues, not for individual candidates
    (B) Their activities are not regulated by the Federal Election Commission (FEC)
    (C) Their activities are limited to national presidential elections
    (D) They raise money to influence federal, state, and local elections
    (E) They may not be formed by corporations, unions, or other special interest groups

22. Which of the following is NOT a way in which the powers of the executive branch are balanced by the legislative branch?

    (A) The Senate may use the filibuster to block an executive order.
    (B) Congress may impeach and convict a president for "high crime and misdemeanors."
    (C) The Senate can decline to ratify a treaty.
    (D) The Senate can decline to approve a president's nominee for the Supreme Court.
    (E) The Congress may refuse the president's request to declare war.

23. The attorney general is the head of which of the following entities?

    (A) The Senate Judiciary Committee
    (B) The Department of Justice
    (C) The Department of State
    (D) The Judge Advocate General's Corps
    (E) The Central Intelligence Agency

24. Which of the following is an example of an implied power of the Congress?

    (A) regulation of interstate commerce
    (B) borrowing money on the credit of the United States
    (C) oversight of executive branch agencies
    (D) declarations of war
    (E) establishment of a post office

25. If no presidential candidate receives a majority of the Electoral College vote, then who becomes the president?

    (A) The candidate who wins the popular national vote
    (B) The incumbent vice president of the United States
    (C) Whomever is selected by the United States Supreme Court
    (D) The president *pro tempore* of the Senate
    (E) The candidate who wins the majority of votes in the House

GO ON TO THE NEXT PAGE.

26. The No Child Left Behind Act, which established educational standards that states must meet to receive federal educational funding, is an example of which of the following?

   (A) A federal mandate
   (B) A constitutional amendment
   (C) Affirmative action
   (D) Tort reform
   (E) A government sponsored enterprise

27. Unlike in a closed primary election, in an open primary election

   (A) voters select the winner by caucus instead of by individual ballots
   (B) the election results are not binding
   (C) any registered voter may participate, regardless of party affiliation
   (D) voters may register to vote on the day of the election
   (E) voters may vote for more than one candidate

28. Political efficacy refers to the idea that

   (A) political parties can provide a check to the political influence wielded by corporations
   (B) individuals believe that they can influence the government through participation in the democratic process
   (C) the system of checks and balances ensures that the government is both efficient and productive
   (D) politicians have a duty to inform their constituents about the democratic process
   (E) government is most effective when the same party controls all three branches of government

29. An inherent power of the president is the power to

   (A) appoint a nominee for the U.S. Supreme Court
   (B) negotiate a treaty with another country
   (C) declare a state of emergency following a natural disaster
   (D) veto a bill passed by the U.S. Congress
   (E) appoint ambassadors while Congress is in recess

30. Which of the following is the most accurate statement about writs of *certiorari*?

   (A) Fewer than 5% of petitions for writs of *certiorari* are granted by the Supreme Court.
   (B) The Supreme Court grants writs of *certiorari* only when there is a "circuit split."
   (C) The lower court's ruling is overturned if the Supreme Court denies a writ of *certiorari*.
   (D) Only the solicitor general may petition for a writ of *certiorari*.
   (E) The attorney general may appeal a decision without petitioning for a writ of *certiorari*.

31. Which of the following statements best characterizes cooperative federalism?

   (A) The executive and legislative branches working on legislation together
   (B) The federal government granting power over a policy area to the states
   (C) Governments working with businesses to address an issue
   (D) Many states working together to address a regional issue
   (E) State and federal governments working on the same issue

32. Which of the following constitutional principles might be violated if the Environmental Protection Agency issued, enforced, and adjudicated all disputes regarding a new regulation?

   (A) Vertical federalism
   (B) Due process of law
   (C) Comity
   (D) Equal protection of the laws
   (E) Separation of powers

33. Which of the following is LEAST likely to explain low voter turnout for an election?

   (A) The preclearance provision of the Voting Rights Act
   (B) Low levels of political efficacy among registered voters
   (C) Regulations that require voters to show identification
   (D) The frequency with which state and local elections occur
   (E) The fact that elections are held on weekdays

GO ON TO THE NEXT PAGE.

34. A "motion for cloture" is used to

    (A) send a bill back to the House
    (B) override a presidential veto in the House
    (C) amend an appropriations bill in the House
    (D) end a filibuster and force a vote on a bill in the Senate
    (E) block a vote on a presidential appointee in the Senate

35. Which of the following statements about presidential elections since 1972 is most accurate?

    (A) Voters increasingly get their information from newspapers.
    (B) Voters have become more focused on individual candidates.
    (C) Elections have become dominated by special interest groups.
    (D) Voters increasingly vote based on a party's platform.
    (E) No candidate has won a majority of the popular vote.

36. The idea that the Bill of Rights applies to both federal and state governments by means of the Fourteenth Amendment is called

    (A) *mandamus*
    (B) *habeas corpus*
    (C) strict constructionism
    (D) comity
    (E) the doctrine of incorporation

37. Which of the following is the primary purpose of "motor voter" laws?

    (A) To increase turnout on election days
    (B) To make it easier for citizens to register to vote
    (C) To require that all voters know how to drive
    (D) To establish voter identification laws
    (E) To automatically register all licensed drivers to vote

38. Why has network news coverage become less diverse in recent years?

    (A) Increasing liberal bias in the news media
    (B) Increasing visibility for individual candidates on TV
    (C) Increasing concentration of ownership in the news media
    (D) Decreasing cost of political ads on TV
    (E) Decreasing cost of newspapers

39. Which of the following is true of appellate courts?

    (A) Appellate judges never use the *stare decisis* principle.
    (B) Appellate trials are usually jury trials.
    (C) Appellate judges usually decide the facts of a case.
    (D) About 90% of appellate cases involve criminal law.
    (E) Appellate judges review decisions of lower courts.

Opinions on Support for Congressional Gun Control Measures

Region	Men Favor	Men Oppose	Women Favor	Women Oppose
Northeast	56%	33%	58%	33%
Midwest	41%	48%	39%	49%
South	31%	56%	31%	57%
West	65%	26%	64%	27%

40. The preceding table most clearly shows a large difference of opinion based on

    (A) gender
    (B) region
    (C) age
    (D) income
    (E) race

41. Which of the following has the Supreme Court held about the death penalty?

    (A) The death penalty may only be imposed upon citizens.
    (B) Under some circumstances, the death penalty may not violate the Eighth Amendment.
    (C) Under some circumstances, the death penalty may violate the Third Amendment.
    (D) States may execute any adult regardless of intellectual disability.
    (E) The death penalty may only be imposed upon men.

GO ON TO THE NEXT PAGE.

42. Which of the following is an example of devolution?

    (A) Allowing states to decide how to meet federally mandated greenhouse gas emissions targets
    (B) A "race to the bottom" in which states compete with each other to have the fewest environmental regulations
    (C) A state that legalizes marijuana possession in conflict with federal law
    (D) A state being prevented from implementing a fuel efficiency standard that is more stringent than that set by the federal government
    (E) The federal government establishing a requirement that a state increase its drinking age to 21 in order to receive federal highway funding

43. An example of a categorical grant would be

    (A) money loaned by the federal government to cities to fund school maintenance
    (B) money given by the federal government to states without conditions
    (C) money loaned by the federal government to a private company to prevent it from failing
    (D) money given by the federal government to states to fund Head Start early education programs
    (E) tax deductions given by the federal government to private citizens who buy fuel efficient automobiles

44. The Voting Rights Act of 1965 has had which of the following effects?

    (A) States have been prohibited from establishing voter identification requirements.
    (B) Voters must now pass literacy tests before voting.
    (C) Voting participation for racial minority voters has increased.
    (D) The voting age was lowered from 21 to 18.
    (E) It overturned *Plessy v. Ferguson.*

45. Which of the following has been true of the Republican Party since the 1980s?

    (A) It has become aligned with civil libertarians.
    (B) It has come to be dominated by labor unions.
    (C) It has become more antagonistic to business interests.
    (D) Its membership has come to include environmental activists.
    (E) It has become more influenced by evangelical Christians.

46. Legislative oversight occurs when

    (A) congressional committees investigate and evaluate the performance of executive agencies and departments
    (B) a court is unwilling to break with precedent to overturn legislative acts
    (C) the Supreme Court declares laws or executive actions unconstitutional
    (D) an amendment to a bill is proposed that softens more objectionable elements of the bill
    (E) a bill passes both the Senate and the House of Representatives with at least a two-thirds majority

GO ON TO THE NEXT PAGE.

INDEPENDENT VOTERS AND PRESIDENTIAL ELECTIONS (1980-2012)

Percent of Independents Voting for Candidates, by Party

	2012	2008	2004	2000	1996	1992	1988	1984	1980
Democratic	42.3	51.1	52.4	44.3	48.7	39.2	42.6	33.0	29.8
Republican	50.1	48.5	47.5	48.6	33.4	30.4	57.1	66.5	55.2

Percent of Popular Vote Won, by Party
(Incumbents' results in *italics*)

	2012	2008	2004	2000	1996	1992	1988	1984	1980
Democratic	*51.1*	52.9	48.3	48.4	*49.2*	40.3	45.7	40.6	*41.0*
Republican	47.2	45.7	*50.7*	47.9	40.7	*37.5*	53.4	*58.8*	50.8
Other	*	*	*	*	8.4	18.9	*	*	6.6

*No third-party candidate won more than 5% of the popular vote in these elections.

47. The table above supports which of the following statements about independent voters during presidential elections?

   (A) Independent voters are more likely to support the incumbent when the incumbent is a Democrat.
   (B) Until 2000, the independent vote generally aligned with the popular vote.
   (C) The unpredictability of the independent voters is why politicians do not try to attract independent voters.
   (D) Republicans have won a plurality of independent votes whenever there was a viable third-party candidate.
   (E) The Republican Party would earn more votes if there were not independent voters.

48. The origination clause of the Constitution states that

   (A) the Bill of Rights must not be infringed upon by any state legislature
   (B) Congress and the president must jointly create the annual federal budget
   (C) revenue bills must be initiated in the House of Representatives
   (D) the Supreme Court has original jurisdiction over all constitutional matters
   (E) international treaties are to be written by the president

49. How many votes in the Senate must a presidential nominee to the Supreme Court receive in order to be confirmed?

   (A) Forty percent
   (B) Fifty-one percent
   (C) Fifty-five percent
   (D) Sixty percent
   (E) Seventy-five percent

50. Federal judges are subject to which of the following disciplinary actions?

   (A) Impeachment, conviction, and removal from office by Congress
   (B) Removal from office by the appointing President
   (C) Removal from office by the president-elect
   (D) Recall elections by citizens residing in the district over which the judge has jurisdiction
   (E) Establishment of an arbitrary term limit

51. Which of the following statements about interest groups is accurate?

   (A) They don't use campaign funding as a tactic to win favor with legislators.
   (B) They are more successful when their members all belong to the same political party.
   (C) They rarely cover issues that appeal to residents of more than one state.
   (D) They focus most of their lobbying efforts on state legislators.
   (E) They generally are not focused on appealing to a broad group of people.

GO ON TO THE NEXT PAGE.

52. Which of the following statements is true regarding delegates to presidential nomination conventions?

    (A) Delegates are generally more likely to register as third party voters at some point.
    (B) The majority of the general population is more educated than are delegates.
    (C) Delegates typically have little interest in politics.
    (D) Typically, the general population is less ideological than are delegates.
    (E) Usually, the general population is wealthier than are delegates.

53. What power was granted to the states by the Articles of Confederation but not by the Constitution?

    (A) Coining money
    (B) Authorizing constitutional amendments
    (C) Having representation in Congress
    (D) Appealing to the president to adjudicate disputes
    (E) Levying taxes

54. Which of the following categories of spending are paid without an appropriations bill?

    (A) Department of Education special acts and authorizations
    (B) Justice department budgets
    (C) Federal budget entitlements
    (D) Department of Defense funding
    (E) Housing and Urban development assistance

55. According to *Brown v. Board of Education* (1954), which of the following amendments was violated by the "separate but equal" doctrine that had been established in *Plessy v. Ferguson* (1896)?

    (A) First Amendment
    (B) Sixth Amendment
    (C) Ninth Amendment
    (D) Thirteenth Amendment
    (E) Fourteenth Amendment

56. Which of the following best predicts how someone will vote in an election?

    (A) The voter's gender
    (B) The voter's political party affiliation
    (C) The voter's socioeconomic status
    (D) The voter's religion
    (E) Where the voter lives

GO ON TO THE NEXT PAGE.

PARTY AFFILIATION IN THE UNITED STATES BASED ON EDUCATIONAL ATTAINMENT

Highest Level of Educational Attainment	Males		Females	
	Republicans	Democrats	Republicans	Democrats
Grade School	12%	85%	13%	87%
High School Diploma	13%	80%	21%	72%
Vocational Degree	24%	72%	28%	58%
College Degree	36%	64%	36%	52%
Master's Degree	49%	51%	30%	61%
Doctoral Degree	56%	34%	19%	70%

57. All of the following can be inferred from the table above EXCEPT:

    (A) Men who have attained a vocational degree are more likely to identify as Republicans than are those with only a high school diploma.
    (B) Men who have attained a doctoral degree are more likely to identify as Democrats than are those with only a college degree.
    (C) Women who have completed grade school and men who have attained a high school diploma are equally likely to identify as Republicans.
    (D) Men who have attained a Master's degree are less likely to identify as Republicans than they are to identify as Democrats.
    (E) Women who have attained a vocational degree are more likely to identify as Republicans than are men who have attained a vocational degree.

58. Which of the following would occur if Congress were to pass legislation and declare a recess, and the president took no action on the bill within ten days of its passage?

    (A) A line-item veto
    (B) A pocket veto
    (C) An adjournment
    (D) A writ of *certiorari*
    (E) Senatorial courtesy

59. Which of the following is not a special position held by a member of Congress?

    (A) President *pro tempore*
    (B) Speaker of the House
    (C) Congressional Management Foundation Chair
    (D) Minority Whip
    (E) Democratic Caucus Chairman

60. Interest groups are barred from taking part in which of the following activities?

    (A) Sending lawmakers to educational seminars
    (B) Giving tangible gifts to lawmakers
    (C) Providing research to government officials
    (D) Staging protests and boycotts
    (E) Filing lawsuits in federal courts

END OF SECTION I

This page intentionally left blank.

UNITED STATES GOVERNMENT AND POLITICS

Section II

Time—1 hour and 40 minutes

Directions: You have 100 minutes to answer all four of the following questions. Unless the directions indicate otherwise, respond to all parts of all four questions. It is suggested that you take a few minutes to plan and outline each answer. Spend approximately one-fourth of your time (25 minutes) on each question. Illustrate your essay with substantive examples where appropriate. Make certain to number each of your answers as the question is numbered below.

1. The framers of the U.S. Constitution created the American government to hinder any single faction from becoming too powerful. As a result, government power and responsibility divides many ways. One of these ways is through federalism, in which the national government has some powers, state governments have other powers, called reserved powers, and many powers are shared. While the framers' conception of division of power remains largely intact, the common source of the government power is the participation of citizens. Since the eighteenth century, some amendments to the U.S. Constitution increase opportunities for political participation by citizens.

    (a) Identify one power the U.S. Constitution expressly gives to the national government, but denies state governments.

    (b) Powers neither specifically granted to the federal government nor denied to state governments are reserved to the states by the Tenth Amendment. Identify one reserved power.

    (c) Identify two constitutional amendments that increased opportunities for political participation by citizens and explain how these amendments increased participation.

GO ON TO THE NEXT PAGE.

2. Citizens' personal characteristics play a large role in determining their political ideologies and attitudes.

    (a)   Define political ideology.

    (b)   Identify the political ideology commonly associated with the Democratic Party and describe one belief commonly held by people with that ideology.

    (c)   Identify the political ideology commonly associated with the Republican Party and describe one belief commonly held by people with that ideology.

    (d)   Choose two of the following factors and describe how each factor you choose influences people's ideology and political attitudes:
- Race/ethnicity
- Gender
- Income level

GO ON TO THE NEXT PAGE.

3. The political party that controls the majority is able to exert great influence on the legislative process. However, there are limits to the power exerted by the party in power.

    (a) Explain how each of the following gives the majority party an advantage in the legislative process.

- Speaker of the House selection
- Control of the Rules Committee
- Germaneness requirement

    (b) Explain how each of the following limits the power of the majority party in the Senate legislative process.

- Filibuster
- Senatorial hold
- Rider

GO ON TO THE NEXT PAGE.

From Where Do Americans Receive the News?

Percent of respondents who receive news
from only traditional media
(Television, radio, and/or print newspapers)

Age	2010	2012
18-24	21%	11%
25-29	32%	20%
30-39	27%	22%
40-49	40%	24%
50-64	46%	42%
65 and older	62%	60%

Source: Pew Research Center

4. News media play an important role in shaping public debate.

(a) Define the following terms.

- Public opinion
- Policy agenda

(b) Explain how the news media affect the policy agenda.

(c) Refer to the table above.

- Describe the difference in news consumption between those 18 to 24 years old and those 65 and older.
- Describe the change in news consumption among all age groups from 2010 to 2012.

END OF EXAMINATION

Chapter 16
Practice Test:
Answers and
Explanations

ANSWER KEY

Section I

1.	B
2.	D
3.	A
4.	E
5.	C
6.	B
7.	A
8.	B
9.	D
10.	C
11.	E
12.	A
13.	B
14.	D
15.	B
16.	E
17.	C
18.	C
19.	D
20.	A
21.	D
22.	A
23.	B
24.	C
25.	E
26.	A
27.	C
28.	B
29.	C
30.	A

31.	E
32.	E
33.	A
34.	D
35.	B
36.	E
37.	B
38.	C
39.	E
40.	B
41.	B
42.	A
43.	D
44.	C
45.	E
46.	A
47.	B
48.	C
49.	B
50.	A
51.	E
52.	D
53.	A
54.	C
55.	E
56.	B
57.	B
58.	B
59.	C
60.	B

EXPLANATIONS

Section I

1. **B** Federalists favored a strong central government, as opposed to the weak Congress created by the Articles of Confederation. Anti-Federalists preferred that power remain with the states. While choices (A) and (C) were issues raised during the Constitutional Convention, they were not the subject of the primary debates between Federalists and Anti-Federalists as states considered ratifying the Constitution.

2. **D** Gerrymandering is the drawing of voting district boundaries to achieve an electoral result that benefits the drawer. One common gerrymandering tactic is to "pack" members of a racial minority into a single district to minimize their effect on other districts; so eliminate choice (E). Another tactic is to "crack" members of a demographic group: in this case, a political party that draws its support from suburban voters may divide the region's urban voters into several districts where they will be outnumbered by suburban voters, thus eliminating the electoral influence of the urban voters; so eliminate choice (B). Districts are usually drawn to protect incumbents and make their seats "safe" from challengers, so eliminate choice (A). While the Supreme Court has placed restrictions on the use of gerrymandering (e.g. districts must be contiguous and must not deny representation to racial minorities), it has never outright banned it; eliminate choice (C). All of these methods of gerrymandering have the effect of reducing voters' influence on their representatives, which is why choice (D) is the best answer.

3. **A** This is the definition of the constitutional principle of federalism. Choice (B) describes how states are represented in the U.S. Senate. Choice (C) is true of the Constitution, but does not define federalism. Choice (D) describes the separation of powers included in the Constitution. Choice (E) is incorrect because while states share powers with the national government, in a federal system they do not give up all power.

4. **E** "Pork barrel" legislation refers to a law that establishes funding for a project in the member's home district in order to benefit his or her constituents. The name "pork barrel" does not refer to farming, so eliminate choices (A) and (B). Nor does it refer to food, so eliminate choice (D).

5. **C** The White House Chief of Staff is appointed by the president to manage White House affairs and advise the president, but is not subject to Senate approval. A president's nominee for any of the other positions must be approved by the Senate before the appointment takes effect.

6. **B** Coalition building is the cooperation of distinct groups with their own interests toward a common purpose. Choice (B) is the best because the ACLU, NAWL, and AFL-CIO believed Samuel Alito was too conservative to be allowed on the Supreme Court and worked together to oppose his nomination. Choice (A) is incorrect because realignment deals with voters switching political parties. Choice (C) is incorrect because impeachment means to remove someone from office. Choice

(D) is incorrect because federal judges and justices are not elected; therefore, they are not subject to recall elections. Choice (E) is incorrect because a voter drive registers people to vote.

7. A   Through its power of judicial review, the Supreme Court has the power to interpret the Constitution but not to override the Constitution or its Amendments; therefore, the best answer is choice (A). The Court's power of judicial review allows it to overturn laws passed by Congress and presidential actions, so eliminate choices (B) and (C). The supremacy clause of the Constitution gives the Supreme Court the power to overturn actions of state governments as well, so eliminate choices (D) and (E).

8. B   Political parties were not anticipated by the framers of the Constitution and are not mentioned in it, so the best answer is choice (B). Choice (A) is incorrect because the electoral college is mentioned in Article II, which explains how the president is elected. Choice (C) is incorrect because the Constitution laid out three branches of government and checks and balances among them. Choice (D) is incorrect because Article I, which addresses Congress, specifies the two-year and six-year terms for representatives and senators, respectively. Choice (E) is incorrect because Article VI, Clause 2 specifies that the Constitution and federal law are "the supreme law of the land;" this is often referred to as the "supremacy clause."

9. D   The First Amendment begins with "Congress shall make no law respecting an establishment of religion, or prohibiting the free exercise thereof…." The Supreme Court has interpreted this to mean that federal, state, and local governments cannot take actions that favor one religion over another or none at all (the establishment clause), and that government cannot interfere with the practice of religion (the free-exercise clause). Choice (D) is the best answer because it accurately describes the precedent established by the decisions in *Engel v. Vitale* (1962) and *Abington School District v. Schempp* (1963). Choice (A) is incorrect because it summarizes the decision in *Schenck v. United States* (1919), which addressed a free-speech issue. Choice (B) inaccurately describes the tax exempt status of religious organizations. Choice (C) is incorrect because Congress can pass a law to dissolve an administrative agency. Choice (E) inaccurately describes religious freedom.

10. C   The Supreme Court's decision in *Marbury v. Madison* was the first to overturn an act of Congress, establishing the precedent of judicial review. Thus, the best answer is choice (C). Choice (A) is incorrect because "one man, one vote" was established by the Court's 1964 decision in *Reynolds v. Sims*. Choice (B) is incorrect because "separate but equal" was established by the Court's 1896 decision in *Plessy v. Ferguson*; it was later overturned by the Court's 1954 decision in *Brown v. Board of Education*. Choice (D) is incorrect because a right to privacy was established in the Court's 1965 decision in *Griswold v. Connecticut*. Choice (E) is incorrect because a freedom of expression in based on the First Amendment's freedom of speech and has been hotly debated for the last century.

11. E   Divided government occurs when the president's political party does not hold a majority in both houses of Congress, creating more friction and less cooperation between the two branches. Because ambassadors are nominated by the president and must be confirmed by the Senate in order to serve, (E) is a frequent result when the president and the Senate are of different parties. Choice

(A) is incorrect because reapportionment occurs on the state level. Choice (B) is incorrect because passage of a constitutional amendment requires a two-thirds majority in each house of Congress, which is not significantly more likely in times of divided government. Choice (C) is incorrect because divided government creates conflict between branches of the federal government (or even bodies of Congress) but not between states and the federal government. Choice (D) is incorrect because during times of divided government, the opposition party in Congress limits the power of the president more than the president's party would.

12. **A**   Choice (A) is the best answer because the decision in *Plessy v. Ferguson* (1896) upheld a state law mandating racial segregation. Choice (B) is incorrect because *McCulloch v. Maryland* (1819) established that the Bank of the United States could not be taxed by the State of Maryland because of the supremacy clause in the Constitution. Choice (C) is incorrect because *Gibbons v. Ogden* (1824) reinforced the federal government's power to regulate interstate trade, citing the Constitution's commerce clause and supremacy clause. Choice (D) is incorrect because *Brown v. Board of Education* (1954) overturned the *Plessy v. Ferguson* decision. Choice (E) is incorrect because *Gideon v. Wainwright* (1963) mandated that states must provide an attorney for a defendant who cannot afford one.

13. **B**   The Constitution divides power among the legislative, executive, and judicial branches. Each branch can restrict, or "check," the actions of the others, establishing a "balance" that prevents tyranny. This makes choice (B) the best. Choice (A) is incorrect because the Constitution creates a republic, or representative democracy, in which decisions are made by elected representatives. Direct democracy empowers voters to make legislative decisions, such as ballot initiatives, referendums, and recall elections. This occurs in some states but not in the federal government. Choice (C) is incorrect because each state has equal representation in the Senate but representation in the House is proportional to population. The president is elected by the Electoral College, in which each state has a number of votes equal to its number of senators and representatives. Choice (D) is incorrect because only a central government exercises power in a unitary system: the Constitution establishes a system of federalism, in which power is shared between the federal government and the states. Choice (E) is incorrect because suffrage is the right to vote, and many people were not permitted to vote in 1787. Since then, the Fifteenth Amendment has extended suffrage to African American men, the Nineteenth Amendment has extended suffrage to women, and the Twenty-sixth Amendment has lowered the voting age to 18.

14. **D**   Precedent is the tradition of deciding cases in a matter consistent with the decisions of past courts. *Stare decisis*, Latin for "the decision stands," is the phrase associated with legal precedent, making choice (D) the best. Choice (A) is incorrect because a writ of *certiorari* is a request from the Supreme Court to a lower court for a case transcript; this writ is issued when the Court is considering hearing a case. Choices (B) and (E) are incorrect because *de jure* means "by law" and *de facto* means "in practice." This distinction has become important in cases dealing with segregation, which may not exist legally (*de jure*) but exist in reality (*de facto*). Choice (C) is incorrect because *ex*

post facto ("after the fact") describes a law that criminalizes an action after it has already occurred; the Constitution prohibits Congress from passing such laws.

15. **B** The Federal Election Campaign Acts of 1971 and 1974 created the Federal Election Commission (FEC). The FEC and subsequent laws have placed limits on how much money may be given to candidates and political parties, so eliminate choice (C). The FEC also requires campaigns to disclose information about their donations and expenditures, so eliminate choices (A) and (D). Presidential candidates who receive more than 10 percent of the vote in primary elections and agree to follow certain spending limits are eligible to receive matching funds for donations under $250; therefore, you should eliminate choice (E). There are no laws or FEC regulations barring "attack" ads, so the best answer is choice (B).

16. **E** Choice (A) is incorrect because all revenue (tax) bills must originate in the House. Choice (B) is incorrect because representation is proportional to population in the House and equal among states in the Senate. Choice (C) is incorrect because the president *pro tempore* of the Senate is a ceremonial role, while the Speaker of the House is a leadership role. Choice (D) is incorrect because the House plays strict time limits on debates, while the Senate allows for unlimited debate, as seen with the filibuster. Choice (E) is the best because the Senate Finance Committee is the equivalent of the House Ways and Means Committee.

17. **C** Article I, Section 4 grants the power to determine the "times, places, and manner of holding elections for senators and representatives" to the state legislatures; this makes choice (C) the best answer. The federal government may take corrective action when state election practices violate voters' rights (such as gerrymandering to reduce the influence of minority voters and literacy tests), but the primary responsibility falls on the states, so eliminate choices (A), (B), (D), and (E).

18. **C** "Iron triangles" are informal alliances that form as rules are developed by bureaucratic agencies. The three parties in an "iron triangle" are 1) the bureaucratic agency that writes the rules, so eliminate choice (D); 2) the congressional committees that oversee the agency, so eliminate choices (A) and (B); and 3) the affected industry and its interest groups, so eliminate choice (E). Choice (C) is incorrect because the courts are not involved in making public policy.

19. **D** Congressional districts are single-member districts: the candidate who wins the most votes is elected to office and the losing parties receive no representation. This is in contrast to party-proportional representation, in which, for example, a party that receives 10 percent of the vote takes 10 percent of the seats in parliament. In this "winner take all" situation, minor parties receive no representation, so eliminate choices (A) and (C). Instead, groups of voters congeal into two major parties in an effort to win a majority, making choice (D) the best answer. Because voters generally have only two choices in an election and the margin of victory doesn't matter, representatives are less responsive to voter demands; therefore, you can eliminate choice (E). Choice (B) is incorrect because single-member districts affect how representatives are elected but not the power they exercise in office.

20.   A   The First Amendment guarantees five freedoms: speech, religion, petition, press, and assembly. Choice (A) is the best answer because *Roe v. Wade* addressed a woman's right to an abortion. *New York Times v. United States*, as one would imagine from the name, deals with freedom of the press, so eliminate choice (B). Choice (C) is incorrect because *DeJonge v. Oregon* addresses freedom of assembly. Choice (D) is incorrect because *Dennis v. United States* addresses freedom of speech. Choice (E) is incorrect because *Engel v. Vitale* prohibited state-sponsored prayer in school.

21.   D   PACs are organized in order to campaign for individual candidates, pieces of legislation, or ballot measures. While PACs may campaign for issues, choice (A) is incorrect as they can do more than *just* campaign for issues. Choice (B) is incorrect as the FEC does regulate PAC activities. Choice (C) is incorrect as PACs may also campaign for state and local elections as well. Choice (E) is incorrect as corporations and unions are permitted to form PACs.

22.   A   The Senate uses the filibuster to block a vote on a bill; it does not affect executive orders. Choices (B), (C), and (D) are incorrect as Article II of the U.S. Constitution grants Congress the power to impeach and convict a president, the Senate the power to ratify treaties, and the Senate the power to refuse to approve a president's appointees. Choice (E) is incorrect as Article I of the U.S. Constitution grants the Senate the power to decline a president's request to declare war.

23.   B   The attorney general is appointed by the president and approved by the Senate to serve as the chief executive officer of the Department of Justice. Choice (A) is incorrect as the head of the Senate Judiciary Committee is a chairman or chairwoman. Choice (C) is incorrect as the Secretary of State heads up the State Department. Choice (D) is incorrect as the head of the Judge Advocate General's Corps is the Judge Advocate General. Choice (E) is incorrect as the head of the Central Intelligence Agency (CIA) is the Director of the CIA.

24.   C   Though Article II of the U.S. Constitution never enumerates oversight as a congressional power, such oversight is implicit in its power to pass laws and to appropriate funds. Choices (A), (B), (D), and (E) are all enumerated powers in Article II.

25.   E   Amendment XII of the U.S. Constitution states that if no candidate wins the majority of the vote in the Electoral College, the top three candidates are presented to the House, and whoever wins a majority becomes president. Choice (A) is incorrect as the popular vote has no official weight. Choices (B) and (D) are incorrect, as they are first and third, respectively, in line of succession if the president dies or is removed from office; their position does not affect the outcome of elections however. Choice (C) is incorrect as the U.S. Supreme Court plays no direct role in selecting the president.

26.   A   No Child Left Behind (NCLB) set requirements for states by the federal government and, therefore, is a federal mandate. Choice (B) is incorrect because NCLB did not change the constitution. Choice (C) is incorrect because affirmative action relates to efforts to remediate the effects of discrimination through admissions or hiring preferences. Choice (D) is incorrect because tort reform

refs to proposed changes in the civil justice system. Choice (E) is incorrect because a government-sponsored enterprise is a type of corporation created by the federal government.

27.   **C**   In an open primary, any registered voter can participate. For example, in an open Republican primary, Republicans, Democrats, and Independents can vote. However, in a closed Republican primary, only voters who are registered Republicans can vote. Choice (A) is incorrect as a caucus is not a type of primary. Choice (B) is incorrect as results of open primaries are binding. Choice (D) is incorrect because there is no difference in the registration deadlines of closed and open primaries. (Most states do not allow for same-day voter registration.) Choice (E) is incorrect as open primaries allow voters to select only one candidate.

28.   **B**   Political efficacy refers to the idea that private citizens can influence the government by voting and otherwise participating in the political process. Choices (A), (C), and (E) are incorrect because political efficacy refers to private citizens, not parties or branches of government. Choice (D) is incorrect because political efficacy does not assume that politicians must educate voters.

29.   **C**   Article II does not explicitly allow the president to declare a state of emergency. Rather, the power to declare a state of emergency is inferred from Article II, Section 3's "take care" clause: the president "shall take care that the laws be faithfully executed." Article II, Section 2 explicitly gives the president the power to appoint Supreme Court nominees, enter into treaties, and make recess appointments; thus, choices (A), (B), and (E) are incorrect. Choice (D) is incorrect because the presidential veto power is explicitly mentioned in the Presentment Clause (Article I, Section 7's description of the law-making process).

30.   **A**   Those who want the Supreme Court to hear their appeal must file a petition for a writ of *certiorari* with the Court. If four justices choose to hear a case, the Court will issue a writ of *certiorari*: the Court's official request for the transcript of a lower court case. The Supreme Court rarely grants writs of *certiorari*; for example, in 2009, the Court granted only 1.1 percent of petitions. Choice (B) is incorrect as the Court may grant a writ whenever it has jurisdiction and four justices decide to grant it. In general, if the Court denies a petition the lower court's ruling stands; eliminate choice (C). Choice (D) is incorrect as any citizen may petition the Court. Choice (E) is incorrect as the attorney general would petition the Court just as any other individual would.

31.   **E**   Cooperative federalism occurs when more than one level of government works together on a policy area. Choices (A), (C), and (D) are incorrect as federalism refers to the relationship between the federal and state governments. Choice (B) is incorrect as it describes "devolution."

32.   **E**   Separation of powers refers to the division of responsibility among the branches of government: the legislative branch creates laws, the executive branch enforces laws, and the judicial branch interprets laws. If the Environmental Protection Agency (EPA), which is an executive branch agency, performed all three functions, it would risk violating the separation of powers. Choice (A) is incorrect as federalism refers to the sharing of powers between levels of government. Choice (B) is incorrect as due process refers to the process required to deprive someone of his or her rights. Choice

(C) is incorrect as comity refers to legal reciprocity: the principle that different jurisdictions respect each other's legislative, executive, and judicial actions. Choice (D) is incorrect as equal protection requires that all citizens be treated the same under the law.

33. **A** The preclearance provision of the Voting Rights Act (VRA) requires that jurisdictions with a history of voter disenfranchisement gain approval from the Department of Justice before making any changes to their voting procedures; this has the effect of increasing, not decreasing, voter turnout. In 2013, the Supreme Court's ruling in *Shelby County v. Holder* put the future of the VRA in doubt. The Court struck down Section 4(b) of the VRA, which determines which states are subject to the preclearance requirement. Until Congress revises Section 4(b), no states are subject to the preclearance requirement. Since the preclearance provision, effective or not, would not reduce voter turnout, choice (A) is the best. Choices (B) is incorrect because "low levels of political efficacy" means voters don't believe they can affect the outcome of an election; therefore, low levels of political efficacy would decrease voter turnout. Because some voters don't have photo identification, laws that require voters to show identification prevent voters from casting their ballots; therefore, choice (C) should be eliminated. Choice (D) is incorrect because voters are less likely to vote when there are frequent elections. Voters are less likely to participate in weekday elections than in weekend elections since they must take time off work to vote on a weekday; therefore, choice (E) should be eliminated.

34. **D** A senator enacts a "motion for cloture" to end a filibuster and force a vote on a bill. Choices (A), (B), and (C) are incorrect as a motion for cloture occurs only in the Senate. Choice (E) is incorrect as it refers to a potential goal of a filibuster.

35. **B** Since 1972, voters have begun to vote more for the candidate than for the party. Choice (A) is incorrect as newspaper readership is on the decline. Choice (C) is incorrect as special interest groups have long played an important role in elections. Choice (D) is incorrect as this is the opposite of what has occurred. Choice (E) is incorrect as multiple presidents have won the majority of the popular vote.

36. **E** The doctrine of incorporation holds that the protections granted by the Bill of Rights apply to both state and federal government actions. Choices (A) and (B) are incorrect as *mandamus* and *habeas corpus* are judicial actions called "prerogative writs:" orders issued by one branch of government to another. Choice (C) is incorrect because this refers to the philosophy that the Constitution should be interpreted closely to the intent of the framers. Choice (D) is incorrect as comity refers to the idea that one court will recognize the decision of a court in a different jurisdiction.

37. **B** Motor voter laws allow individuals to register to vote when applying for a driver's license, thus making voter registration easier. Choice (A) is incorrect as "motor voter" laws are not directly related to voter turnout. Choice (C) is incorrect as there is no requirement that voters must drive. Choice (D) is incorrect as voter identification laws are separate from motor voter laws. Choice (E) is incorrect as both non-citizen residents and citizens under 18 can be licensed to drive but not eligible to vote.

38.   **C**   Choice (C) is the best answer because less diversity of media ownership leads directly to less diversity of news coverage. For example, a newspaper, radio station, and television channel may choose to cover three different events or provide three different perspectives on an issue. However, if they share the same owner, they're more likely to cover the same events and express the same ideas. The cost of political ads on TV is increasing, as is the cost of newspapers, so you can eliminate (D) and (E) right away. An increased presence of individual candidates giving individual viewpoints contributes to diversity in news coverage, so eliminate choice (B) too. Choice (A) is controversial—conservative media critics tend to see liberal bias in news media, for example, because most reporters hold liberal views. However, liberal critics point to the ownership of media outlets by large corporations and see a resulting conservative bias. Therefore, (A) is not the best choice and you can eliminate it.

39.   **E**   The use of the word "never" in choice (A) is too strong and should make you very suspicious of that choice. Appellate judges usually try to keep their decisions consistent with the decisions of past judges, a principle known as *stare decisis,* so eliminate (A). Appellate trials are decided by judges, not juries, and the judges decide issues of law, not the facts of the case, so (B) and (C) can go. While appellate cases are split between criminal law and civil law, the split is not as lopsided as 90/10 percent, so cross out (D). You should be left with (E), the correct answer, since a party who wants to appeal the decision of a lower court can bring the case to a higher appellate court.

40.   **B**   The chart measures opinions on support for congressional gun control measures as broken down by gender and region, so get rid of choices (C), (D), and (E). There isn't much gender difference within the regions: men's and women's results are within 1–2 percent of each other. The chart shows large differences among the regions (high support for gun control in the Northeast and West, low support in the Midwest and South), so go with choice (B).

41.   **B**   The Supreme Court has held that while the death penalty might constitute "cruel and unusual punishment" under some circumstances and thus violate the Eighth Amendment, in many cases it does not. Choices (A) and (E) are incorrect as the Supreme Court has held that noncitizens and women may be executed. Choice (C) is incorrect as the Third Amendment has to do with billeting troops and thus has nothing to do with the death penalty. Choice (D) is incorrect as the Supreme Court has held that the "mentally retarded" may not be executed.

42.   **A**   Devolution is the process by which the federal government allows states to make decisions that would otherwise be made at the federal level. Choice (B) is incorrect as it does not deal with a transfer of power. Choices (C) and (D) are incorrect because they deal with states attempting to act in conflict with federal law. Choice (E) is incorrect as the federal government is imposing a requirement upon the state by means of its Article I spending power.

43.   **D**   Categorical grants are grants given by the federal government that can be spent for specific purposes only. Choices (A) and (C) are incorrect because they describe loans instead of grants. Choice (B) is incorrect because it describes block grants. Choice (E) is incorrect because a tax deduction is not a grant.

44. **C** The Voting Rights Act removed restrictions that had prevented access to voting for many African Americans and other racial minorities. Choice (A) is incorrect as many states still have identification requirements. Choice (B) is incorrect as the Voting Rights Act actually prohibited literacy tests. Choice (D) is incorrect as the voting age was changed by the Twenty-sixth Amendment. Choice (E) is incorrect as *Plessy v. Ferguson* was overturned by *Brown v. Board of Education*.

45. **E** Since the 1980s, evangelical Christians have exerted more and more influence upon the positions of the Republican Party. Choice (A) is incorrect as civil libertarians are not necessarily associated with the Republicans more than Democrats. Choices (B) and (D) are incorrect as labor unions and environment activists are more associated with the Democratic Party. Choice (C) is incorrect as the Republican Party is generally considered more sympathetic to business interests.

46. **A** One of Congress's most important tasks, legislative oversight is used as a way of checking the power of the executive branch by having congressional committees investigate and evaluate the performance of executive agencies and departments. Choice (B) is incorrect as it describes the process of judicial restraint. Choice (C) is incorrect as it outlines the process of judicial review. Choice (D) is incorrect as it describes the function of a saving amendment. Choice (E) is incorrect because it doesn't relate the legislative branch to the executive branch in any way.

47. **B** The data in the tables show that the winner of the popular vote won a plurality (more than any other candidate) among independent voters from 1980 to 1996: the Republican candidates won the popular vote and a plurality of independent voters in 1980, 1984, and 1988; the Democratic candidate won the popular vote and a plurality of independent voters in 1992 and 1996. Then in 2000, correlation ends. The Democratic candidates won the popular vote in 2000, 2008, and 2012; however, a plurality of independent voters supported the Republican candidates in 2000 and 2012. In 2004, the Republican candidate won the popular vote in 2004, but a plurality of independents supported the Democratic candidate. Choice (A) is incorrect because incumbents ran in six of these nine elections: Democrats were incumbents in 1980, 1996, and 2012, but a plurality of independents supported them only in 1996; Republicans were incumbents in 1984, 1992, 2004, but a plurality of independents supported them only in 1984. Choice (D) is incorrect because third-party candidates won more than 5 percent of the popular vote in 1980, 1992, and 1996, and the Democratic candidates won a plurality of independent votes in two of those elections: 1992 and 1996. Choices (C) and (E) are incorrect because there are no data in the table to support them.

48. **C** The origination clause is found in Article I, Section 7 of the Constitution and states that all bills for raising revenue shall originate in the House of Representatives. Choice (A) can be eliminated because it refers to the incorporation doctrine. The president sets a budget request as required by the Budget and Accounting Act of 1921, and Congress then passes appropriations bills for the spending of money in the approved budget; therefore, eliminate choice (B). Article II, Section 2 gives the Supreme Court original jurisdiction over cases affecting ambassadors, other public ministers and consuls, and those in which a state shall be party; therefore, you may eliminate choice (D).

Choice (E) is incorrect because the treaty clause in Article II, Section 2 grants the president the power to make treaties.

49. **B** A nominee must be confirmed by a simple majority (51 percent) in order to be confirmed. Forty percent is insufficient to confirm a nominee, so eliminate choice (A). Choices (C) and (E) are incorrect because they are more than what is necessary to confirm a nominee. Choice (D) is incorrect because it describes the super majority (three-fifths) that must be obtained in order to end a filibuster.

50. **A** Article II, Section 4 of the Constitutions states that federal judges can be removed from office on impeachment for, and conviction of, treason, bribery, or other high crimes and misdemeanors. Judges cannot be removed by presidents, are neither elected nor recalled by citizens, and aren't subject to imposition of an arbitrary term limit. Accordingly, eliminate all choices except choice (A).

51. **E** Interest groups are organizations of people who share a common interest and want to promote that interest among government officials. Their cause is generally very narrow in nature, although people across many states could share that common interest, so select choice (E) and eliminate choice (C). Many large, highly successful interest groups have many members from different political affiliations and lobby federal lawmakers as much as or more than state lawmakers; therefore, you may eliminate choices (B) and (D). Finally, funding for contributions, advertisements, research, etc., is an important part of becoming a successful interest group, so eliminate choice (A).

52. **D** Delegates to presidential nomination conventions are more ideological than the general population; therefore, choice (D) is the best. Eliminate choices (A), (B), (C), and (E) because they all state the opposite of what is true.

53. **A** Although the Articles of Confederation gave both the federal government and the states the power to coin money, Article I, Section 8 of the Constitution reserves that power for the federal government alone. Choice (B) is incorrect because the Articles of Confederation and the Constitution each gave the states the power of amendment. States still have representation in Congress, although in different numbers than outlined in the Articles of Confederation, so eliminate choice (C). The president has never been an adjudicator of disputes among states. Congress had that role under the Articles of Confederation and the Supreme Court has it now; therefore, you may eliminate choice (D). Finally, states have the power to levy taxes under both the Articles of Confederation and the Constitution, so eliminate choice (E).

54. **C** Federal budget entitlements are automatically paid to any qualified person. Congress does not need to pass an appropriations bill as it does for spending by all other agencies or programs listed. After the annual budget is set, appropriations committees approve bills to actually spend the money outlined in the budget. Entitlements, such as Medicare or Social Security, are not part of this extra approval process.

55. **E** The Fourteenth Amendment includes the equal protection clause which states that no person within a single jurisdiction shall be denied equal protection of the laws in that jurisdiction. *Brown v.*

Board of Education found that separate educational facilities were inherently unequal. None of the other amendments contain the equal protection clause, so all other choices can be eliminated.

56. **B** A voter's political party affiliation is the best predictor of which candidate an individual will vote for. Some correlation can be found between a voter's choice and his or her gender, socioeconomic status, religion, and geography, but far stronger correlations can be found for Democrats voting for Democratic candidates and Republicans voting for Republican candidates.

57. **B** Choice (B) is a false statement: 64 percent of men with a college degree identify as Democrats, while only 34 percent of men with a doctoral degree do. Therefore, men with a doctoral degree are less likely to identify as Democrats, making choice (B) is the credited response to this EXCEPT question. The other choices can be eliminated because they are true statements. Choice (A) is a true statement: 24 percent of men with a vocational degree identify as Republican, compared with 13 percent of men with a high school diploma. Choice (C) is a true statement: 13 percent of women who completed grade school identify as Republican, just as 13 percent of men with high school degrees do. Choice (D) is a true statement: 49 percent of men with a Master's degree identify as Republican, compared with 51 percent who identify as Democrats. Choice (E) is a true statement: 28 percent of women with vocational degrees identify as Republican, compared with 24 percent of men with vocational degrees.

58. **B** The question accurately defines a pocket veto. A line-item veto occurs when the president vetoes only certain parts of a bill before signing it, so eliminate choice (B). (In 1998, the Supreme Court ruled that the presidential line-item veto is unconstitutional.) Adjournment is the term for taking a recess, so eliminate choice (C). A writ of *certiorari* is issued when the Supreme Court agrees to hear a case; eliminate choice (D). Senatorial courtesy occurs when the president consults a senator on nominations to be made for positions within that senator's state; eliminate choice (E).

59. **C** The Congressional Management Foundation is a nonpartisan, nonprofit organization that works with members of Congress, but is not part of Congress and not run by members of Congress. The president *pro tempore* is the most senior member of the Senate and the Speaker of the House is elected by the majority in the House of Representatives; therefore, eliminate choices (A) and (B). Both the House and the Senate have a minority whip and a Democratic (and Republican) Caucus Chairman, so eliminate choices (D) and (E).

60. **B** Lawmakers and other government officials are prohibited from accepting outright gifts from lobbyists and others who might have a political agenda. Sometimes educational trips may be construed as gifts, but that line is not black and white, so choice (A) is incorrect. Choices (C), (D), and (E) all describe activities that comprise a large portion of what interest groups have done in the past and do now, in addition to lobbying. Accordingly, they can all be eliminated.

Section II

Question 1

This question offers six possible points, one in part (a), one in part (b), and four in part (c).

You get one point in part (a) for identifying a power the U.S. Constitution gives to the national government, but not to state governments. Possible answers include the power to declare war, the power to sign treaties, the power to create federal courts, and the power to coin money.

You get another point in part (b) for naming a reserved power. Examples include regulating intrastate business, issuing licenses, and running and financing federal elections.

There are several Constitutional Amendments that increased opportunities for political participation by citizens. Identifying two of the following gets you two points for part (c), while one point is awarded for each of the two accompanying explanations:

- The Fifteenth Amendment, which granted voting rights to males of all races,
- The Seventeenth Amendment, which changed the election of senators from votes by state legislatures to votes by the general voting public,
- The Nineteenth Amendment, which granted voting rights to women,
- The Twenty-third Amendment, which allowed the residents of Washington, D.C. to vote in elections,
- The Twenty-fourth Amendment, which eliminated poll-taxes, and
- The Twenty-sixth Amendment, which lowered the voting age from 21 to 18.

Question 2

This question is worth seven points: one from part (a), two from part (b), two from part (c), and two from part (d).

The correct definition in part (a) is that an ideology is a coherent set of thoughts and beliefs about politics and government. You don't have to be quite that exact on the exam to get the point, but you should be able to note that an ideology represents beliefs that make up a political view.

The first point in part (b) comes from identifying that liberal ideology is associated with the Democratic Party. The second point comes from describing a belief held by liberals: support of government regulation of the economy, separation of church and state, and affirmative action programs, to name a few. You don't need to name a few; just one from each category to get two more points.

The first point in part (c) comes from identifying that conservative ideology is associated with the Republican Party. The second point comes from describing a belief held by conservatives, such as smaller government, lower taxes, and support of government regulation of social issues (such as gay marriage and abortion).

You may earn one point for describing how each factor you choose in part (d) influences political beliefs.

- Broadly speaking, minority populations tend to be more liberal and support Democrats, while the majority white population leans conservative and tends to vote for Republican candidates. However, this is not true in all cases: you can still pick up the point by noting that, for example, Cuban-Americans are a minority population that tend to support Republicans or that highly educated whites tend to support Democrats.
- In the gender category, more women are liberal or Democrats, while more men are conservative or Republicans.
- As for income level, richer Americans tend to be fiscally conservative, while poorer Americans often support government intervention in economic matters.

Question 3

Students may earn a total of six points on this question. Three points are available for part (a) and three for part (b).

Part (a) asks you to explain how each of the three House features mentioned gives the majority party an advantage in the legislative process. You'll earn one point for each of the three you explain. Here are the points you need to make.

- The Speaker is the leader of the majority party in the House. The majority party selects the chairs of all the House committees and holds a majority on all of the House committees, effectively controlling the legislative process. As the leader of the majority party, the Speaker is thus able to exert great influence in setting the House agenda.
- The Rules Committee sets the rules for how a bill will be debated and when it will be voted on. The majority party selects the chair and a majority of the members of the Rules Committee. This makes it easier for the majority party to pass bills that it likes and prevent passage of bills that it does not like. The Rules Committee decides how long a bill will be debated before its vote. The Rules Committee also decides whether amendments to a bill will be allowed (open rule) or will not be allowed (closed rule).
- The germaneness requirement is the rule that amendments to a bill be germane (relevant) to the bill. This limits the possible "killer" amendments (a "killer" amendment is one that changes a bill in such a way to ensure that members of Congress will not vote for the bill) that can be added and maintains the focus of House debate.

Part (b) asks you to explain how each of the three Senate features mentioned limits the power of the majority party in the legislative process. You'll earn one point for each of the three you explain. Here are the points you need to make.

- The filibuster is a Senate procedure that allows one or more senators to debate indefinitely. A senator can use the filibuster to prevent or delay action on a particular bill or to prevent or delay all action in the Senate, which effectively stops the Senate from functioning. The only way to end a filibuster is through cloture, in which 60 senators vote to end debate. Rarely does one party hold 60 seats in the Senate; therefore, even the majority party usually lacks the ability to stop a filibuster.
- A senatorial hold prevents action from being taken on a bill, and senators of either party can place a hold on a bill. Like the filibuster above, a hold can be overridden only with cloture (60 senators vote to proceed) and can prevent or significantly delay action on a bill. This limits the power of the majority party in the Senate because any senator, including one of the minority party, can place a hold on a bill.

- A rider is an amendment to a bill. The Senate has no germaneness requirement for amendments; therefore, senators can attach riders to bills (make amendments) that are unrelated to the subject of the bill. By attaching an unattractive rider to a bill (see "killer" amendments above), a senator can prevent passage of a bill because a majority will not support the bill with the rider. This limits the power of the majority party in the Senate because any senator, including one of the minority party, can add a rider to a bill.

Question 4

This question is scored on a five-point scale. Students can earn two points for part (a), one point for part (b), and two points for part (c).

Part (a) asks you to define public opinion and policy agenda. You will receive one point for each correct definition.

- Public opinion is what the public thinks about a given issue.
- Policy agenda is a set of issues or subjects that policymakers (government officials) view as important.

Part (b) asks that you explain how the news media may affect the policy agenda. News media may affect the policy agenda by providing information to or raising awareness of an issue with the public and/or government policymakers.

Part (c) refers you to the table and asks you to identify the difference between young and old news consumers as well as the change over time of all age groups. You may receive a total of two points for part (c), one point for identifying each of the following:

1. A higher percentage of older Americans receive news from traditional media only (television, radio, and/or print newspaper) than do younger Americans, or a lower percentage of younger Americans receive news from traditional media only (television, radio, and/or print newspaper) than do older Americans.
2. A lower percentage of Americans in all age groups received news from traditional media only (television, radio, and/or print newspaper) in 2012 than in 2010.

PRACTICE TEST SCORING WORKSHEET

Section I: Multiple-Choice

_____ × 1.0000 = _____
Number of Correct   Weighted
(out of 60)   Section I Score
                                     (Do not round)

Section II: Free Response

Question 1   _____ × 2.5000 = _____
              (out of 6)   (Do not round)

Question 2   _____ × 2.1428 = _____
              (out of 7)   (Do not round)

Question 3   _____ × 2.5000 = _____
              (out of 6)   (Do not round)

Question 4   _____ × 3.0000 = _____
              (out of 5)   (Do not round)

AP Score Conversion Chart U.S. Government and Politics

Composite Score Range	AP Score
93-120	5
82-92	4
66-81	3
48-65	2
0–47	1

Sum = _____
       Weighted Section II
       Score (Do not round)

Composite Score

_____ + _____ = _____
Weighted   Weighted   Composite Score
Section I Score   Section II Score   (Round to nearest
                                            whole number)

The Princeton Review

1. YOUR NAME:
(Print)
Last   First   M.I.

SIGNATURE: _____ **DATE:** _____ / _____ / _____

HOME ADDRESS: _____
(Print)   Number and Street

_____ **E-MAIL:** _____
City   State   Zip

PHONE NO.: _____ **SCHOOL:** _____ **CLASS OF:** _____
(Print)

IMPORTANT: Please fill in these boxes exactly as shown on the back cover of your test book.

OpScan *i*NSIGHT™ forms by Pearson NCS EM-255325-1:654321
Printed in U.S.A.

© TPR Education IP Holdings, LLC

2. TEST FORM

3. TEST CODE

4. PHONE NUMBER

5. YOUR NAME

First 4 letters of last name				FIRST INIT	MID INIT

6. DATE OF BIRTH

MONTH	DAY	YEAR
○ JAN		
○ FEB		
○ MAR	⓪ ⓪	⓪ ⓪
○ APR	① ①	① ①
○ MAY	② ②	② ②
○ JUN	③ ③	③ ③
○ JUL	④ ④	④ ④
○ AUG	⑤ ⑤	⑤ ⑤
○ SEP	⑥ ⑥	⑥ ⑥
○ OCT	⑦ ⑦	⑦ ⑦
○ NOV	⑧ ⑧	⑧ ⑧
○ DEC	⑨ ⑨	⑨ ⑨

7. SEX
○ MALE
○ FEMALE

8. OTHER
1 Ⓐ Ⓑ Ⓒ Ⓓ Ⓔ
2 Ⓐ Ⓑ Ⓒ Ⓓ Ⓔ
3 Ⓐ Ⓑ Ⓒ Ⓓ Ⓔ

Begin with number 1 for each new section of the test. Leave blank any extra answer spaces.

SECTION 1

1 Ⓐ Ⓑ Ⓒ Ⓓ Ⓔ	26 Ⓐ Ⓑ Ⓒ Ⓓ Ⓔ	51 Ⓐ Ⓑ Ⓒ Ⓓ Ⓔ	76 Ⓐ Ⓑ Ⓒ Ⓓ Ⓔ
2 Ⓐ Ⓑ Ⓒ Ⓓ Ⓔ	27 Ⓐ Ⓑ Ⓒ Ⓓ Ⓔ	52 Ⓐ Ⓑ Ⓒ Ⓓ Ⓔ	77 Ⓐ Ⓑ Ⓒ Ⓓ Ⓔ
3 Ⓐ Ⓑ Ⓒ Ⓓ Ⓔ	28 Ⓐ Ⓑ Ⓒ Ⓓ Ⓔ	53 Ⓐ Ⓑ Ⓒ Ⓓ Ⓔ	78 Ⓐ Ⓑ Ⓒ Ⓓ Ⓔ
4 Ⓐ Ⓑ Ⓒ Ⓓ Ⓔ	29 Ⓐ Ⓑ Ⓒ Ⓓ Ⓔ	54 Ⓐ Ⓑ Ⓒ Ⓓ Ⓔ	79 Ⓐ Ⓑ Ⓒ Ⓓ Ⓔ
5 Ⓐ Ⓑ Ⓒ Ⓓ Ⓔ	30 Ⓐ Ⓑ Ⓒ Ⓓ Ⓔ	55 Ⓐ Ⓑ Ⓒ Ⓓ Ⓔ	80 Ⓐ Ⓑ Ⓒ Ⓓ Ⓔ
6 Ⓐ Ⓑ Ⓒ Ⓓ Ⓔ	31 Ⓐ Ⓑ Ⓒ Ⓓ Ⓔ	56 Ⓐ Ⓑ Ⓒ Ⓓ Ⓔ	81 Ⓐ Ⓑ Ⓒ Ⓓ Ⓔ
7 Ⓐ Ⓑ Ⓒ Ⓓ Ⓔ	32 Ⓐ Ⓑ Ⓒ Ⓓ Ⓔ	57 Ⓐ Ⓑ Ⓒ Ⓓ Ⓔ	82 Ⓐ Ⓑ Ⓒ Ⓓ Ⓔ
8 Ⓐ Ⓑ Ⓒ Ⓓ Ⓔ	33 Ⓐ Ⓑ Ⓒ Ⓓ Ⓔ	58 Ⓐ Ⓑ Ⓒ Ⓓ Ⓔ	83 Ⓐ Ⓑ Ⓒ Ⓓ Ⓔ
9 Ⓐ Ⓑ Ⓒ Ⓓ Ⓔ	34 Ⓐ Ⓑ Ⓒ Ⓓ Ⓔ	59 Ⓐ Ⓑ Ⓒ Ⓓ Ⓔ	84 Ⓐ Ⓑ Ⓒ Ⓓ Ⓔ
10 Ⓐ Ⓑ Ⓒ Ⓓ Ⓔ	35 Ⓐ Ⓑ Ⓒ Ⓓ Ⓔ	60 Ⓐ Ⓑ Ⓒ Ⓓ Ⓔ	85 Ⓐ Ⓑ Ⓒ Ⓓ Ⓔ
11 Ⓐ Ⓑ Ⓒ Ⓓ Ⓔ	36 Ⓐ Ⓑ Ⓒ Ⓓ Ⓔ	61 Ⓐ Ⓑ Ⓒ Ⓓ Ⓔ	86 Ⓐ Ⓑ Ⓒ Ⓓ Ⓔ
12 Ⓐ Ⓑ Ⓒ Ⓓ Ⓔ	37 Ⓐ Ⓑ Ⓒ Ⓓ Ⓔ	62 Ⓐ Ⓑ Ⓒ Ⓓ Ⓔ	87 Ⓐ Ⓑ Ⓒ Ⓓ Ⓔ
13 Ⓐ Ⓑ Ⓒ Ⓓ Ⓔ	38 Ⓐ Ⓑ Ⓒ Ⓓ Ⓔ	63 Ⓐ Ⓑ Ⓒ Ⓓ Ⓔ	88 Ⓐ Ⓑ Ⓒ Ⓓ Ⓔ
14 Ⓐ Ⓑ Ⓒ Ⓓ Ⓔ	39 Ⓐ Ⓑ Ⓒ Ⓓ Ⓔ	64 Ⓐ Ⓑ Ⓒ Ⓓ Ⓔ	89 Ⓐ Ⓑ Ⓒ Ⓓ Ⓔ
15 Ⓐ Ⓑ Ⓒ Ⓓ Ⓔ	40 Ⓐ Ⓑ Ⓒ Ⓓ Ⓔ	65 Ⓐ Ⓑ Ⓒ Ⓓ Ⓔ	90 Ⓐ Ⓑ Ⓒ Ⓓ Ⓔ
16 Ⓐ Ⓑ Ⓒ Ⓓ Ⓔ	41 Ⓐ Ⓑ Ⓒ Ⓓ Ⓔ	66 Ⓐ Ⓑ Ⓒ Ⓓ Ⓔ	91 Ⓐ Ⓑ Ⓒ Ⓓ Ⓔ
17 Ⓐ Ⓑ Ⓒ Ⓓ Ⓔ	42 Ⓐ Ⓑ Ⓒ Ⓓ Ⓔ	67 Ⓐ Ⓑ Ⓒ Ⓓ Ⓔ	92 Ⓐ Ⓑ Ⓒ Ⓓ Ⓔ
18 Ⓐ Ⓑ Ⓒ Ⓓ Ⓔ	43 Ⓐ Ⓑ Ⓒ Ⓓ Ⓔ	68 Ⓐ Ⓑ Ⓒ Ⓓ Ⓔ	93 Ⓐ Ⓑ Ⓒ Ⓓ Ⓔ
19 Ⓐ Ⓑ Ⓒ Ⓓ Ⓔ	44 Ⓐ Ⓑ Ⓒ Ⓓ Ⓔ	69 Ⓐ Ⓑ Ⓒ Ⓓ Ⓔ	94 Ⓐ Ⓑ Ⓒ Ⓓ Ⓔ
20 Ⓐ Ⓑ Ⓒ Ⓓ Ⓔ	45 Ⓐ Ⓑ Ⓒ Ⓓ Ⓔ	70 Ⓐ Ⓑ Ⓒ Ⓓ Ⓔ	95 Ⓐ Ⓑ Ⓒ Ⓓ Ⓔ
21 Ⓐ Ⓑ Ⓒ Ⓓ Ⓔ	46 Ⓐ Ⓑ Ⓒ Ⓓ Ⓔ	71 Ⓐ Ⓑ Ⓒ Ⓓ Ⓔ	96 Ⓐ Ⓑ Ⓒ Ⓓ Ⓔ
22 Ⓐ Ⓑ Ⓒ Ⓓ Ⓔ	47 Ⓐ Ⓑ Ⓒ Ⓓ Ⓔ	72 Ⓐ Ⓑ Ⓒ Ⓓ Ⓔ	97 Ⓐ Ⓑ Ⓒ Ⓓ Ⓔ
23 Ⓐ Ⓑ Ⓒ Ⓓ Ⓔ	48 Ⓐ Ⓑ Ⓒ Ⓓ Ⓔ	73 Ⓐ Ⓑ Ⓒ Ⓓ Ⓔ	98 Ⓐ Ⓑ Ⓒ Ⓓ Ⓔ
24 Ⓐ Ⓑ Ⓒ Ⓓ Ⓔ	49 Ⓐ Ⓑ Ⓒ Ⓓ Ⓔ	74 Ⓐ Ⓑ Ⓒ Ⓓ Ⓔ	99 Ⓐ Ⓑ Ⓒ Ⓓ Ⓔ
25 Ⓐ Ⓑ Ⓒ Ⓓ Ⓔ	50 Ⓐ Ⓑ Ⓒ Ⓓ Ⓔ	75 Ⓐ Ⓑ Ⓒ Ⓓ Ⓔ	100 Ⓐ Ⓑ Ⓒ Ⓓ Ⓔ

The Princeton Review

1. YOUR NAME: _____
(Print)
Last   First   M.I.

SIGNATURE: _____   **DATE:** _____ / _____ / _____

HOME ADDRESS: _____
(Print)
Number and Street

_____   **E-MAIL:** _____
City   State   Zip

PHONE NO.: _____   **SCHOOL:** _____   **CLASS OF:** _____
(Print)

IMPORTANT: Please fill in these boxes exactly as shown on the back cover of your test book.

OpScan *i*NSIGHT™ forms by Pearson NCS EM-255325-1:654321
Printed in U.S.A.

© TPR Education IP Holdings, LLC

2. TEST FORM

3. TEST CODE

4. PHONE NUMBER

5. YOUR NAME

First 4 letters of last name				FIRST INIT	MID INIT

Bubbles A–Z

6. DATE OF BIRTH

MONTH	DAY	YEAR
JAN		
FEB		
MAR		
APR		
MAY		
JUN		
JUL		
AUG		
SEP		
OCT		
NOV		
DEC		

7. SEX
- MALE
- FEMALE

8. OTHER
1. A B C D E
2. A B C D E
3. A B C D E

Begin with number 1 for each new section of the test. Leave blank any extra answer spaces.

SECTION 1

1 A B C D E   26 A B C D E   51 A B C D E   76 A B C D E
2 A B C D E   27 A B C D E   52 A B C D E   77 A B C D E
3 A B C D E   28 A B C D E   53 A B C D E   78 A B C D E
4 A B C D E   29 A B C D E   54 A B C D E   79 A B C D E
5 A B C D E   30 A B C D E   55 A B C D E   80 A B C D E
6 A B C D E   31 A B C D E   56 A B C D E   81 A B C D E
7 A B C D E   32 A B C D E   57 A B C D E   82 A B C D E
8 A B C D E   33 A B C D E   58 A B C D E   83 A B C D E
9 A B C D E   34 A B C D E   59 A B C D E   84 A B C D E
10 A B C D E   35 A B C D E   60 A B C D E   85 A B C D E
11 A B C D E   36 A B C D E   61 A B C D E   86 A B C D E
12 A B C D E   37 A B C D E   62 A B C D E   87 A B C D E
13 A B C D E   38 A B C D E   63 A B C D E   88 A B C D E
14 A B C D E   39 A B C D E   64 A B C D E   89 A B C D E
15 A B C D E   40 A B C D E   65 A B C D E   90 A B C D E
16 A B C D E   41 A B C D E   66 A B C D E   91 A B C D E
17 A B C D E   42 A B C D E   67 A B C D E   92 A B C D E
18 A B C D E   43 A B C D E   68 A B C D E   93 A B C D E
19 A B C D E   44 A B C D E   69 A B C D E   94 A B C D E
20 A B C D E   45 A B C D E   70 A B C D E   95 A B C D E
21 A B C D E   46 A B C D E   71 A B C D E   96 A B C D E
22 A B C D E   47 A B C D E   72 A B C D E   97 A B C D E
23 A B C D E   48 A B C D E   73 A B C D E   98 A B C D E
24 A B C D E   49 A B C D E   74 A B C D E   99 A B C D E
25 A B C D E   50 A B C D E   75 A B C D E   100 A B C D E

NOTES